# The Virgin Discography: the 1970s

## Caroline, WATT, JCOA, Front Line, Dindisc, Oval, Atra, Butt, ECM & more

# The Virgin Discography: the 1970s

## Caroline, WATT, JCOA, Front Line, Dindisc, Oval, Atra, Butt, ECM & more

Mark Jones

This edition published 2013 by

The Record Press

The Record Press is an imprint of Bristol Folk Publications
www.bristol–folk.co.uk

ISBN 978–1–909953–00–0



Layout, design and digital realisation by Bristol Folk Publications.
Printed and bound on demand by Lulu.com.

# Contents

**Introduction** ... 1
**Virgin in the 1970s: a short history** ... 3
Section sources and endnotes ... 17
**Discographies** ... 19
Sources used in the discography ... 19
Release and deletion dates ... 19
Recommended retail price ... 19
Original label designs ... 20
Tape releases ... 21
Discography structure ... 21
***Virgin*** ... ***22***
V 2000 series LPs ... 22
VC 500 series LPs ... 50
QV/QVQS 2000 series quadraphonic LPs ... 51
VCL 5000 series 10" LPs ... 52
VP 2000 series picture disc LPs ... 52
VR series LPs ... 53
VD 2500 series 2–LPs ... 53
VGD 3500 series 2–LPs ... 57
Custom catalogue LPs ... 58
VS 100 series 7" singles ... 59
VS 100–12 series 12" singles ... 75
VEP 1000 series 7" EPs ... 78
VOLE series 12" singles ... 79
SIXPACK series 7" picture disc EPs ... 80
Promotional records (all formats) ... 81
***Caroline*** ... ***86***
C 1500 series LPs ... 86
CA 2000 series LPs ... 90
CAD 3000 series 2–LPs ... 92
***Oval*** ... ***93***
OVL 3000 series LPs ... 93
OVLM 5000 series LPs ... 93
OVAL 1000 series 7" singles ... 94
***WATT and JCOA*** ... ***95***
WATT series LPs ... 95
J 2000 series LPs ... 96
JD 3000 series 2–LP ... 97
JD 4000 series 3–LP ... 97
***Atra*** ... ***98***
ATRALP 1000 series LPs ... 98
ATRA series 7" singles ... 98
***The Front Line*** ... ***100***
FL 1000 series LPs ... 100
FCL 5000 series 10" LPs ... 106
FLB 3000 series LPs ... 106
FLX 4000 series LPs ... 107
FLD 6000 series 2–LPs ... 107
FLS 100 series 7" singles ... 108
FLS 100–12 series 12" singles ... 110
VOLE series 12" single – slight reprise ... 110

***Butt***......111
NOTT series LPs......111
BUTT series LP......111
***Ice***......112
ICE series LP......112
GUY series 7” singles......112
GUY series 12” singles......112
***DinDisc***......113
DIN series 7” singles......113
***Odds and sods***......114
No Bad/The Record Company......114
Quiet Records......114
Disques Clouseau......115
Smirksongs......115
Fast Product......115
Custom catalogue number......115
***ECM and JAPO***......116
ECM LPs......116
JAPO LPs......120
***Virgin artists on other labels***......122
**Appendices: summary listings**......124
Quadraphonic releases......124
Picture discs......124
Coloured, luminous and clear vinyl releases......124
12” singles......125
Flexidiscs......126
8-track cartridges......126
Cassettes......127
Caroline label artists on Virgin VS 100 series 7” singles......128
UK–only Virgin set numbers assigned to ECM multi–LPs......129
Known export–only packages/releases......129
Releases including the Caroline Exports [U.K.] logo......129
Virgin Films......129

# Introduction

Nowadays, Virgin is a globally–recognised brand and the Virgin record label has been home to some of the world's best–selling artists. The beginnings, however, were rather more humble. Virgin started life as an offshoot of Richard Branson's *Student* magazine, selling records at discount prices by mail–order. The postal strike of 1971 forced Virgin to find a physical retail outlet, which, in turn, led to a string of Virgin shops around the UK. Richard Branson was keen to branch out from retail to other areas in the music industry and to this end the Manor was kitted out as a recording studio. A record label was a logical progression – the missing link between the recording of artists at one end of the chain and the retail of the subsequent records at the other. Indeed, all had been planned since early days – for example, Roger Dean had been commissioned to come up with a record label design over a year in advance of the record label's existence.

This discography covers the 1970s, from Virgin's beginnings as the ultimate left–field, progressive label through its embracing of reggae, punk and new wave, before industry downturn and near insolvency drove the company to market more commercial product. To become a mainstream competitor meant that Virgin needed to sign artists based on potential record sales and marketability rather than continuing to back esoteric outsiders. The fact that Virgin managed to compete with the majors and still retain a certain amount of kudos as both a label and a retailer during the 1980s says a lot about the way in which the company was perceived by the record buying public.

During the 1970s it was hip to hang around in Virgin's record shops and buy Virgin label records (that records were cheaper there than elsewhere undoubtedly helped). The odd thing is that during the early 1980s when Virgin turned, to all intents and purposes, into a mainstream pop label it was *still* the done thing to hang out in Virgin's record shops and buy Virgin label records – perhaps because it was Virgin that was breaking many of the current pop acts – still defining tastes rather than confirming them.

When all's said and done, though, there's something very special about Virgin's first six years. Whilst most of the ephemeral, quick–buck, pop product pushed out by the company in the 1980s and beyond has long gone from public consciousness, many of Virgin's early records are now considered important cultural reference points. Never mind whether it's *Tubular Bells* or *Camembert Electrique* or *Never Mind the Bollocks* or *Metal Box* or *The Front Line*, having Virgin records in your collection was a statement about you. And Virgin changed, just like you did – and that's probably why there are so many record collections out there with albums by both Henry Cow and PIL nestling together – but less, I would imagine, with both Faust and Culture Club!

So, have a read through the discographies to remind yourself of what was and have a hunt around your record collection (even if it does mean going up to the attic to find your old vinyl) and pull out and play some of those old favourites. What the hell, pull out your stash of old *Fabulous Furry Freak Brothers* or *Sniffin' Glue* or *Zigzag* or *Black Music* or *NME* whilst you're at it. Go on, you know you want to.

Meanwhile, the most often asked question – why no pictures? Well, it's all down to copyright and cost. From experience, I know that negotiating to reproduce sleeves can add years to a project and incur silly costs – e.g. EMI once tried to charge me £1,000 (plus VAT) to reproduce fifteen Wurzels sleeves. It does mean that these books remain cheap and cheerful, though. For illustrations of sleeves and labels try discogs.com and the exemplary 45cat.com – think of it as an exercise in blended learning.

## Thanks to

In alphabetical order: Pete Barnes; Ian McCann at *Record Collector*; Mike Tobin, ex–regional promotion for Virgin (whether he knows it or not, I ended up with plenty of his old Virgin singles and albums he'd unloaded at Tony's Records in Clifton Village – what a shame it all got sold over the years) ... and let's not forget the unknown medical student at Bristol Maternity Hospital, as was way back then, who, very kindly, gave me his spare *Rotter's Club* sticker. His spare one, mind – the other was stuck to his jacket.

# *Virgin in the 1970s: a short history*

In the beginning, there was *Student* magazine. Then came the Student Advisory Centre. Both of these existed in a constantly precarious financial state, which necessitated a more stable income stream. Then, in 1969, the Retail Price Maintenance Agreement appertaining to the sale of records was abolished. Until this point, records had to be sold at the price the manufacturers stipulated, but now retailers were free to decide their own pricing structures. These were the factors behind the setting up of Virgin Records. The plan was to sell records at discount prices by mail–order and then to use the income to bolster the magazine and advisory centre. However, things didn't quite work out that way.

To go back a bit, Richard Branson was the product of a privileged background and was educated at Scaitcliffe Preparatory School and Stowe. His family encouraged self–reliance and independence from an early age, which was just as well because these are excellent traits for surviving both at public school and in business. At Scaitcliffe Branson excelled at sports but was academically weak and, once he'd moved up to Stowe, his continuing academic weakness spurred a nascent entrepreneurial spirit into being. This manifested itself in several ludicrous schemes for making money, including growing and selling Christmas trees and breeding budgies.

A later idea, developed along with school friend, Johnathan Holland–Gems, was to create an alternative school magazine – Stowe had the aptly titled (not to mention stuffy–sounding) *The Stoic*. The scope was quickly widened, once the disadvantages of deliberately limiting the target market were considered, to that of a magazine for all schools, technical colleges and universities. Of this first step on the road to what became Virgin Richard Branson says:

> ... with contributors, advertisers, distributors and costs all in place – at least on paper – I had written my first business plan [but the] numbers looked too small to work, so [we] decided to involve more schools, and technical colleges and universities: it would open up the magazine to more people, and encourage advertisers. We thought that if we aimed the magazine at university students then sixth–formers would buy it; but if we published a magazine for sixth–formers then students wouldn't be interested.[1]

So at the age of 15, with the first issue of *Student* becoming a reality, Richard Branson learned how to hustle big business for advertising revenues and politicians and celebrities for interviews. It took well over a year to get the first issue of the magazine to print and it was circulated in January 1968, by which time Branson and Holland–Gems had both left school.

Over the next couple of years, *Student* included interviews and contributions from the likes of Gerald Scarfe, Harold Wilson, Mick Jagger, Jean Paul Satre, John Lennon, John Peel, Peter Blake, Dudley Moore, Bertrand Russell, David Hockney, Alan Aldridge, Harold Pinter and R. D. Laing. There was just one problem, really, and that was that *Student* wasn't making money, though as Branson says:

> Above all, you want to create something you are proud of. That has always been my philosophy of business. I can honestly say that I have never gone into any business purely to make money. If that is the sole motive then I believe you are better off not doing it. A business has to be involving; it

> has to be fun, and it has to exercise your creative instincts. Running *Student* was certainly fun.[2]

Although the magazine wasn't making money, Branson saw *Student* as the first stage in a wider scheme – the creation of a brand, if you like – where the *Student* name could be used in other business areas, such as in servicing student demand for term–time accommodation and travel. The seeds were set for Virgin's later related and non–related diversification. A business can't generally get away with non–related diversification, but a brand can pretty much make up the rules as it goes along, as Virgin later proved – but we're running ahead of ourselves here. Back with *Student*, an early casualty was Branson's intention to be a journalist, which was swept aside because he was too busy attending to the myriad tasks involved in getting the next issue to print and ensuring that the bills got paid.

The first expansion of the *Student* name was the opening of the Student Advisory Centre, which soon started taking up more time than the magazine. The advisory centre introduced Branson to the joys of prosecution for offering counselling on venereal disease. This, it seems, violated both the Indecent Advertisements Act 1889 and the Venereal Disease Act 1917. Branson was fined a small amount, but the positive publicity generated by the case caused the law to be amended and Branson received a letter of apology for his prosecution from the Home Secretary. Branson's next court appearance was not destined to have such a happy ending, except, perhaps, as a learning point.

Meanwhile, the next stepping stone to the creation of a record label appeared on the horizon. Branson, in *Losing My Virginity*, says he noticed that one of the major influencing factors on young people was the music to which they listened and that *Student* was run to a constant background of LPs on the communal record player. LPs were expensive, with price determined by the manufacturer under the U.K. Retail Price Maintenance Agreement. In 1964 the Resale Prices Act was passed, which aimed to remove such agreements unless it could be proved that specific price agreements were in the public interest. In late 1969 the Retail Price Maintenance Agreement on records was abolished, but the price–cutting war between retail outlets that many had predicted didn't materialise and LP records remained expensive luxury items.

Branson planned the setting up of a discount record retail business, based on the fact that *Student* magazine would make an excellent – and 'free' – medium for advertising cut price records. Despite wanting to widen the *Student* brand, Branson decided that the mail–order business should have a different name to disassociate it from the magazine in which the records were to be advertised – although those with reading skills might have noticed that the Virgin and *Student* addresses were one and the same – to whit, 10, South Wharf Road, London, W.2.

It was, according to Branson, one of the girls on the *Student* staff who came up with the name 'Virgin' in celebration of the fact that none of them knew anything about business[3] . As things turned out, the first Virgin advertisement came out in spring, 1970, in what was became the last edition of *Student* (Vol. 2, No. 4). The advertisement said, in large letters, "Name any record you want and we'll sell it to you 10% to 25% cheaper than anybody else" and then asked for a list of readers' wants. The response confirmed one thing, which was that a lot of people were very interested in paying less for records.

Nik Powell, Branson's childhood friend, who had been ousted from *Student* after a failed 'coup d'état' against Branson, was invited back into the fold to take charge of Virgin's finances with a 40% stake in the new company. As the mail–order business expanded *Student* fell dormant and Branson tried to sell the magazine as a going concern. Talks fell through and *Student* didn't so much die as get quietly pushed aside to give Virgin the increasingly large amount of time that it required.

The model for the mail–order business was quite interesting in that people paid up–front for their records, only at which point did Virgin order the record from the distributors. This is a very good way to ensure that money is not tied up in stock but, on the downside, Virgin missed out on discount offered for bulk orders. The business model had other flaws – if you are competing on cost–leadership, then you have no option but to keep your overheads down. However, the half page adverts that started to appear in the music press ate into an already reduced margin and Virgin also took the cost of postage onto themselves, thus cutting margin further. This could further be abused by naughty individuals who worked out that they could get multiple copies by pretending that they hadn't received their records. To turn a small margin per item into real money required selling lots of individual units – and the 'stack 'em high and sell 'em cheap' model requires a lot of effort for even small gains. As Branson later stated in *Music Week*:

> Record companies were unwilling to give us the sort of margins we needed on product – I don't think they really approved of what we were doing anyway – so that our profit on each sale was very small. Against that as the business began to grow, our overheads increased with it – we had to employ more staff, there were extra postage costs and we found ourselves spending more and more money on advertising ...[4]

As if this wasn't enough, Virgin was almost finished off in January 1971 when the Post Office went on strike. The weak point of running a mail–order business is that you are wholly dependent on a third party for continued business success. Thanks to what turned into a six–week strike Virgin was unable to get records already paid for out to customers but, more importantly, from point of view of cash flow – the life blood of any organisation – it was unable to receive any further payments.

Branson says that he and Nik Powell estimated that they would be broke in a week unless they found another sales channel[5], which realistically meant a shop. The first shop was above a shoe shop at the less–exclusive end of Oxford Street, and they even got it rent–free. A day or so before the shop was ready to open, Richard Branson's South African second cousin, Simon Draper, turned up looking for a job, whilst he was in–between degree courses. He started the next day, despite no knowledge of the record retail trade and never did get back to University. We'll hear more of him throughout.

The advisory centre was still running in Piccadilly, though it had taken second stage to Virgin in Branson's day–to–day activities. The charity was soon renamed as HELP! and Branson's direct involvement seems to have dwindled to somwhere between minimal and non–existent as he concentrated on planning future horizontal and vertical integration within the music industry. This intention was based on the fact that record companies tended to make much better margins than did the companies at the retail end of the chain. As regards the retail end, which was currently limited to the shop in Oxford Street, the shop was made comfortable, informal and welcoming to customers, which was a far cry from the functional job racks in Boots and Woolworths.

Branson also had the idea that the recording experience could also be made more pleasurable than was currently the case and started to look for somewhere nice in the country that could be turned into a recording studio. The Manor at Shipton–on–Cherwell was a serendipitous find and cost £30,000 with loans from the bank and an accomodating aunt. Tom Newman and Phil Newell worked on putting the studio together, which started to eat into the money that Virgin did not have – by early–1971 Virgin was £15,000 overdrawn. A lot of money in those days.

It was at this point that Branson discovered that selling records in the UK that were meant for export created a much larger margin per record. This was because records bought for export didn't incur Purchase Tax. The initial discovery had been a pure accident: Branson had arrived in France with a batch of export records for Belgium – Customs in Dover had stamped the relavent paperwork – but the French wouldn't allow the records through because Branson was missing a specific document to say that the records would not be sold on French soil. Branson was forced to return to the UK with the export records, but also with the paperwork that said that they had been exported. Branson decided that this could be a good way to get the company and himself out of debt – the extra income that could be made on this batch alone was around £5,000. H. M. Customs and Excise, however, was well aware of this scam – Branson was not the only person that had discovered this lucrative 'option' – and pounced on Virgin's warehouse and shops for evidence of the fraud. News of Branson's arrest even appeared in the US trade magazine, *Billboard*:

> Court proceedings have been started by Customs & Excise against London dealer Richard Branson, owner of Virgin Records discount shop who was accused at Dover last week of making a false declaration about records intended for export. It is alleged that on May 28 Branson made an untrue statement to Dover customs officials concerning 10,000 albums due to be exported.[6]

After a taste of police custody, Branson negotiated an out–of–court settlement that added £60,000 to Virgin's debt. This debt had to be paid in instalments over the next three years, so things had to change to make Virgin profitable.

The first thing done – based on Branson's stated preference of expanding out of a crisis, rather than retrenching – was that Virgin started to open shops around the country, the first being in Brighton. The second thing that Virgin had to do was to learn how to manage the shops in a way that made them both attractive to customers and profitable to the company. Simon Draper, meanwhile, was dong well in his role as record buyer for both the shops and mail–order arm by using his own musical taste as a yardstick to define an image for Virgin. This was done through a deliberate policy of stocking certain types of music and not others. What was 'in' included progressive and experimental records imported from Europe and the US, which would otherwise have been difficult to find. Easy listening and middle–of–the–road pop was most definitely 'out'.

One other thing, however, that was 'in' was bootleg albums and Virgin very openly sold these illicit items. As *Music Week* reported:

> ... not all aspects of Branson's operation have been admired by his competitors in the record industry, and one in particular – his involvement in selling bootleg albums – provoked, not surprisingly, a lot of criticism [7]

The same article went on to report that Branson had claimed that Virgin, as at August 1973, was no longer selling bootlegs, although he vigorously defended his right to do so on the decidedly dodgy moral (and even dodgier legal) grounds of giving fans access to live versions of songs that were often better than the studio performances offered by the record companies. In further defense of his position, he stated that Virgin had never manufactured bootlegs, but that they bought them from (unspecified) wholesalers at £2.00 a shot and that they only ever made between 25p and 50p per record[8]. Oh well, that's all right, then. Whilst we're at it, let's just remember that one of Richard Branson's Irish wolfhounds was called Bootleg, not that Virgin was rubbing it in, or anything.

Meanwhile, a new face, Chris Stylianou, joined as sales manager, but some of the names that crop up at Virgin during these early years had been around for quite a while. John Varnon, who dealt with promoting Virgin's shops and the mail–order side, had been assistant editor of *Student* and Max Handley, who had been deputy editor of *Student*, recorded an album at the Manor in sessions ranging from 1971 to 1974 (released on Virgin's Caroline subsidiary in 1974). Adverts for the album in the music press referred to Handley as "... one mad novelist".

One new name that cropped up in 1971 was Mike Oldfield – he and his sister, Sally, were at the Manor doing some backing recordings during the September. Whilst there, Tom Newman and Simon Hayworth got to hear the tape that Oldfield had been recording on a reel–to–reel tape recorder borrowed from ex–boss, Kevin Ayers. Newman played the tape to Simon Draper, who also liked what he heard. The record label was still in the planning stage and that Virgin would go ahead with the idea was still in doubt, but Draper took Oldfield's contact details in case.

By mid–1972 plans had firmed up and Richard Branson asked Simon Draper to head the planned record label for a 20% stake in a new company, Virgin Music, which was to be separate from the Virgin Records retail company. There was the slight problem, however, of finding artists to sign. Draper phoned Mike Oldfield to see if he'd had any luck with getting a recording contract. The answer was no, so Virgin got him down to record his album, liked the results and, according to Oldfield's autobiography, signed him *after* they'd released the album! No–one at Virgin knew what a recording contract should look like and they famously copied Sandy Denny's recent solo contract with Island.

It is, perhaps, fitting that an Island contract should have been used as the template for Virgin's first signing because Simon Draper considered Island to be the perfect blueprint on which to model the new label:

> In my view, Island were far and away the best record label in the world at the time and it was definitely the company we modeled ourselves on. I think that, at a certain point, Island became an entirely different sort of company and in the '80s we took off into another area and became a mainstream international competitor with the big corporate companies, but in the '70s we were more alike. I just don't think we did it as well as Island.[9]

It was also to Island that Virgin turned for a manufacturing and distribution deal, with EMI acting as co–distributor. The usual deal for a small company like Virgin was to entrust marketing and promotion to the manufacturing and distribution company, but Branson decided that, with a chain of shops around the country, Virgin could deal with the marketing and promotion side itself. This was a gamble, but one that, if Virgin was successful, would provide it with a much greater proportion of income per record sale. As Branson said, "Our gamble that we could promote [Tubular Bells] ourselves made us our first fortune."[10] This fortune went to pay off the various debts, including that for Customs and Excise, and also went towards increasing Virgin's roster.

The label was incorporated in September 1972, the latest in a spate of recent music–related companies to be spun–off under the Virgin umbrella. As *Music Week* reported: "... the Virgin label [is] the latest addition to a remarkable organisation embracing mail–order, managements agency, exporting, publishing, retailing and a recording studio complex, which is the brainchild of an equally remarkable man, Richard Branson ..."[11]

To promote the first releases on the new record label, Richard Branson sent out a press release to retailers in early May 1973, advising them of what was going on:

> You will probably have discovered by now from Music Week or your Island and EMI rep that we are about to launch our own independent label. Wethought that we would let you know clearly what will be happening with our label before you get snowed under by all the leaflets, brochures and general publicity that the reps will thrust upon you. Naturally we shall be doing our best to promote and publicise our records. As retailers ourselves ... we have often been painfully reminded that even the best publicised records are not fully backed by a grass roots sales service [but we] are confident that Island's excellent distribution, backed by EMI, will get you the records you want. [12]

As regards the record label, Richard Branson has described Simon Draper's development of an artist roster as his "building his own record collection"[13], but Draper has refuted this. His own current taste ran to American bands like Little Feat and The Band, but British bands just didn't make this type of music (even when they tried), so Draper used his knowledge of what sold well in the shops and by mail–order to sign similar artists to Virgin. His intimate knowledge of the level of import sales made by European groups such as Faust, Tangerine Dream, Gong and, a little later, Wigwam led him to either sign these outright to Virgin or to license them for the UK and other available territories. As Draper said:

> Richard had asked me to start this label without really knowing what I was going to do, no one else really questioned what I was up to. The direction to take initially was fairly clearly indicated by the demand we were getting through the retail and mail order company ...[14]

As the time approached for Virgin's first record releases, the price for records on the main V 2000 series was pegged in line with Island's ILPS LP series (currently £2.19), but Virgin also came up with a gimmick for the promotional push for their first LP releases in May 1973, which was to sell Faust's first album for the label at the price of a single, which was currently 48p. This marketing ploy worked very well and *Music Week*, a fortnight after the album's release, reported:

> Virgin Records claims that the Faust Tapes ... has already sold 40,000 copies in the first week [and is] is planning to press a further 40,000 to cope with the demand. The cut–price album will however be withdrawn before the release of the next full–price album from Faust in the autumn.[15]

However, someone somewhere hadn't done their sums properly and a fortnight later, *Music Week* reported the somewhat hasty deletion of the album in advance of the planned deletion:

> The Faust Tapes ... has proved so successful that Virgin is being forced to delete the item on June 20. Simon Draper, head of the label, told Music Week that although costs were being kept to a minimum, Virgin is losing about 2p on the sale of each copy of the LP. The album was originally released at a low price, Dreaper [sic] continued, as a publicity exercise ... but sales have far exceeded expectations ... according to Virgin, around 60,000 copies of the album have been sold this month and by July 20, sales are expected to reach the 100,000 mark. Rather than re–issue the LP at a normal full–price, it has been decided to delete it.[16]

The article went on to mention that Faust, "As part of an effort to keep down overheads ... agreed not to collect any royalties from sales of the LP."[17] – which was very nice of them. There seems to have been a certain amount of incredulity in the music press at the number of sales that Virgin claimed, if you read between the lines, though there is certainly evidence that the LP sold well enough to chart.

> The Faust Tapes ... currently at number 18 in the MM chart will be deleted on July 20. Reason? Well, it was too popular. At 48p a go, the album costs more to produce than the price it sells for. So, on 60,000 sales Virgin have already LOST £2,000. Such are the crazy economics of the business ... or so they say.[18]

Notwithstanding the fact that 60,000 multiplied by 2p comes to £1,200 and not £2,000, this didn't stop Virgin from trying the same trick again a little later with Gong's *Camembert Electrique*, but by this time they must have revisited their sums – besides singles had gone up by 11p at that point, presumably allowing Virgin to now make at least a few pence per copy. Talking of Faust and Gong, not to mention Mike Oldfield, Virgin promoted their releases with promotional appearances by all three artists:

> Promotion for [The Faust Tapes] is being backed up by a tour of the band making their first live appearance in this country ... The other Virgin albums are also being promoted. The whole of Tubular Bells, by Mike Oldfield, has been played on the John Peel Show and is being backed up by a star studied [sic] concert at Queen Elizabeth Hall on June 25. Gong, have been supplementing their current tour with performances at Virgin record shops to promote their album ...[19]

Not content with starting one label, Virgin also started another especially for budget offerings. Although nothing on the Virgin label proper could exactly be described as mainstream, Virgin created a separate outlet for various esoteric offerings for which they felt that they couldn't justify a full price tag. The name Caroline was already in use as Virgin's export company and was also used for the new budget imprint label.

Carolione Exports used a 'moonface' logo, first used in *Student* magazine, whilst the Caroline record label used a new – and extremely attractive – Roger Dean label design. The original C 1500 catalogue sequence sold at £1.49 per album, in line with Island's budget HELP series). Despite the low prices, intended to stimulate impulse puirchase, sales were often miniscule and many Caroline albums now represent the hardest to find of Virgin's early output. And thinking back to Faust's first album, if sales stood at 100,000 copies, why is it so bloody hard to find a copy[20]?

To return to Roger Dean, he had been introduced to Virgin in 1970 and his main task in the early years was to design the graphics for Virgin adverts in the music press. It was either late 1970 or early 1971 when he was asked to come up with a label design, even though there wasn't yet a record label. The importance of the overall image created by Dean for Virgin cannot be understated – and for those lucky enought to own a copy, a selection of Dean's early advertisement graphics, logos and labels can be viewed in his book, *Views*[21]. His record sleeve designs were becoming very well known thanks mainly to the success of Yes, with whom Dean had worked since 1971, and it was albums by progressive bands like Yes that sold in large numbers in Virgin's shops. The fact that Roger Dean's designs appeared on Virgin's product helped to position that product in the minds of progressive rock consumers. This was the era when the sleeve and label designs had become an important indicator of the sort of music contained on the record within and many records sold on spec based solely on the fact that they were on the Virgin label.

The mirrored girl idea was hit upon very early, although the design as used on the first Virgin label design bore slight resemblance to the original designs. Dean went on to create all of the label designs up until 1977, and even later label designs (mostly) incorporated a small mirrored girl logo. Even in 1979 the mirrored girl logo was used in trade advertisements in preference to the then current 'handwritten' logo. Of these various designs, Carla Capalbo and Dominy Hamilton, writing in Roger Dean's *Views*, said:

> Dean used the mirror–image repeatedly for Virgin; often the pictures were mirror–images, but sometimes they only appeared to be. All of the graphics were originally done in black and white. The first label ... to be used on a record was black and white, and it was not coloured until after the first few records came out. The design combines a photograph and a drawing ...[22]

Meanwhile, there was news of events on the recording side of Virgin's business as *Music Week* reported on the creation of a mobile studio, currently named "The Monster" but later to be better known "Manor Mobile":

> It was Phil Newell who had the idea of putting a mobile studio on the road but it took Richard Branson and the backing of Virgin records to transform Newell's idea of being a nomadic producer into a reality that included 24 tracks and the most ambitious mobile to date – built into a freightliner container that can be shipped abroad and placed on a satisfactory transporter anywhere in the world ... Branson was just launching the Virgin label and appreciat[ed] the problem of recording bands like Gong who are basically live acts, so he and Newell formed a joint company and put the studio together. Says Branson: "The other thing we are going to do is take the studio out to the artists [sic] houses where they can record on their own instruments in the comfort of their own homes.["] [23]

Newell, before he was enticed to The Manor, had been a studio engineer with Pye and was backed up by Alan Perkins, who had been running the Pye mobile for the past eighteen months. Indeed, The Monster had started life as the Pye mobile studio before Virgin bought it. It was later dismantled and set up at Mike Oldfield's Herefordshire house so that he could record what became *Ommadawn* in splendid isolation away from the hustle and bustle of life at the Manor.

In November 1973 there was some interesting and, as things turned out, old and slightly misleading news:

> WATT Records ... will have [its] debut releases in Britain distribute[d] by Island Records, though logo identification will be shared ... Wider distribution is being handled by the German firm ECM throughout continental Europe.[24]

First off, the first two WATT label records had already been released in either July or August (depending on which source you believe) on the joint Virgin/WATT label. Also, the listed distributor was Virgin, rather than Island, though in real terms this meant distribution via the Island/EMI set–up hence the confusion, no doubt. It's worth pointing out that there must have been some piggery jokery going on with the current Island/ECM link–up. At this point West German ECM product was distributed in the UK by Island/EMI, but in 1976 distribution moved to Virgin, which soon after switched its manufacturing and distribution deal from Island/EMI to CBS.

Meanwhile, back in 1973, not content with being a one–hit wonder (two, if you count *The Faust Tapes*' brief reign in the UK *Melody Maker* chart), Branson decided that it was time for Virgin to go international based on the UK success of *Tubular Bells*. He met with Atlantic's Ahmet Ertegun to organise a licence agreement for the US and Canada and Virgin even went as far as to open an office in Atlantic's New York headquarters. This was run by Annie Shand, who had previously handled licensing for Virgin in the UK. However, *Tubular Bells* was the only hit in the US, this after the music was used *The Exorcist*, and there was little success for any of the other US releases. Licensing deals were also set up in Europe via (mostly) Ariola, in Australia via Festival and in South Africa via Gallo.

On the performance side, there was yet another spin–off company, Virgin Concerts Ltd., whose managing director was Martin Cole – flyers for the 1973 Faust tour cited "Virgin Concerts and Martin Cole present" – with Richard Branson and Nik Powell listed as directors. This company organised, as one might expect from the name, concerts for Virgin artists as well as for similarly–left–field, non–Virgin artists, such as Magma, who had recorded at the Manor and for whom Virgin Concerts' Laurie Small booked Bristol's Colston Hall for 24 June 1974 for a booking fee of £225, of which a quarter was paid by Virgin Concerts up–front – by cheque, if you really need to know[25].

In August 1974 Simon Draper announced that Virgin was going to distribute Michael Mantler and Carla Bley's US Jazz Composer's Orchestra Association (JCOA) label in the UK. According to Draper, import sales of JCOA records via Virgin had been good, hence the cherry–picking of JCOA's back catalogue for full UK release along with the release of new product [26].

In the lead up to Christmas, Virgin began its largest promotional campaign to date and dabbled for the first time in television and radio advertising. They even went as far as hiring John Cleese to do the voice–overs [27]. However, by late 1974 it was dawning on Virgin that, despite a great deal of early success, they were still viewed very much as a 'one trick pony'. Simon Draper said:

> Our come–uppance came in the mid–'70s when we found that to survive we had to mature as a label and broaden our roster and somehow avoid disappearing down the blind alley of only pursuing one type of music, one direction, so we spent a lot of energy in '75 trying to sign credible rock

> acts – still sticking to our principles – we were still very idealistic. We definitely weren't about to completely surrender to commercialism...[28]

To make the jump to the 'big time' Virgin tried to sign the Rolling Stones, the Who, Pink Floyd and 10CC, but none of these attempts was successful. The Rolling Stones' manager went on to use the then vast amount ($4,000,000) that Virgin had managed to scrape together as leverage to gain an even bigger sum from the mainstream bidders. EMI finally won with a $5,000,000 bid. As Simon Draper later said:

> They were impressed by Richard's boldness in trying to make the big jump. And they were impressed by the fact that we could come up with the money, which Richard did by going 'round and tapping all of the licensees and trying to get a kind of co–operative thing going. But I don't think any of those bands really took us seriously, however, because in spite of Tangerine Dream [and] *Tubular Bells*, we were still really a very small company at that time.[29]

Meanwhile, technologically, things were, as always, moving fast and Virgin decided to update the studios at the Manor. The studio was eventually reopened on 1 August 1976.

> In 1975 it was decided to totally rebuild and re–equip the studio bringing in Westlake Audio for the design and a new 32 into 24 console was ordered from Helios. The wraparound Helios console frame also housed four Kepexes, two DBX companders, two UA compressors, two Teletronix LA3a, four A&D F760s, an Eventide Phaser Little Dipper notch filter and two Neve compressors ... The new Helios cost £50,000 and had the wrap around style to meet the symmetrical requirement of the Westlake room. It was a 32 into 24, with 4 band eq (with variable Q) [with] 2 EMT plates, 2 Master Room reverbs and all Ampex tape machines. [30]

In late 1975, Virgin began co–distributing the small, independent Atra reggae label. Previously, Atra seems to have distributed its own product and it is possible that Virgin's co–distribution only went as far as album releases. This deal would have remained as a footnote were it not for the fact that Atra's owners hired a 'heavy' and went, on the night of 1 March 1976, to Richard Branson's home, where they pulled him out of bed and beat him up. During this the two Clarke brothers, who owned Atra, demanded that Branson paid them £5,000. Branson went to the police, who set up a sting operation with Branson's co–operation and arrested the brothers. In court, Council had said that "... there was a dispute between Atra which claimed it was owed £1,000 and Virgin, which agreed to only £320 of that sum." [31]

In early 1976, not having been put off distribution deals by Branson's recent ordeal, Virgin signed a deal with the German ECM and JAPO labels to distribute their West German–manufactured albums in the UK. This certainly brought in some welcome cash but, even more so than Virgin, these two labels were selling to a very narrow, niche, modern jazz market. Virgin was also, at this point, still co–running Mike Mantler and Carla Bley's WATT label in the UK but, after a handful of new releases in 1976, further WATT product ceased to be issued, other than as imports via ECM, that is.

By mid–1976, Ken Berry, who had joined as a clerk, had progressed to Virgin's 'inner sanctum'. He broke the news that most of Virgin's artists were losing them money and that the whole company was basically being bank–rolled by Mike Oldfield and Tangerine Dream. The hard reality was that Virgin had to make some decisions as to which artists to keep and which to drop, whilst the hunt went on for profitable new artists.

There were other changes afoot in August 1976. The manufacturing and distribution deal with Island/EMI, which had been in place since the beginning, was superceded by a new deal with CBS. Richard Branson said, "We have had a good relationship with Island, but have reached a situation where we were being competitive with each other,"[32] which may have been a contributing factor to the change, but the main reason was that Virgin had signed a new sales deal with Anchor Records and the switch to CBS had been one of the conditions:

> Long predicted, but regarded as being idealistic rather than viable, an alliance of independent labels in a joint sales operation took a significant step towards reality this week. Virgin ... has signed a new deal which gives CBS manufacturing and distribution rights – and Anchor total sales responsibility. At this stage, stressed Anchor managing director Ian Ralfini, the deal with Virgin merely gives the British independent the use of Anchor's sales team, over which the American–owned company retains control ... "The addition of the Virgin repertoire will give our sales force additional credibility with the dealers and the only stipulation I made was that the distribution and manufacture should be through CBS, which handles Anchor product. Any other arrangement would have been far too complicated ...["] said Ralfini.[33]

CBS began manufacturing and distributing Virgin product on 1 September and this arrangement continued well into the 1980s. The sales side, however, wasn't quite so successful and in January 1977 *Music Week* announced that the arrangement with Anchor was to come to an end in the March. When asked by *Music Week* if Anchor had done a good job, Richard Branson remained enigmatic – "Anchor has a certain way of doing things, Virgin has a certain way of doing things ..."[34] which, given the circumstances, presumably meant no. Virgin's way of doing things was soon formalised by the setting up of their own sales team:

> Virgin Records is to launch its own national sales force on March 1 and has cancelled plans to go into a sales partnership with Anchor, with which it has had a sales agreement since August. The news coincides with reports that the company is now seriously considering taking on established acts. Handling Virgin, Caroline, ECM and Oval product, the new team will report to marketing manager Darrol Edwards and sales manager Ann Green ... Virgin's arrangement with Anchor ... was made last August, since which Virgin have paid a service fee for Anchor's work ...[35]

Ann Green was soon to be the subject of an in–depth article in *Music Week*, based on the fact that she was, at this point, the first ever female UK record company sales manager[36]. And just in case any randy record retailers liked the look of what they saw in the accompanying photo, the article went on quash any hopes in that direction by pointing out that Miss Green was getting married in the near future.

Meanwhile, the process of signing potentially lucrative new artists went on. 1977 was the year that Virgin failed to sign Dire Straits, who chose Phonogram instead, and, if stories are true, turned down The Police, other than for a publishing deal. Earlier in the year, however, Virgin had gained overnight notoriety when they signed the Sex Pistols after both EMI and A&M had signed and, almost immediately, dropped the band. This certainly represented a new image for Virgin, and the publicity potential of signing such a notorious group was not lost on the company. Simon Draper had the following to say about the Sex Pistols:

> I went to see the Sex Pistols and really didn't like it at all. I was very against signing them, which we could have done because Malcolm McLaren offered them to me straightaway. What a mistake, eh? A few weeks later, I heard 'Anarchy in the U.K.[',] which was clearly an absolute classic, and obviously deeply regretted not having signed them the first time around.[37]

Richard Branson, probably with a great deal of truth behind the jocular comment, remarked, "However other record companies might protest, I think practically everyone in the UK would have liked to sign the Sex Pistols.["][38].

1977 was also the year that Virgin started to put out singles in much larger quantities than hitherto. The company recognised that the music scene in the UK was changing, with a groundswell of punk bands taking a DIY approach to record making. This coincided with a general downturn in the record industry. It was getting harder to sell large quantities of albums so Virgin started to sign bands that could give them hit singles and a series of welcome short–term cash injections.

Meanwhile, things were happening on the Caroline export front. The handful of reggae artists that Virgin had signed between 1975 and 1977 began to clock up big export sales in Nigeria. In Africa it seems that anyone could set up as a record retailer and Caroline's main customer in Nigeria imported fridges for his 'day job'. To satisfy this new market more reggae artists were signed in almost industrial quantities. The records were released on Virgin's new Front Line label imprint – as Simon Draper said:

> We started to get huge orders from Nigeria ... so that's when Richard went off on his trip to Jamaica with suitcases stuffed with money, to sign as many reggae artists as possible. Then we started the Front Line label ... so that it didn't flood Virgin. We had acres of it, and in the end we were chartering jumbo jets to take all these records out to Nigeria. All that seemed to stop. It was: a) maybe the market was being flooded; and, perhaps more to the point, b) there was a military coup, and they stopped all imports.[39]

Notice of the setting up of the Front Line label appeared in *Music Week* in February 1978 under the heading of "Virgin puts reggae in the Front Line"[40]. Many Front Line albums were manufactured in Nigeria for the local market, and the arrangement that Virgin came to about these Nigerian–manufactured records has led to much confusion for collectors over the intervening thirty–odd years. The label has lots of gaps in its main FL 1000 catalogue number sequence and for years it was assumed that the gaps related to records that were planned but not issued. However, research for this discography discovered that most, if not all, of the 'unused' numbers were assigned to reggae records that had been released previously in the UK on the Virgin label proper. These records were manufactured in, and only made available in, Nigeria on Front Line. Sadly, only one catalogue number has been confirmed.

To return to Caroline Exports at this point, in the early years turnover had been fairly low and sales were easily handled by a staff of two but, by 1978, Chris Stylianou was running the company with a staff of thirty and turnover had increased to around £12m, about a quarter of which came from Virgin's own product. Most export sales were accounted for by the US, Africa, Australia, Japan and other more far–flung territories. Europe, for the most part, was excluded from Caroline's operations because there was too much in the way of competition to make the effort financially worthwhile. As regards what sold where – Nigeria's previously mentioned penchent for Jamaican toasters aside – Japan and Australia were very interested in punk imports, whilst Morocco, it seems, was importing Peter Frampton LPs in silly quantities[41]. Lucky Morocco.

By the end of 1978 Virgin consisted of various core companies: the record shops were run by Nik Powell , the record company was run by Simon Draper and Ken Berry, the music publishing company was run by Carol Wilson and there was also the recording studio at the Manor. Apart from these, Virgin had recently set up a new London–based studio, The Town House Studios, and in October opened The Venue, in Victoria Street, though this latter venture was not necessarily successful and it had been closed by the mid–1980s. Richard Branson had also bought a pub frequented by Virgin's staff, but this too is featured amongst the small number of Virgin's unsuccessful entrepreneurial episodes. Also, in August 1979, Virgin acquired Eddy Grant's Ice label from under the noses of WEA.

As regards Carol Wilson at Virgin Music, change was in the air. In late August 1979 *Music Week* got hold of the news that Virgin was setting up a new record label and a new music publishing company, named DinDisc and DinSong respectively. By the following week they had hold of some firm information:

> ... Virgin has formed Dindisc and Dinsong as a means of continuing the expansion of the company's interests without overloading the existing companies ... The new companies have arisen from Virgin's music publishing operation and Carol Wilson – head of Virgin Music – is managing director. She heads an executive staff of four which comprises Nicki Davies – previously London promotions manager Island Records – as marketing manager, Donna Thompson – from Virgin Music – as promotions manager, Dave Fudger – also from Virgin Music – as A&R manager, and Eugene Manzi – previously of Berserkely – as press officer. Nick Garnett who was professional manager at Virgin Music becomes general manager of the new publishing company Dinsong, while Rob Gold, former managing director of Logo Music, will replace Carol Wilson as managing director of Virgin Music ... Retail outlets in the UK will be serviced by the Virgin salesforce and distribution is through CBS. Dindisc will be handled in the US by Virgin's Independent operation and worldwide by Virgin's licensees ...[42]

The two new companies were run from Vernon Yard and the plan was to move them around the corner, to 61–63 Portobello Road, W11, near the end of September[43]. Despite the optimism as regards US distribution, Virgin America, which had been set up in 1978, in New York, closed its office soon after the above announcement.

With a noticeable increase in output in terms of both singles and albums Virgin's sales team was increased during mid–1979. The team moved into the limelight several times at the tail end of 1979, firstly because of its involvement in *Music Week's* Record

Dealer Tour and secondly because of what looks like some amusing non–communication within Virgin's press and publicity team. Of the Dealer Tour, the following was said:

> The industry's smallest and most feminine, and one of its most effective sales managers Ann Kelly will be at every venue, with her assistants Hilary Routledge, Belinda Hillier, and Bron Palmer. Tele–sales girl Veronica Hopkins, area managers Mike Lawrence and Des Fraser, and members of Virgin's recently enlarged sales force will be on hand at some of the dates. As well as promoting the established acts ... Virgin will be talking about new signings ... plus the newly–acquired Ice label ...[44]

Two weeks later Ann Kelly – Ann Green as was – got another namecheck when *Music Week* announced a hook–up between Virgin and Stiff's sales teams:

> Independent companies Stiff and Virgin have formed a joint sales force. In future Stiff product will be sold in and serviced to UK retail outlets by the 14 strong Virgin sales team, which will continue to report to head of sales Ann Kelly who will remain based at Virgin. Stiff will continue to be distributed by Island but will no longer be sold by the EMI sales team. Commenting on the deal Ann Kelly says: "It seems only natural that the country's two most energetic and successful indies should enter into a mutually benficial arrangement."[45]

This however, provoked an interesting response from Al Clark, Virgin's director of press and publicity, and an equally interesting rejoinder from *Music Week's* editor. The following from Clark:

> The Virgin/Stiff sales team, to which you referred two weeks ago as "recently formed", has been in existence for over two years as the Virgin sales team. The fact that Stiff is now paying good money to use this prodigious aggregation of experienced unit–shifters does not mean that its formation is either recent, or indeed prompted solely by the nation's need for more Jona Lewi albums.[46]

*Music Week's* rejoinder was, "... Funny, we could have sworn that we were sent a press release announcing a "new joint Virgin/Stiff sales team"." Could it be a coincidence that the following edition of *Music Week* included a vacancy at Virgin for "an enthusiastic ... sales representative"? Had someone been fired for sending misleading press releases? Had there been the unmistakable whiff of cordite as someone took the honourable way out? Well no, the vacancy was for someone to sell Virgin singles in Scotland. Interested parties were requested to phone Hilary on 01–727–8070 and were informed that the post came with a good rate of pay, performance–based bonuses and a company car or van.

Despite the last year of the old decade seeing Virgin expanding its sales team, buying, or otherwise spinning off, new companies and, in Oxford Street, on June 30, opening the largest record shop in Europe[47], bad financial news was a near constant companion. The various acquisitions and expansions of the last year or so fitted well with Richard Branson's oft–quoted preference for expanding out of a crisis rather than retrenching, but nothing could hide the fact that, during 1979 especially, interest rates soared and there was a major downturn in sales across the entire record industry.

The recession bit deeper and Virgin started the 1980s with backs against the wall and the very real threat of a major pre–tax loss ... and on this cliffhanger we have to end because we have left the 1970s behind. At the start of the new decade it was Phil Collins, Gillan and Japan, amongst others, to the rescue – but that's another story, and one that I'll leave to someone else.

## Section sources and endnotes

1. Branson, R. 1998. *Losing My Virginity*, London, Virgin, p.43.
2. Ibid, p.57.
3. Ibid, p.79.
4. No author attributed. 1973. Richard Branson and the virgins which came up trumps. *Music Week*, 18 August 1973, p.15.
5. *Losing My Virginity*, op. cit., p.76.
6. Partridge, R. 1971. U.K. Raid on Tax Dodgers/U.K. Hitting On Evasion of Export Tapes. *Billboard*, 31 July 1971, p.1 and p.45.
7. No author attributed. 1973. Richard Branson and the virgins which came up trumps. *Music Week*, 18 August 1973, p.15.
8. Ibid.
9. Southern, T. (1995) *Virgin: A History of Virgin Records*. A Publishing Company, Axminster, p.242.
10. *Losing My Virginity*, op. cit., p.131.
11. Richard Branson and the virgins which came up trumps, op. cit.
12. Branson, R. May 1973. RE: Label launch. Press release to retailers.
13. *Virgin: a history of Virgin Records*, op. cit., p.20.
14. *Virgin: a history of Virgin Records*, op. cit., p.9.
15. No author attributed. 1973. Virgin success. *Music Week*, 9 June 1973, p.3.
16. No author attributed. 1973. Faust LP deletion. *Music Week*, 20 June 1973, p.2.
17. Ibid.
18. The Raver. 1973. Del LP that was TOO Popular. *Melody Maker*, July 1973, Page and exact date unknown – from clipping.
19. No author attributed. 1973. Virgin success. *Music Week*, 9 June 1973, p.3.
20. My first copy was given to me in the late 1970s by Jane Hanney, a schoolfriend who lived around the corner and along a bit, who had been given it by an ex–boyfriend. She gave it to me on the condition that she never saw or heard it again. Can't think why – great little album!
21. Dean, R. 1975. *Views*, London, Dragon's Dream.
22. Ibid, p.85.
23. No author attributed. 1973. Virgin on the move. *Music Week*, 28 July 1973, p.SSII.
24. No author attributed. 1973. Watt's first releases distributed by Island. *Music Week*, 24 November 1973, p.3.
25. Small, L. 19 April 1974. RE: Hiring agreement to Colston Hall, Bristol, for 'Magma'. Letter to Muir, R. W.
26. No author attributed. 1974. Virgin to distribute JCOA jazz label - releases soon. *Music Week*, 31 August 1974, p.3.
27. No author attributed. 1974. Virgin tele-push hinge on Oldfield. *Music Week*, 14 December 1974, p.1.
28. *Virgin: a history of Virgin Records*,op. cit., p.242.
29. Ibid, p.245.
30. Burns, P. & Harris, T. 2011. The Manor Studios [Online]. Available: http://www.philsbook.com/manor.html [Accessed 6 July 2013].
31. No author attributed. 1977. Virgin's Branson assaulted. *Music Week*, 22 October 1977, p.4.
32. Brian Mulligan. 1976. Virgin-Anchor tie-up brings independents sales alliance nearer. *Music Week*, 21 August 1976, p.1.
33. Ibid.
34. Hayward, J. 1977. Virgin plans sales force. *Music Week*, 29 January 1977, p.1.
35. Ibid.
36. Hayward, J. 1977. Ann Green: sales manager on Virgin territory. *Music Week*, 26 February 1977, p.26.
37. *Virgin: a history of Virgin Records*, op. cit., p.245.
38. Hayward, J. 1977. Virgin broadside for Sex Pistols. *Music Week*, 21 May 1977, p.1.
39. *Virgin: a history of Virgin Records*, op. cit., p.74.
40. No author attributed. 1978. Virgin puts reggae in the Front Line. *Music Week*, 4 February 1978, p.3.
41. No author attributed. 1978. Expansion Plans Reign in Export/Import. *Billboard*, 25 March 1978, p.UK-8. Note that Chris Stylianou's name is miscredited as "Spirianou" in the article.
42. No author attributed. 1979. Virgin's Dindisc venture. *Music Week*, 1 September 1979, p.2.

43. Ibid.
44. No author attributed. 1979. Music Week Record Dealer Tour '79 Supplement: Into the Eighties! Virgin. *Music Week*, 22 September 1979.
45. No author attributed. 1979. Virgin and Stiff form joint sales team. *Music Week*, 6 October 1979, p.4.
46. No author attributed. 1979. Stiff reproach. Music Week, 10 November 1979, p.50.
47. Anderson, T. 1979. Virgin to open superstore. *Music Week*, 9 June 1979, p.1.

# Discographies

In a previous book in *The Great British Record Label* series – the Transacord one, I think – I compared compiling a discography to putting together a giant, complicated jigsaw, where various key pieces are missing and where some of the pieces turn out to be from different jigsaws. I see no reason to alter this comparison – if anything this current discography was even more so thanks to Virgin's propensity for not bothering to advise trade publications of whole swathes of releases. Therefore, the research net had to widen, which threw up a lot more anomalies than usual. Have fun spotting them.

## Sources used in the discography

[1] *The New Records* (published monthly)
[2] *The New Cassettes and Cartridges/The New Cassettes* (published monthly)
[3] *The New Singles* (published weekly)
[4] *Music Master 1976* (2nd edition)
[5] *Music Master 1979* (5th edition)
[6] *Music Master 1984* (10th edition)
[7] *Music Master 1985* (11th edition)
[8] *Music Master British Pop Singles 1975–84: Title Index* (1st edition)
[9] *Music Master Labels List '89* (9th edition)
[10] *Music Master Singles Catalogue* (3rd edition)
[11] *Music Week* (published weekly)
[12] *Melody Maker* (published weekly)
[13] *New Musical Express* (published weekly)
[14] *Record Mirror* (published weekly)
[15] Virgin sticker including RRP (or RRP printed directly on sleeve)
[16] Promotional materials (specified in the accompanying notes)
[17] *Cassettes and Cartridges* (published monthly)
[18] *The Pop Singles* (published quarterly
[19] *Budget Records* (published quarterly)

The first three sources above, along with *Budget Records*, were published by Francis Antony, whilst the *Music Master* series was published by John Humphries. Each source is represented in the listings by superscript numbers: e.g. **Rel:** Apr 1975[1] indicates that the release was advised in the April 1974 edition of *The New Records*.

## Release and deletion dates

If only the year of release is shown, this is as listed on record labels. Release dates are sourced, where possible, from contemporary trade publications, *The New Records* and *The New Cassettes/The New Cassettes and Cartridges*, which were issued monthly, and *The New Singles*, which was issued weekly, plus relevant *Music Master* publications, which were published annually. *Music Master 1976* includes details for LPs only, whilst subsequent editions include listings of all formats, including tape versions. Dates sourced from *The New Records* and *The New Cassettes/The New Cassettes and Cartridges* tend to be a month out. This is because both publications were issued mid–month so, for example, an April release would generally be notified in March, by which time the April edition would have gone to publication, so the listing would appear in the May edition instead – which came out mid–April! Wherever there is a discrepency in release date between different publications, all conflicting sources are listed.

Deletion dates are sourced from *Music Master 1976* (deletions advised between 1973 and the end of 1975), *Music Master 1979* (deletions advised up to the end of 1978), and *Music Master 1984* (deletions advised up to the end of 1983).

## Recommended retail price

Prices for LPs and tapes are sourced from *The New Records*, *The New Cassettes/The New Cassettes and Cartridges* and the *Music Master* publications. Generally, the prices shown in *The New Records* and *The New Cassettes/The New Cassettes and Cartridges* are correct and so these are used as the main source. *Music Master* prices are shown only where no other price source was available or where it differs from that in *The New Records* et al.

One interesting point to note is that prices sourced from adverts in music papers, such as *Melody Maker*, are a few pence lower than listed in trade publications or shown on generic Virgin price stickers. Possibly these represent the price if buying the record in a Virgin shop. Also, Virgin's own adverts listed a second, much lower price, for buying from their mail–order arm: for example, the *Melody Maker* for 16 November, 1974 lists V 2000 series LPs (and the lone QV 2000 LP) at £1.95 (RRP £2.45), VC 500 series LPs at 55p (RRP 59p), VD 2500 series double LPs at £2.35 (RRP £2.99) and VS 100 series singles at 45p (RRP 48p). As regards Caroline, the C 1500 series LPs are listed at £1.35 (RRP £1.49) and CA 2000 series LPs at £1.65 (RRP £1.99).

## Original label design

The list below shows acronyms used in the discography. Labels not listed – such as Caroline, WATT, JCOA, Oval, Ice and Dindisc – either did not change over time or, if the design did change, individual records did not appear on more than one design.

**V1** – Girl and dragon (black and white) – LP (1973) and 7" single (1973 to 1976)
**V2** – Girl and dragon (colour) – LP only (1974 to 1975 and 1975 to 1976)
**V3** – Mirrored girl (beige with white rim) – LP only (1975)
**V4** – Mirrored girl (red with white rim) – LP only (1976)
**V5** – Mirrored girl (green with white rim) – LP only (1976)
**V6** – Mirrored girl (red without white rim) – LP and 12" single (1976)
**V7** – Mirrored girl (green without white rim) – LP and 12" single (1976 to 1978)
**V8** – Mirrored girl (blue) – 7" single only (1976)
**V9** – Blue with 'neon' flash – LP, 7" and 12" singles (1977)
**V10** – Green (side 1) and red (side 2) – LP, 7" and 12" singles (1978 onward)
**V11** – Grey and white, variation of V10 – 7" single only (Devo)
**V12** – White and red, variation of V10 – 7" single only (Skids)
**V13** – White and blue, variation of V10 – 7" and 12" single (Oldfield)
**CUS** – Custom – LP, 7" and 12" singles (mostly late 1970s)
**PRO** – Yellow with red rim – 12" promotional 'disco' singles (1975)
**FL1** – Front Line (fist and barbed wire) – LP, 7" and 12" single (1978 to 1979)
**FL2** – Front Line (yellow) – LP, 7" and 12" single (1979)

## Tape releases

Sadly, Virgin seems, on various occasions, to have been reluctant to inform trade publications when they issued tape versions of albums (even more so than with LPs and singles). Some early tapes have a July 1974 release date in the listings even though they are known to have been issued earlier, but this listing in *Cassettes and Cartridges* appears to be the only notification there is. In fact the July 1974 date represented a change from Island to Virgin distribution – see below for further details on this – hence all currently available product was repromoted along with newly–available tapes at this point.

There are a few anomalies, in that some early albums are listed in *Cassettes and Cartridges* as being released on both cassette and cartridge, when it is almost certain that only cassette versions were issued. The fact that *Cassettes and Cartridges* later relisted these with no mention of 8–track version would suggest that the original listing was down to the erroneous assumption that where tape versions were issued, these appeared on both formats. Not so, with Virgin, and it is clear that each album release was assessed for tape sales viability first and then the decision was taken whether to issue on tape, and if so, on which format or formats. In some cases, later in the 1970s, cassette versions seem to have been issued sometimes a year or so after the original album release – and, of course, Virgin doesn't seem to have bothered telling anyone. In many instances, the only way to confirm whether a particlar album was issued on tape is down to finding a copy – and even then it might first have been issued in this format in the 1980s.

No tape versions were released for Caroline, JCOA or Oval labels, whilst only two WATT and one Front Line albums had cassette versions released.

Early tapes were listed in *Cassettes and Cartridges* as being distributed by Island. This credit was changed to Virgin by the time the July 1974 edition came out, which probably represents the move, as regards 8–track versions, from hard plastic case outers with wraparound inlay to card slipcase outers. Where RRP for tape versions up to July 1974 state a probable price, e.g. **RRP:** prob. £2.65, then this represents the current Island price, as listed in *The New Cassettes and Cartridges*, based on the assumption that tape versions were pegged in line with Island prices as were LPs.

## Discography structure

The listings concentrate on one record label at a time, listed in chronological order of first release on each label. Within each label section LP catalogue sequences are listed first – single LP sequences followed by 2–LP sequences, etc., with LPs on one–off catalogue numbers (including multi–LP sets) rounded up at the end. Following this come the various 7" and 12" single catalogue sequences. The Virgin section finishes up with promotional–only records of all formats. Apart from these promotional releases or one–off catalogue numbers individual catalogue sequences are listed in chronological order of first release where possible – though this gets difficult from the very start because both the first V 1000 and VC 500 sequence LPs were issued the same day. Still, there were three V 1000 sequence LPs to one VC 500 sequence LP, so VC 500 LPs come second!

Only artist, title, release/deletion and RRP details (if known) are listed in the ECM and JAPO label section because these records were not UK pressings and were only distributed in the UK by Virgin. In fact for a while I hemmed and hawed about including any details whatsoever, but decided that these records should be included, if only in summary form, because UK trade releases regularly listed these as Virgin UK releases.

# Virgin

## V 2000 series LPs

The V 2000 sequence, when first introduced, had its RRP pegged to Island's main ILPS sequence. As the years went on. however, new releases often had a lower price to stimulate sales, which explains some of the fluctuations in the listings. The sequence is fairly straightforward with only one or two variations, such as the odd quadraphonic release or free bonus record. Of more interest are the gaps where no record was issued.

One cause of confusion relates to what constitutes the original label design for certain records because a short–term change in 1975 to the beige, mirrored girl design and subsequent reversion to the previous design has made a few things uncertain, such as what represents an original copy of *Ommadawn*. Research for this book shows that, against the belief of many Virgin collectors, beige label copies represent the original press of *Ommadawn*. However, the later coloured girl and dragon version is harder to find and commands a higher price tag.This raises an interesting issue. Collectors usually spend their time seeking out original copies of records but, with Virgin, several repressings command a higher value than the original release, such as blue 'neon' label design copies of *Ommadawn* and *Boxed* and red, mirrored girl label copies of *Hatfield and the North*. The nice (or, depending on your point of view, most annoying) thing for Virgin collectors is that, what with so many changes of label design between 1975 and 1977, some very nice variations turn up when you least expect them – red, mirrored girl label copy of *Tubular Bells*, anybody? No, I've never seen one either, but you never know.

---

***V 2001*** ***MIKE OLDFIELD: Tubular Bells***

| | | |
|---|---|---|
| 1. Side One | 1. Side Two | **Label:** V1 |
| | | **Rel:** 25 May '73[16] |
| | | **RRP:** £2.19[4] |

| | | |
|---|---|---|
| **Cassette:** TCV 2001 | **Rel:** Jul 1974[17] | **RRP:** prob. £2.65 |
| **8–track:** 8X V2001 | **Rel:** Jul 1974[17] | **RRP:** prob. £2.65 |

Original and early V2 label copies came in a gloss, laminated sleeve with "13 Notting Hill Gate" credit. Later matt sleeves included the amended "119 Portabello Road" credit. Fairly rare copies exist on the beige mirrored girl label design and there is one stupidly rare oddity: normal stereo copies (with matrix numbers "A–16U"/"B–15U") appeared on the white–rimmed, green mirrored girl label design but with quadraphonic credits on the labels. These sell for silly amounts. Two one–sided white label test pressings are known to exist. *A* Virgin promotional handout for retailers states a release date of 25 May. The original cassette issue had white labels with black overprinting. The original 8–track version came in clear hard plastic cover with wraparound inlay. Release date above for tape versions represents a repromotion date with probable RRP as at repromotion.

An SQ Quad version with model aeroplane engine noise added was issued in 1975 (QV 2001) and a different Quad mix with different version of *The Sailor's Hornpipe* section, was released in the *Boxed* 4–LP set (VBOX 1). Two versions were issued on picture disc (VP 2001): one version seems to be a stereo mix of the original 1975 SQ Quad release complete with model aeroplane engine noise and the other seems to be the normal stereo mix without aeroplane noise.

---

***V 2002*** ***GONG: Radio Gnome Invisible Part 1 Flying Teapot***

| | | |
|---|---|---|
| 1. Radio Gnome Invisible | 1. The Pot Head Pixies | **Label:** V1 |
| 2. Flying Teapot | 2. The Octave Doctors And The Crystal Machine | **Rel:** 25 May '73[16] |
| | 3. Zero the Hero And The Witch's Spell | **RRP:** £2.19[4] |
| | 4. Witch's Song/I Am Your Pussy | |

| | | |
|---|---|---|
| **Cassette:** TCV 2002 | **Rel:** Jul 1974[17] | **RRP:** prob. £2.65 |

***V 2003*** ***STEVE YORK'S CAMELO PARDALIS: Manor Live***

1. See The Light
2. Keep On
3. Hey God
4. Full Time Love
5. Black Note Meets White Note
6. Trouble, Trouble

1. Male Chauvinist Pig Song
2. Slidin' Sideways
3. Women's Lib Song
4. I'll Be Home
5. Do What You Feel

**Label:** V1
**Rel:** 25 May '73[16]
**RRP:** £2.19[4]

---

***V 2004*** ***FAUST: Faust IV***

1. Krautrock
2. The Sad Skinhead
3. Jennifer

1. Just A Second
2. Picnic On A Frozen River, Deuxieme Tableau
3. Giggy Smile
4. Läuft ... Heisst Das Es Läuft Oder Es Kommt Bald ... Läuft
5. It's A Bit Of A Pain

**Label:** V1
**Rel:** 21 Sep' 73[13]
**RRP:** £2.19[4]

**Cassette:** TCV 2004 **Rel:** Nov 1973[17] **RRP:** not advised
**8–track:** 8XV 2004 **Rel:** Nov 1973[17] **RRP:** not advised
The original 8–track version came in clear, hard plastic cover with a wraparound inlay.

---

***V 2005*** ***HENRY COW: The Henry Cow Legend***

1. Nirvana For Mice
2. Amygdala
3. Teenbeat Introduction
4. Teenbeat

1. Extract From 'With The Yellow Half–Moon And Blue Star'
2. Teenbeat Reprise
3. The Tenth Chaffinch
4. Nine Funerals Of The Citizen King

**Label:** V1
**Rel:** Oct 1973[1]
**RRP:** £2.19[1]

**Cassette:** TCV 2005 **Rel:** Nov 1973[17] **RRP:** not advised
**8–track:** 8XV 2005 **Rel:** Nov 1973[17] (may not exist – see below)
No title on labels or front/back of sleeve. Title above from sleeve spine. An advert for Faust and Henry Cow's new LPs in the *NME* (date unknown) gives the Faust release date as 21 September and says the Henry Cow LP is already available. Cassette only relisted with July 1974 issue of *Cassettes and Cartridges*, which squares with Virgin's 1975 catalogue not mentioning an 8–track issue.

---

***V 2006*** ***LINK WRAY: Beans And Fatback***

1. Beans And Fatback
2. I'm So Glad
3. Shawnee Tribe
4. Hobo Man
5. Georgia Pines
6. Alabama Electric Circus

1. Water Boy
2. From Tulsa To North Caroline
3. Right Or Wrong (You Lose)
4. In The Pines
5. Take My Hand (Precious Lord)

**Label:** V1
**Rel:** 1973
**RRP:** £2.45[4]
**Del** 1977[5]

**Cassette:** TCV 2005 **Rel:** Nov 1973[17] **RRP:** not advised
**8–track:** 8XV 2006 **Rel:** Nov 1973[17] (may not exist – see below)
The segue of *Beans and Fatback* and *I'm So Glad* from this LP was later issued on the *Dead On Arrival* compilation (VD 2508) credited as "I'm So Glad I'm So Proud". The July 1974 edition of *Cassettes and Cartridges* only lists a cassette version of this album.

---

***V 2007*** ***GONG: Radio Gnome 2 Angels Egg***

1. Other Side Of The Sky
2. Sold To The Highest Buddha
3. Castle In The Clouds
4. Prostitute Poem
5. Givin My Luv To You
6. Selene

1. Flute Salad
2. Oily Way
3. Outer Temple
4. Inner Temple
5. Percolations
6. Love Is How Y Make It
7. I Niver Glid Before
8. Eat That Phone Book Coda

**Label:** V1
**Rel:** 1973
**RRP:** £2.19[4]

**Cassette:** TCV 2007 **Rel:** Jul 1974[17] **RRP:** prob. £2.65

Early copies included a booklet that documented Zero the Hero's adventures to date. Beware of facsimiles from the Gong Appreciation Society in the early 1990s. Original copies also included a sticker on the front of the sleeve to cover a certain piece of female anatomy. The sticker said "i am an angel's egg RIP ME OFF HERE". Sadly, for completist collectors, most people did.

---

### *V 2008 HATFIELD AND THE NORTH: Hatfield And The North*

| | | |
|---|---|---|
| 1. The Stubbs Effect | 1. Fol De Rol | **Label:** V2 |
| 2. Big Jobs (Poo Poo Extract) | 2. Shaving Is Boring | **Rel:** Apr 1974[11] |
| 3. Going Up To People And Tinklling | 3. Licks For The Ladies | **RRP:** £2.30[4] |
| 4. Calyx | 4. Bossa Nochance | |
| 5. Son Of "There's No Place Like Homerton" | 5. Big Jobs No. 2 (By Poo And The Wee Wees) | |
| | 6. Lobster In Cleavage Probe | |
| 6. Aigrette | 7. Gigantic Land–Crabs In Earth Takeover Bid | |
| 7. Rifferama | 8. The Other Stubbs Effect | |

**Cassette:** TCV 2008 **Rel:** Jul 1974[17] **RRP:** prob. £2.65
**8–track:** 8XV 2008 **Rel:** (may not exist – see below)

Various sources state that original copies exist on the first label design, but the date of issue would suggest not (the LP was released in 1974 despite the 1973 publication date on labels) and that second label copies represent the original release. A small number of copies were issued on the later red mirrored girl label design and these are very rare. 8–track version listed in *Music Master 1979* but not in *Cassettes and Cartridges* or other contemporary trade listings.

This is, perhaps, the definitive early Virgin album, with exemplary musicianship and quirky time signatures, all underpinned by Richard Sinclair's very English vocals – the Canterbury Scene's Bud Flanagan (to Kevin Ayers' Chesney Allen) perhaps.

---

### *V 2009 CHILI CHARLES: Busy Corner*

| | | |
|---|---|---|
| 1. Busy Corner | 1. Country Slicker | **Label:** V2 |
| 2. High School | 2. Speedy Jones | **Rel:** Apr[11]/May'74[1] |
| 3. Sunrise! | 3. Five | **RRP:** £2.30[1] |
| 4. The World Just Keep Us Turning On | 4. City Slicker | **del** 1977[5] |

**Cassette:** TCV 2009 **Rel:** Jul 1974[17] **RRP:** prob. £2.65

---

### *V 2010 TANGERINE DREAM: Phaedra*

| | | |
|---|---|---|
| 1. Phaedra | 1. Mysterious Semblance At The Strand Of Nightmares | **Label:** V2 |
| | | **Rel:** Apr 1974[11] |
| | 2. Movements Of A Visionary | **RRP:** £2.30[4] |
| | 3. Sequent C | |

**Cassette:** TCV 2010 **Rel:** Jul 1974[17] **RRP:** prob. £2.65
**8–track:** 8XV 2010 **Rel:** Jul 1974[17] **RRP:** prob. £2.65

Some copies with A–1U/B–2U matrix numbers had the catalogue number misprinted in the top, left–hand corner of the front of the gatefold sleeve instead of on the rear. These are extremely rare and tend to sell for quite a lot. A different LP, recorded August 1973 at Skyline Studio, Berlin, was almost issued as Tangerine Dream's first Virgin album. However, the group came over to the UK and recorded what became *Phaedra* at the Manor in December 1973. The unreleased album was given a remix in 1984 and was issued in the UK on the Jive label in 1986 as *Green Desert* (HOP 226).

---

### *V 2011 HENRY COW: Unrest*

| | | |
|---|---|---|
| 1. Bittern Storm Over Ulm | 1. Solemn Music | **Label:** V1 |
| 2. Half Asleep, Half Awake | 2. Linguaphone | **Rel:** May[11]/Jun '74[1] |
| 3. Ruins | 3. Upon Entering The Hotel Adlon | **RRP:** £2.30[1] |
| | 4. Arcades | |
| | 5. Deluge | |

**Cassette:** TCV2011 **Rel:** Jul[2]/Aug 1974[11] **RRP:** prob. £2.65

Virgin deliberately reverted to the original label design for this. An excerpt from *Bittern Storm Over Ulm* was remixed in 1984, titled *Bittern Storm Revisited*, and included on a benefit album for striking miners and their families, titled *The Last Nightingale* (Re 1984). To show solidarity, and because I could do bugger all else to help to fight rampant, bully–boy Thatcherism at its most thuggish, I bought a copy. And I joined COHSE. There, that'll show 'em.

---

***V 2012*** ***KEVIN COYNE: Blame It On The Night***

| | | |
|---|---|---|
| 1. River Of Sin | 1. Blame It On The Night | **Label:** V2 |
| 2. Sign Of The Times | 2. Poor Swine | **Rel:** Apr/May[11]/ Jun 74[1] |
| 3. I Believe In Love | 3. Light Up Your Little Light | **RRP:** £2.30[1] |
| 4. Don't Delude Me | 4. Choose | |
| 5. Wanting You Is Not Easy | 5. Witch | |
| 6. Take A Train | 6. Right On Her Side | |

**Cassette:** TCV 2012 **Rel:** Jul 1974[17] **RRP:** prob. £2.65
Insert. No cassette version available as at 1978 according to the inner sleeve of the Virgin/Record Mirror *Half Pounder* promotional compilation (RM BURG 1).

---

***V 2013*** ***MIKE OLDFIELD: Hergest Ridge***

| | | |
|---|---|---|
| 1. Side One | 1. Side Two | **Label:** V2 |
| | | **Rel:** Aug[4]/Sep '74[11] |
| | | **RRP:** £2.50[4] |

**Cassette:** TCV 2013 **Rel:** not advised **RRP:** not advised
**8–track:** 8XV 2013 **Rel:** not advised **RRP:** not advised
Many original copies were poor pressings and were returned. I've never seen a A–1U/B–1U copy, if any existed in the first place. So which matrix number, I wonder, represents a first press?

---

***V 2014*** ***SLAPP HAPPY: Slapp Happy***

| | | |
|---|---|---|
| 1. Casablanca Moon | 1. The Secret | **Label:** V2 |
| 2. Me And Parvati | 2. A Little Something | **Rel:** Apr[11]/May[11]/ Jun 74[1] |
| 3. Half Way There | 3. The Drum | **RRP:** £2.30[1] |
| 4. Michelangelo | 4. Haiku | |
| 5. Dawn | 5. Slow Moon's Rose | |
| 6. Mr. Rainbow | | |

**Cassette:** TCV 2014 **Rel:** Jul 1974[17] **RRP:** prob. £2.65
Booklet.

---

***V 2015*** ***CAPTAIN BEEFHEART AND THE MAGIC BAND: Unconditionally Guaranteed***

| | | |
|---|---|---|
| 1. Upon the My–Oh–My | 1. Full Moon, Hot Sun | **Label:** V2 |
| 2. Sugar Bowl | 2. I Got Love On My Mind | **Rel:** May 1974[1] |
| 3. New Electric Ride | 3. This Is The Day | **RRP:** £2.30[1] |
| 4. Magic Be | 4. Lazy Music | |
| 5. Happy Love Song | 5. Peaches | |

**Cassette:** TCV2015 **Rel:** May[11]/Jul 1974[17] **RRP:** prob. £2.65
**8–track:** 8XV 2015 **Rel:** Jul 1974[17] **RRP:** prob. £2.65
The sleeve credits "Captain Beefheart and The Magic Band", whilst the labels credit only "Captain Beefheart". The single released to promote the album also credits only "Captain Beefheart".

---

***V 2016*** ***EDGAR FROESE: Aqua***

| | | |
|---|---|---|
| 1. Aqua | 1. NGC 891 | **Label:** V2 |
| 2. Panorphelia | 2. Upland | **Rel:** Jun 1974[4] |
| | | **RRP:** £2.50[4] |

**Cassette:** TCV 2016 **Rel:** Aug 1974[17] **RRP:** not advised

***V 2017*** ***ROBERT WYATT: Rock Bottom***

| | | |
|---|---|---|
| 1. Sea Song | 1. Alifib | **Label:** V2 |
| 2. A Last Straw | 2. Alife | **Rel:** Jul[4/11]/Sep '74[1] |
| 3. Little Red Riding Hood Hit The Road | 3. Little Red Robin Hood Hit The Road | **RRP:** £2.50[1] |

**Cassette:** TCV 2017 — **Rel:** Jul 1974[17] — **RRP:** not advised
**8–track:** 8XV 2017 — **Rel:** not advised — **RRP:** not advised
8–track version confirmed despite non–appearance in trade listings.

---

***V 2018*** ***COMUS: To Keep From Crying***

| | | |
|---|---|---|
| 1. Down (Like A Movie Star) | 1. So Long Supernova | **Label:** V2 |
| 2. Touch Down | 2. Perpetual Motion | **Rel:** Sep 1974[4/11] |
| 3. Waves And Caves | 3. Panophany | **RRP:** £2.50[4] |
| 4. Figure In Your Dreams | 4. Get Yourself A Man | **Del** 1977[5] |
| 5. Children Of The Universe | 5. To Keep From Crying | |
| | 6. After The Dream | |

**Cassette:** TCV 2018 — **Rel:** Oct[11]/Nov 1974[17] — **RRP:** not advised

---

***V 2019*** ***GONG: You***

| | | |
|---|---|---|
| 1. Thought For Naught | 1. Perfect Mystery | **Label:** V2 |
| 2. A P.H.P.'s Advice | 2. The Isle Of Everywhere | **Rel:** Oct[4]/Nov '74[11] |
| 3. Magick Mother Invocation | 3. You Never Blow Yr Trip Forever | **RRP:** £2.45[4] |
| 4. Master Builder | | |
| 5. A Sprinkling Of Clouds | | |

**Cassette:** TCV 2019 — **Rel:** Nov 1974[17] — **RRP:** not advised
**8–track:** 8XV 2019 — **Rel:** not advised — **RRP:** not advised
Insert. Mail–order price listed as £1.95 in the *Melody Maker* for 16 November 1974 ... though if you look further down the page it also appears again in Virgin's "Top 50" listings with a mail–order price of £1.89. Never let your middle hand know what your right left hand is doing. 8–track version confirmed despite non–appearance in trade listings.

---

***V 2020*** ***DAVID BEDFORD: Star's End***

No track credits on labels or sleeve.

**Label:** V2
**Rel:** Sep[4]/ Nov 1974[4/11]
**RRP:** £2.45[4]

**Cassette:** TCV 2020 — **Rel:** Nov 1974[17] — **RRP:** not advised
**8–track:** 8XV 2020 — **Rel:** (may not exist – see below)
Included a sleeve sticker pointing out the inclusion of Mike Oldfield and Chris Cutler. The original title was intended to be "The Heat Death of the Universe". Mail–order price listed as £1.95 in the *Melody Maker* for 16 November 1974 but, as per V 2019 above, it also appears again in Virgin's "Top 50" listings with a mail–order price of £1.89. *Music Master 1976* has two listings for this album, one under "David Bedford" and one under "Mike Oldfield", both of which include different release dates. 8–track version listed in *Music Master 1979* but not in *Cassettes and Cartridges* or any other contemporary trade listings.

### *V 2021* *IVOR CUTLER: Dandruff*

| Side 1 | Side 2 | |
|---|---|---|
| 1. Solo On Mbira (Bikembe) In 5:3 Time | 1. Men | **Label:** V2 |
| 2. Dad's Lapse | 2. Trouble Trouble | **Rel:** Oct[4]/Nov '74[11] |
| 3. I Worn My Elbows | 3. I Love You | **RRP:** £2.45[4] |
| 4. Hair Grips | 4. Vein Girl | |
| 5. I Believe In Bugs | 5. Five Wise Saws | |
| 6. Fremsley | 6. Life In A Scotch Sitting Room | |
| 7. Goozeberries And Bilberries | 7. The Painful League | |
| 8. Time | 8. Piano Tuner Song 2000 AD | |
| 9. I'm Walking To A Farm | 9. Self Knowledge | |
| 10. The Railway Sleepers | 10. An Old Oak Tree | |
| 11. Life In Scotch Sitting Room, Vol. 2 Ep. 1 | 11. The Aimless Dawnrunner | |
| 12. Three Sisters | 12. Face Like A Lemon | |
| 13. Baby Sits | 13. A Bird | |
| 14. Not Big Enough | 14. A Hole In My Toe | |
| 15. A Barrel Of Nails | 15. My Mother Has Two Red Lips | |
| | 16. I Like Sitting | |
| | 17. The Forgetful Fowl | |
| | 18. If Everybody | |
| | 19. For Sixpence | |
| | 20. I Used To Lie In Bed | |
| | 21. If All The Cornflakes | |
| | 22. My Sock | |
| | 23. When I Entered | |
| | 24. Two Balls | |
| | 25. Miss Velvetlips | |
| | 26. Lean | |
| | 27. Fur Coats | |
| | 28. The Darkness | |
| | 29. A Beautiful Woman | |
| | 30. Making Tidy | |

| | | |
|---|---|---|
| **Cassette:** TCV 2021 | **Rel:** Nov 1974[17] | **RRP:** not advised |

---

### *V 2022* *TOM NEWMAN: Fine Old Tom*

| Side 1 | Side 2 | |
|---|---|---|
| 1. Susie | 1. Sad Sing | **Label:** V2 |
| 2. Poor Bill | 2. Nursery Rhyme | **Rel:** Jan[1]/Feb '75[4] |
| 3. Will You Be Mine In The Morning | 3. Song For S.P. | **RRP:** £2.45[1] |
| 4. Ma Song | 4. Superman | **Del:** 1977[5] |
| 5. Penny's Whistle Boogie | 5. Alison Says | |
| 6. She Said, She Said | 6. Day Of The Percherons | |

| | | |
|---|---|---|
| **Cassette:** TCV 2022 | **Rel:** Feb 1975[17] | **RRP:** not advised |

Die–cut sleeve. Inner sleeve. "Nursery Ryme" is the spelling on both sleeve and inner sleeve with correct spelling on label. Release date credited as 14 February 1975 in sleeve notes of the *V* compilation (VD 2502), so the *Music Master* date looks to be the more accurate.

---

### *V 2023* *CAPTAIN BEEFHEART AND MAGIC BAND: Bluejeans And Moonbeams*

| Side 1 | Side 2 | |
|---|---|---|
| 1. Party Of Special Things To Do | 1. Rock 'N' Roll's Evil Doll | **Label:** V2 |
| 2. Same Old Blues | 2. Further Than We've Gone | **Rel:** Nov[4]/Dec 1974[1/11] |
| 3. Observatory Crest | 3. Twist Ah Luck | **RRP:** £2.50[1] |
| 4. Pompadour Swamp | 4. Bluejeans And Moonbeams | |
| 5. Captain's Holiday | | |

| | | |
|---|---|---|
| **Cassette:** TCV 2023 | **Rel:** Dec 1974[17] | **RRP:** not advised |
| **8–track:** 8XV 2023 | **Rel:** Dec 1974[17] | **RRP:** not advised |

Sleeve credits "Captain Beefheart & Magic Band". Labels credit "Captain Beefheart". Advert in 9 November 1974 edition of the *NME* credits "Captain Beefheart & The Magic Band" just for variety!

### *V 2024* — *SLAPP HAPPY/HENRY COW: Desperate Straights*

| 1. Some Questions About Hats | 1. Apes In Capes | **Label:** V2 |
|---|---|---|
| 2. The Owl | 2. Strayed | **Rel:** Feb[4]/Mar '75[1] |
| 3. A Worm Is At Work | 3. Giants | **RRP:** £2.50[1] |
| 4. Bad Alchemy | 4. Excerpt From The Messiah | |
| 5. Europa | 5. In The Sickbay | |
| 6. Desperate Straights | 6. Caucasian Lullaby | |
| 7. Riding Tigers | | |
| **Cassette:** TCV 2024 | **Rel:** Feb 1975[17] | **RRP:** not advised |

Front of sleeve and spine credit "Slapp Happy/Henry Cow" whilst the rear of the sleeve and the labels credit just "Slapp Happy" (no credit is given to Henry Cow in *The New Records*). Oddly, the *V* compilation (VD 2502) credits *Extract from the Messiah* to Slapp Happy and *A Worm is at Work* to Henry Cow. *V* also lists the date of release as 21 February. 1975.

---

### *V 2025* — *TANGERINE DREAM: Rubycon*

| 1. Part I | 1. Part II | **Label:** V2 |
|---|---|---|
| | | **Rel:** Mar 1975[1/4] |
| | | **RRP:** £2.50[1] |
| **Cassette:** TCV 2025 | **Rel:** Mar[2]/Apr 1975[17] | **RRP:** £2.65 |
| **8–track:** 8XV 2025 | **Rel:** Mar[2]/Apr 1975[17] | **RRP:** £2.65 |

---

### *V 2026* — *THE ROYAL PHILHARMONIC ORCHESTRA/MIKE OLDFIELD/ DAVID BEDFORD: The Orchestral Tubular Bells*

| 1. Part 1 | 1. Part 2 | **Label:** V2 |
|---|---|---|
| | | **Rel:** Jan 1975[4] |
| | | **RRP:** not advised |
| **Cassette:** TCV 2026 | **Rel:** Feb 1975[17] | **RRP:** not advised |
| **8–track:** 8XV 2026 | **Rel:** Feb 1975[17] | **RRP:** not advised |

Original copies have the front sleeve illustration glued on a plain black background. Later copies have the image printed directly on the sleeve. Title above is taken from the sleeve spine. The front cover has the following credits: "Composed by Mike Oldfield. Arranged for Orchestra by David Bedford. Performed by The Royal Philharmonic Orchestra. With Mike Oldfield On Guitar. Conducted by David Bedford". The label has the following credits: "Performed by The Royal Philharmonic Orchestra. With Mike Oldfield On Guitar. Conducted by David Bedford". White label test pressings known to exist.

---

### *V 2027* — *HENRY COW/SLAPP HAPPY: In Praise Of Learning*

| 1. War | 1. Beginning: The Long March | **Label:** V1/CUS |
|---|---|---|
| 2. Living In The Heart Of The Beast | 2. Beautiful As The Moon – Terrible | **Rel:** May[5]/Jun '75[1] |
| | As An Army With Banners | **RRP:** £2.75[1] |
| | 3. Morning Star | |
| **Cassette:** TCV 2027 | **Rel:** May[17]/Jun 1975[2] | **RRP:** £2.90[2] |

Relisted in the July 1975 edition of *The New Records* credited to "Henry Cow". One label is the original white and black design, though with red instead of black text, whilst the other label is custom. Relisted in the July 1975 edition of *The New Cassettes and Cartridges* under "Henry Cow", with RRP of £2.75.

---

### *V 2028* — *CHILI CHARLES: Quickstep*

| 1. Hip | 1. Where Are You Robert? | **Label:** V2 |
|---|---|---|
| 2. Quickstep | 2. Yesterday | **Rel:** Mar 1975[4] |
| 3. Miles | 3. Nomad | **RRP:** not advised |
| 4. Jumpin' | 4. Sunset | |
| 5. Semba | | |
| **Cassette:** TCV 2028 | **Rel:** not advised | **RRP:** not advised |

Issued 28 March 1975 according to the *V* compilation LP (VD 2502). Cassette listed by Music Master[5].

**_V 2029_** **_CLEAR LIGHT SYMPHONY: Clear Light Symphony_**

| | | |
|---|---|---|
| 1. Part I | 1. Part II | **Label:** V2 |
| | | **Rel:** Mar[4]/Apr'75[1/4] |
| | | **RRP:** £2.75[1] |

**Cassette:** TCV 2029 — **Rel:** Feb[17]/Apr 1975[2] — **RRP:** £2.90
**8–track:** 8XV 2029 — **Rel:** Feb[17]/Apr 1975[2] — **RRP:** £2.90

PVC sticker on front of sleeve with artist credit. I seem to remember seeing second–hand copies in the late 1970s with a second PVC sticker stating the inclusion of Gong members. Is my memory accurate? *Music Master 1976* has two separate listings for this album, both with different release dates. According to the V compilation (VD 2502) this was scheduled for release on 28 February 1975.

---

**_V 2030_** **_HATFIELD AND THE NORTH: The Rotters' Club_**

| | | |
|---|---|---|
| 1. Share It | 1. Underdub | **Label:** V2 |
| 2. Lounging There Trying | 2. Mumps: | **Rel:** Mar 1975[1/4] |
| 3. (Big) John Wayne Socks Psychology On The Jaw | i. Your Majesty Is Like A Cream Donut (Quiet) | **RRP:** £2.50[1] |
| 4. Chaos At The Greasy Spoon | ii. Lumps | |
| 5. The Yes No Interlude | iii. Prenut | |
| 6. Fitter Stoke Has A Bath | iv. Your Majesty Is Like A Cream Donut (Loud) | |
| 7. Didn't Matter Anyway | | |

**Cassette:** TCV 2030 — **Rel:** Mar 1975[2] — **RRP:** £2.65

Relisted in the April 1975 edition of *The New Records*, priced at £2.75. The *V* compilation LP (VD 2502) lists this as being released on 7 March 1975. *Fitter Stoke Has a Bath* is not the same version as included on the single (VS 116). Promotional stickers exist for the album showing a cartoon of a horrid, freckled oik of a child. You can see the sticker on Richard Sinclair's lyric book on the *Bedrock* TV special from 1990. Also listed in the April 1975 edition of *The New Cassettes and Cartridges* at £2.90 in the Folk and Country section. The mind boggles.

---

**_V 2031_** **_STEVE HILLAGE: Fish Rising_**

| | | |
|---|---|---|
| 1. Solar Musick Suite | 1. The Salmon Song | **Label:** V2 |
| i. SunSong (I Love Its Holy Mystery) | i. Salmon Pool | **Rel:** May 1975[1/4] |
| ii. Canterbury Sunrise | ii. Solomon's Atlantis Salmon | **RRP:** £2.75[1] |
| iii. Hiram Afterglid Meets The Dervish | iii. Swimming With The Salmon | |
| iv. SunSong (Reprise) | iv. King Of The Fishes | |
| 2. Fish | 2. Aftaglid | |
| 3. Meditation Of The Snake | i. SunMoon Surfing | |
| | ii. The Big Wave And The Boat Of Hermes | |
| | iii. The Silver Ladder | |
| | iv. Astral Meadows | |
| | v. The Lafta Yoga Song | |
| | vi. Glidding | |
| | vii. The Golden Vibe / Outglid | |

**Cassette:** TCV 2031 — **Rel:** May 1975[2] — **RRP:** £2.90

According to the *V* compilation (VD 2502) this was planned as an April 1975 release.

---

**_V 2032_** **_WHITE NOISE: White Noise 2_**

| | | |
|---|---|---|
| 1. Concerto For Synthesizer: | 1. Concerto For Synthesizer: | **Label:** V2 |
| i. Movement I | i. Movement II (Continued) | **Rel:** Apr[4]/Jun[4]/May 75[1] |
| ii. Movement II | ii. Movement III | **RRP:** £2.75[1] |

**Cassette:** TCV 2032 — **Rel:** Apr 1975[17] — **RRP:** not advised
**8–track:** 8XV 2032 — **Rel:** Apr 1975[17] — **RRP:** not advised

According to the *V* compilation (VD 2502) this was scheduled for release on 4 April 1975. 8–track listed in *Cassettes and Cartridges*, but no copies have come to light in over thirty years of research.

***V 2033*** ***KEVIN COYNE: Matching Head And Feet***

| | | |
|---|---|---|
| 1. Saviour | 1. Mrs Hooley Go Home | **Label:** V2 |
| 2. Lucy | 2. It's Not Me | **Rel:** Apr[4]/Jun '75[1] |
| 3. Lonely Lovers | 3. Turpentine | **RRP:** £2.75[1] |
| 4. Sunday Morning Sunrise | 4. Tulip | |
| 5. Rock 'N' Roll Hymn | 5. One Fine Day | |

| | | |
|---|---|---|
| **Cassette:** TCV 2033 | **Rel:** Jun 1975[2] | **RRP:** £2.90 |
| **8–track:** 8XV 2033 | **Rel:** Jun 1975[2] | **RRP:** £2.90 |

No cassette version available as at 1978 according to the inner sleeve of the *Half Pounder* promotional compilation (RM BURG 1).

---

***V 2034*** ***ROBERT WYATT: Ruth Is Stranger Than Richard***

| | | |
|---|---|---|
| 1. Soup Song | 1. Muddy Mouse (A | **Label:** V2 |
| 2. Sonia | 2. Solar Flares | **Rel:** May[4]/Jul '75[1] |
| 3. Team Spirit | 3. Muddy Mouse (B) | **RRP:** £2.75[1] |
| 4. Song For Che | 4. 5 Black Notes And 1 White Note | |
| | 5. Muddy Mouse (C) | |
| | 6. Muddy Mouth | |

| | | |
|---|---|---|
| **Cassette:** TCV 2034 | **Rel:** Jul 1975[2/17] | **RRP:** £2.90 |
| **8–track:** 8XV 2034 | **Rel:** Jul 1975[2/17] | **RRP:** £2.90 |

Side 1 credited as "Ruth side" and Side 2 as "Richard side" on sleeve: labels credit "Ruth" and "Richard" above track listings. Label lists *Muddy Mouse (c)* and *Muddy Mouth* as two tracks whilst the sleeve says "Muddy Mouse (c) which in turn leads into Muddy Mouth".

---

***V 2035*** ***WIGWAM: Nuclear Nightclub***

| | | |
|---|---|---|
| 1. Nuclear Nightclub | 1. Do Or Die | **Label:** V2 |
| 2. Freddie Are You Ready | 2. Simple Human Kindness | **Rel:** Jun[4]/Aug '75[1] |
| 3. Bless Your Lucky Stars | 3. Save My Money And My Name | **RRP:** £2.75[1] |
| 4. Kite | 4. Pig Storm | |

| | | |
|---|---|---|
| **Cassette:** TCV 2035 | **Rel:** Jul[17]/Aug 1975[2] | **RRP:** £2.90 |

*Music Week* ran a Virgin competition that provided dealers with incentives to promote and sell this album. Judging by the number of copies that turn up for sale, this huge promotional push was not a spectacular success. Licensed from Love Records in Finland, following fairly heavy imports (via Caroline) of their 1973 album, *Being* (UK imports were good enough for Love to translate the booklet into English for later import copies).

---

***V 2036*** ***PEKKA POHJOLA: B The Magpie***

| | | |
|---|---|---|
| 1. The Beginning | 1. Bialoipokku's War | **Label:** V2 |
| 2. The First Morning | 2. The Madness Subsides | **Rel:** Sep[4]/Oct '75[1] |
| 3. Bad Weather – Bialoipokku Dances | 3. Life Goes On | **RRP:** £2.99[1] |
| 4. Bialoipokku's War Dream | | |

**Cassette:** TCV 2036 (most likely does not exist – see below)

Licensed from Love Records in Finland, where it had been issued in 1974 under the title, *Harakka Bialoipokku*. According to the 1975 Virgin catalogue this was not issued in tape format. However, a cassette issue is listed, probably erroneously, in *Music Master 1979*.

### *V 2037* — *IVOR CUTLER: Velvet Donkey*

| 1. If Your Breasts | 1. A Nuance | **Label:** V2 |
|---|---|---|
| 2. I Got No Common Sense | 2. Go And Sit Upon The Grass | **Rel:** Sep[4]/Oct '75[1] |
| 3. Useful Cat | 3. The Even Keel | **RRP:** £2.99[1] |
| 4. Oho My Eyes | 4. Pearly Gleam | |
| 5. The Dirty Dinner | 5. The Best Thing | |
| 6. Yellow Fly | 6. Life In A Scotch Sitting Room Vol. 2, Ep. 7 | |
| 7. Mother's Love | 7. Once Upon A Time | |
| 8. The Meadows Go | 8. There's Got To Be Something | |
| 9. Phonic Poem | 9. The Purposeful Culinary Implements | |
| 10. Life In A Scotch Sitting Room Vol. 2, Ep. 2 | 10. Gee, Amn't I Lucky | |
| 11. Birdswing | 11. The Curse | |
| 12. Nobody Knows | 12. I Think Very Deeply | |
| 13. Uneventful Day | 13. I, Slowly | |
| 14. Little Black Buzzer | 14. Sleepy Old Snake | |
| 15. Bread And Butter | 15. Titchy Digits | |
| | 16. The Stranger | |

**Cassette:** TCV 2037 — **Rel:** not advised — **RRP:** not advised

Cassette listed by Music Master[5].

---

### *V 2038* — *DAVID BEDFORD: Rime Of The Ancient Mariner*

No track credits on labels or sleeve.

**Label:** V3
**Rel:** Sep[4]/Oct '75[1]
**RRP:** £2.99[1]

---

### *V 2039* — *CLEARLIGHT: Forever Blowing Bubbles*

| 1. Chanson | 1. Ergotrip | **Label:** V3 |
|---|---|---|
| 2. Without Words | 2. Et Pendant Ce Temps La | **Rel:** Oct[4]/Nov[4]/ Dec 1975[1] |
| 3. Way | 3. Narcisse Et Goldmund | **RRP:** £2.99[1] |
| | 4. Jungle Bubbles | |

---

### *V 2040* — *EDGAR FROESE: Epsilon In Malaysian Pale*

| 1. Epsilon In Malaysian Pale | 1. Maroubra Bay | **Label:** V3 |
|---|---|---|
| | | **Rel:** Sep[4]/Nov '75[1] |
| | | **RRP:** £2.99[1] |

**Cassette:** TCV 2040 — **Rel:** Oct 1975[17] — **RRP:** not advised

Later – and quite rare – copies appeared on the white–rimmed green mirrored girl label.

---

### *V 2041* — *CAN: Landed*

| 1. Full Moon On The Highway | 1. Red Hot Indians | **Label:** V3 |
|---|---|---|
| 2. Half Past One | 2. Unfinished | **Rel:** Sep[4]/Oct '75[1] |
| 3. Hunters And Collectors | | **RRP:** £2.99[1] |
| 4. Vernal Equinox | | |

**Cassette:** TCV 2041 — **Rel:** 1975[5]. — **RRP:** not advised

---

### *V 2042* — *TOM NEWMAN: Live At The Argonaut (NOT RELEASED)*

Listed as a forthcoming release in the 1975 Virgin catalogue. Subsequently unreleased although test pressings are rumoured to exist. In the early 1990s alternative versions of the tracks were released on the Voiceprint label because the original masters were said to have been lost.

---

### *V 2043* — *MIKE OLDFIELD: Ommadawn*

| 1. Part 1 | 1. Part 2 | **Label:** V3 |
|---|---|---|
| | | **Rel:** Nov[4]/Dec '75[1] |
| | | **RRP:** £2.99[1] |

**Cassette:** TCV 2043 **Rel:** Nov 1975[17] **RRP:** not advised
**8–track:** 8XV 2043 **Rel:** Nov 1975[17] **RRP:** not advised

Inner sleeve. *Music Master 1976* has two listings for this LP, with different months (the October one is most likely erroneous). It has long been assumed that original copies were those on the coloured girl/dragon label, but the first press is on the short–lived beige label, prior to Virgin reverting to the previous label for a couple more months. Certainly, the rarer of these two is the girl/dragon label version. Original copies exist with "Factory sample not for sale" stickers on one label. Copies on the blue 'neon' label design were in matt–finished sleeves instead of the more usual laminated version.

---

***V 2044*** ***TANGERINE DREAM: Ricochet***

1. Part One

1. Part Two

**Label:** V3
**Rel:** Nov 1975[4]/ Jan 1976[1]
**RRP:** £2.99[1]

**Cassette:** TCV 204 **Rel:** Dec 1975[17]/Jan 1976[2] (del 1979[6]) **RRP:** £3.15
**8–track:** 8XV 2044 **Rel:** Dec 1975[17]/Jan 1976[2] **RRP:** £3.15

Original copies were given incorrect matrix numbers, "VS 2044 A1"/"VS 2044 B1", with the "S" scratched out. A slightly later pressing, still on original label design, has "V 2044 A4 GM" / "V 2044 B3 GM" matrix numbers. *Music Master 1976* credits the LP title as "Live in various cathedrals".

---

***V 2045*** ***MALLARD: Mallard***

1. Back On The Pavement
2. She's Long And She's Lean
3. Road to Morocco
4. One Day Once
5. Yellow
6. Desperados Waiting For A Train

1. A Piece Of Me
2. Reign Of Pain
3. South Of The Valley
4. Winged Tuskadero
5. Peon

**Label:** V2
**Rel:** Feb[5]/Apr '76[1]
**RRP:** £2.99[1]

Copies also confirmed on the white–rimmed red mirrored girl label design.

---

***V 2046*** ***GONG: Shamal***

1. Wingful Of Eyes
2. Chandra
3. Bambooji

1. Cat In Clark's Shoes
2. Mandrake
3. Shamal

**Label:** V2
**Rel:** Feb[5]/Apr '76[1]
**RRP:** £2.99[1]

**Cassette:** TCV 2046 **Rel:** Feb[5]/Mar 1976[17] **RRP:** £3.15[5]

---

***V 2047*** ***KEVIN COYNE: Heartburn***

1. Strange Locomotion
2. Don't Make Waves
3. Happy Band
4. I Love My Mother
5. Shangri–La

1. America
2. Big White Bird
3. Games Games Games
4. My Mother's Eyes
5. Daddy

**Label:** V5?
**Rel:** Feb 1976[5]
**RRP:** £2.99[5]

Green, white–rimmed label confirmed, but may exist on V2 label design. No cassette version available as at 1978 according to the *Half Pounder* promotional compilation (RM BURG 1).

---

***V 2048*** ***U ROY: Dread In A Babylon***

1. Runaway Girl
2. Chalice In The Palace
3. I Can't Love Another
4. Dread Locks Dread
5. The Great Psalms

1. Natty Don't Fear
2. African Message
3. Silver Bird
4. Listen To The Teacher
5. Trench Town Rock

**Label:** see below
**Rel:** Feb[5]/Apr '76[1]
**RRP:** £2.99[1]

Promotional copies are on the coloured girl and dragon label design, whilst stock copies are confirmed on the white–rimmed, red label design. All girl and dragon label copies viewed have been promotional copies, so are there any stock copies on this label design? Ah, perhaps the same goes for *Shamal*?

***V 2049*** ***BOXER: Below the Belt***

| Side 1 | Side 2 | |
|---|---|---|
| 1. Shooting Star | 1. Waiting For A Miracle | **Label:** V2 |
| 2. All The Time In The World | 2. Loony Ali | **Rel:** Feb[5]/Mar '76[1] |
| 3. California Calling | 3. Save Me | **RRP:** £2.99[1] |
| 4. Hip Kiss | 4. Gonna Work Out Fine | |
| 5. More Than Meets The Eye | 5. Town Drunk | |

**Cassette:** TCV 2049 **Rel:** Feb 1976[5] **RRP:** £3.15

Original issue included a naked lady on the rear sleeve. This was withdrawn and a Boxer logo added to cover up a certain portion of sleeve. Copies also exist on the white–rimmed red label, though these are extremely rare.

---

***V 2050*** ***LINK WRAY: Stuck In Gear***

| Side 1 | Side 2 | |
|---|---|---|
| 1. Southern Lady | 1. Midnight Lover | **Label:** V5 |
| 2. Tecolote | 2. Cottoncandy Apples | **Rel:** Mar[5]/Jun '76[1] |
| 3. Quicksand | 3. Bo Jack | **RRP:** £2.99[5]/ |
| 4. I Know You're Leaving Me Now | 4. Jack The Ripper | £3.25[1] |
| 5. Did You See The Man | | |

Track 3, side 2 credited as "BoJack" on sleeve (no space) and "Bo Jack" on the label.

---

***V 2051*** ***WIGWAM: Lucky Golden Stripes And Starpose***

| Side 1 | Side 2 | |
|---|---|---|
| 1. Sane Again | 1. Lucky Golden Stripes And Starpose | **Label:** V4 |
| 2. International Disaster | 2. June Maybe Too Late | **Rel:** Mar[5]/May'76[1] |
| 3. Timedance | 3. Never Turn You In | **RRP:** £2.99[1] |
| 4. Colossus | 4. In A Nutshell | |
| 5. Eddie And The Boys | | |

Embossed sleeve. Fold–out lyric insert.

---

***V 2052*** ***THE MIGHTY DIAMONDS: Right Time***

| Side 1 | Side 2 | |
|---|---|---|
| 1. Right Time | 1. I Need A Roof | **Label:** V4 |
| 2. Why Me Black Brother Why | 2. Go Seek Your Rights | **Rel:** May[5]/Jul '76[1] |
| 3. Shame And Pride | 3. Have Mercy | **RRP:** £3.25[1] |
| 4. Gnashing Of Teeth | 4. Natural Natty | |
| 5. Them Never Love Poor Marcus | 5. Africa | |

**Cassette:** TCV 2052 (see below) **Rel:** Aug 1976[5] **RRP:** £3.50[5]

No cassette version available according to the *Half Pounder* compilation (RM BURG 1). Perhaps it was deleted by the time that album was issued. A dub version of this album was issued as *Well Charged* (V 2055).

---

***V 2053*** ***SUPERCHARGE: Local Lads Make Good***

| Side 1 | Side 2 | |
|---|---|---|
| 1. Lonely And In Love | 1. Get Down Boogie | **Label:** V4 |
| 2. Hole Town | 2. Only You | **Rel:** Apr[5]/Jun '76[1] |
| 3. Everyone! Everywhere! | 3. Gimme Your Love | **RRP:** £3.25[1] |
| 4. I Beleieve In You | 4. You've Gotta Get Up And Dance | |
| | 5. She Moved The Dishes First | |

What can I say about the last track? Nothing is probably best.

---

***V 2054*** ***DAEVID ALLEN AND EUTERPE: Good Morning***

| Side 1 | Side 2 | |
|---|---|---|
| 1. Children Of The New World | 1. French Garden | **Label:** V4 |
| 2. Good Morning | 2. Wise Man In Your Heart | **Rel:** May 1976[5] |
| 3. Spirit | 3. She Doesn't She... | **RRP:** £3.25[5] |
| 4. Song Of Satisfaction | | |
| 5. Have You Seen My Friend? | | |

***V 2055*** ***VITAL DUB: Well Charged***

1. Roof Top Dub
2. Ital Dub
3. Fence Dub
4. Ishens Dub
5. Total Dub

1. Merciful Dub
2. Cell Block 11
3. Killer Dub
4. Blacka Blacka Dub

**Label:** V6
**Rel:** Jan[5]/Mar '77[1]
**RRP:** £2.99[1]/ £3.49[5]

Jamaican copies on the Well Charge label credited to "The Revolutionaries" and titled *Vital Dub Strictly Rockers*. This is a dub version of *Right Time* (V 2052). Copies also known to exist on the green mirrored girl label design.

---

***V 2056*** ***KEITH HUDSON: Too Expensive***

1. Smoking
2. Introduce Me
3. Civilisation
4. Thank You Baby

1. Too Expensive
2. Where Is Your Love
3. We Can Work It Out
4. Civilisation (Instrumental)

**Label:** V4
**Rel:** Jul[5]/Aug '76[1]
**RRP:** £3.25[1]

---

***V 2057*** ***ANTHONY MOORE: Out (NOT RELEASED)***

Unreleased by Virgin. First issued in the UK in 1998 by Voiceprint. Wonderful album!

---

***V 2058*** ***JOHNNY CLARKE: Rockers Time Now***

1. Rockers Time Now
2. Ites Green And Gold
3. African Roots
4. Be Holy, My Brothers And Sisters
5. Satta Massagna
6. Stop the Tribal War

1. Declaration of Rights
2. Lets Give Jah, Jah Praise
3. I Wish It Could Go On Forever
4. Natty Dreadlocks Stand Up Rip
5. Prophecy A–Fullfilled
6. Them Never Love Poor Marcus

**Label:** V4
**Rel:** Jul 1976[5]
**RRP:** £3.25[5]

Mono.

---

***V 2059*** ***U ROY: Natty Rebel***

1. Babylon Burning
2. Natty Rebel
3. So Jah Jah Say
4. Natty Kung Fu
5. If You Should Leave Me

1. Do You Remember
2. Travelling Man
3. Have Mercy
4. Badie Boo
5. Go There Natty
6. Fire In A Trenchtown

**Label:** V5
**Rel:** Aug[5]/Sep '76[1]
**RRP:** £3.25[1]

**Cassette:** TCV 2059 **Rel:** Aug 1976[5] **RRP:** £3.50[5]

Later issued on the Front Line label as FL 1038 on Nigerian–manufactured copies. Other reggae records from this era were also assigned most of the otherwise 'missing' FL 1000 catalogue numbers. Does anyone out there know which Virgin label records reappeared on which FL catalogue numbers?

---

***V 2060*** ***DELROY WASHINGTON: I–Sus***

1. Jah Wonderful
2. Generation Game
3. Midnight Ravers
4. Stoney Blows
5. Freedom Fighters

1. Gotta Keep On Movin'
2. Observance
3. Time Passage
4. Clean Hearted People
5. This Ya Reggae Music
6. The Streets Of Ladbrook Grove

**Label:** V4
**Rel:** Aug[5]/Sep '76[1]
**RRP:** £3.25[1]

Insert.

---

***V 2061*** ***PETER TOSH: Legalize It***

1. Legalize It
2. Burial
3. Whatcha Gonna Do
4. No Sympathy
5. Why Must I Cry

1. Igziabeher (Let Jah Be Praised)
2. Ketchy Shuby
3. Till Your Well Runs Dry
4. Brand New Second Hand

**Label:** CUS/V7
**Rel:** Aug 1976[1/5]
**RRP:** £2.99[1]/ £3.25[5]

**Cassette:** TCV 2061 **Rel:** Oct 1976[5/17] **RRP:** £3.59[5]
One custom, one green mirrored girl label. *The New Records* price is incorrect. Relisted in the September 1976 edition with the correct price of £3.25.

---

***V 2062*** ***GLADIATORS: Trenchtown Mix Up***

1. Mix Up
2. Bellyful
3. Look Is Deceiving
4. Chatty Chatty Mouth
5. Soul Rebel

1. Eli Eli
2. Hearsay
3. Rude Boy Ska
4. Know Yourself Mankind
5. Thief In The Night
6. Hello Carol

**Label:** V4
**Rel:** Aug 1976[5]
**RRP:** £3.25[5]

Also confirmed on the non–white–rimmed red mirrored girl label design. No cassette version issued according to the *Half Pounder* promotional compilation (RM BURG 1).

---

***V 2063*** ***MATAYA CLIFFORD: Star Fell From Heaven***

1. Star Fell From Heaven
2. Black Woman
3. Things Are Going My Way
4. Amazing Grace
5. Mama (Stay A Little While)

1. Just A Little Love
2. Running
3. Little Girl
4. Lost Child

**Label:** V6
**Rel:** Sep 1976[5]
**RRP:** £3.25[5]

---

***V 2064*** ***KLAUS SCHULZE: Moon Dawn (NOT RELEASED)***

This was not issued on Virgin, although it must have been a close thing because release was advised to *Music Master* and it appears in the 1979 edition with a release date of August 1976, priced at £3.25.

---

***V 2065*** ***IVOR CUTLER: Jammy Smears***

1. Bicarbonate of Chicken
2. Filcombe Cottage, Dorset
3. Squeeze Bees
4. The Turn
5. Life In A Scotch Sitting Room, Vol. 2 Ep. 11
6. A Linnet
7. Jumping And Pecking
8. The Other Half
9. Beautiful Cosmos
10. The Path
11. Barabadabada
12. Big Jim
13. In The Chestnut Tree
14. Dust
15. Rubber Toy
16. Fistyman

1. Unexpected Join
2. A Wooden Tree
3. When I Stand On An Open Cart
4. High Is The Wind
5. The Surly Buddy
6. Pearly–Winged Fly
7. Garden Path At Filcombe
8. Paddington Town
9. Cage Of Small Birds
10. Life In A Scotch Sitting Room, Vol. 2 Ep. 6
11. Irk
12. Lemon Flower
13. Red Admiral
14. Everybody Got
15. The Wasted Call

**Label:** V6
**Rel:** Sep 1976[5]
**RRP:** £3.25[5]

---

***V 2066*** ***STEVE HILLAGE: L***

1. Hurdy Gurdy Man
2. Hurdy Gurdy Glissando
3. Electrick Gypsies

1. Om Nama Shivaya
2. Lunar Musick Suite
3. It's All Too Much

**Label:** V7
**Rel:** Sep1976[5]
**RRP:** £3.25[5]

**Cassette:** TCV 2066 **Rel:** Oct 1976[5/17] **RRP:** £3.59[5]

---

***V 2067*** ***SUPERCHARGE: Horizontal Refreshment***

1. Play Some Fire
2. After The Show
3. Limbo Love
4. Last Train

1. Bad Time
2. Let The Feeling Grow
3. Mess You Made
4. Really Quite Easy
5. Purple Avenger

**Label:** V7
**Rel:** Feb 1977[5]
**RRP:** £3.49[5]

Insert.

***V 2068*** ***TANGERINE DREAM: Stratosphere***

| Side 1 | Side 2 | |
|---|---|---|
| 1. Stratosphere | 1. 3am At The Border Of The Marsh From Okefenokee | **Label:** V7 |
| 2. The Big Sleep In Search Of Hades | 2. Invisible Limits | **Rel:** Oct 1976[5] |
| | | **RRP:** £3.49[5] |

**Cassette:** TCV 2068 **Rel:** Oct[5]/Nov 1976[17] **RRP:** £3.59[5]
**8–track:** 8XV 2068 **Rel:** Oct[5]/Nov 1976[17] **RRP:** £3.59[5]

***V 2069*** ***PETER BAUMANN: Romance '76***

| Side 1 | Side 2 | |
|---|---|---|
| 1. Bicentennial Present | 1. Meadow Of Infintity (Part 1) | **Label:** V7 |
| 2. Romance | 2. The Glass Bridge | **Rel:** Feb 1977[5] |
| 3. Phase By Phase | 3. Meadow Of Infintity (Part 2) | **RRP:** £3.49[5] |

White label test pressings known to exist.

***V 2070*** ***DAVID BEDFORD: The Odyssey***

| Side 1 | Side 2 | |
|---|---|---|
| 1. Penelope's Shroud (i) | 1. Scylla And Charybdis | **Label:** V7 |
| 2. King Aelous | 2. Penelope's Shroud (iv) | **Rel:** Oct 1976[5] |
| 3. Penelope's Shroud (ii) | 3. Circe's Island | **RRP:** £3.49[5] |
| 4. The Phaeacian Games | 4. Penelope's Shroud Completed | |
| 5. Penelope's Shroud (iii) | 5. The Battle In The Hall | |
| 6. The Sirens | | |

Insert.

***V 2071*** ***CAN: Flow Motion***

| Side 1 | Side 2 | |
|---|---|---|
| 1. I Want More | 1. Babylonian Pearl | **Label:** V7 |
| 2. Cascade Waltz | 2. Smoke (E.F.S. Nr. 59) | **Rel:** Oct 1976[5] |
| 3. Laugh Till You Cry – Live Till You Die (O.R.N.) | 3. Flow Motion | **RRP:** £3.49[5] |
| 4. ... And More | | |

**Cassette:** TCV 2071 **Rel:** Oct 1976[5/17] **RRP:** £3.59[5]
Some copies include a sticker with, "Featuring the Hit Single I Want More".

***V 2072*** ***DAVID BEDFORD/SCOTTISH NATIONAL ORCHESTRA/STEVE HILLAGE: The Orchestral Hergest Ridge (NOT RELEASED)***

This was almost certainly assigned to *The Orchestral Hergest Ridge*, which was recorded by BBC Radio Clyde on 5th May 1976 at the Kelvin Hall, Glasgow. The performance was by the Scottish National Orchestra, conducted by David Bedford, with Steve Hillage on guitar. Virgin purchased the rights to the recording, but it was never issued. Parts of the the recording were almost released on LP on the soundtrack to *Space Movie*, but this too remained unreleased. Parts can, however, be heard on the VHS video for *Space Movie*, which was first issued in 1983.

It has also been mooted, though with no real conviction, that this catalogue number might have been assigned to Captain Beefheart's *Bat Chain Puller*, parts of which were originally recorded in 1976. The album was subsequently unissued and the tracks later released on *Shiny Beast (Bat Chain Puller)*, issued by Virgin in 1980, were re–recordings from 1978.

***V 2073*** ***BOXER: Bloodletting***

| Side 1 | Side 2 | |
|---|---|---|
| 1. Hey Bulldog | 1. Why Pick On Me | **Label:** V7 |
| 2. The Blizzard | 2. Love Has Got Me | **Rel:** Oct 1976[5] |
| 3. Rich Man's Daughter | 3. Dinah–Low | **RRP:** £3.49[5] |
| 4. Big City Fever | 4. Teachers | |
| 5. The Loner | | |

Supposedly withdrawn, though listed as still on catalogue at the end of 1978[5]. Label includes special thanks credit to Boz Burrell, Bobby Tench and Tim Hinkley, which was not exactly normal practice.

**_V 2074_ _GONG: Gazeuse_**

| Side 1 | Side 2 | |
|---|---|---|
| 1. Expresso | 1. Shadows Of | **Label:** V7 |
| 2. Night Illusion | 2. Esnuria | **Rel:** Feb 1977[5] |
| 3. Percolations Part 1 | 3. Mireille | **RRP:** £3.49[5] |
| 4. Percolations Part 2 | | |

**Cassette:** TCV 2074 **Rel:** Feb[5]/Mar 1977[17] **RRP:** £3.59[5]

Memory says this included a poster – memory may be wrong. The last two tracks on side 1 run together with no track band and with a combined timing on the label even though listed and numbered as two separate tracks. Tracks on side 2 follow on numerically from those on the front, so are listed as "4", "5" and "6". Released with the title *Expresso* in the US, hence the next Gong LP released as *Expresso II*. White label test pressings in plain, white sleeves known to exist.

---

**_V 2075_ _I ROY: Musical Shark Attack_**

| Side 1 | Side 2 | |
|---|---|---|
| 1. Semi–Classical Natty Dread | 1. Skyjuice And Festival Dumping | **Label:** V7 |
| 2. Musical Shark Attack | 2. Run For Your Life | **Rel:** Feb 1977[5] |
| 3. Drum Sound | 3. Tribute To Michael Holding | **RRP:** £3.49[5] |
| 4. Is Love I Deal With | 4. Everybody Ballin' | **Del** 1980[6] |
| 5. Social Development | 5. Tribute To Marcus Garvey | |
| 6. Jamboree | | |

Mono. Not issued on cassette[6]. Dub version pressed with white labels and matrix number VDJ 19.

---

**_V 2076_ _JOHNNY CLARKE, Authorized Version_**

| Side 1 | Side 2 | |
|---|---|---|
| 1. Roots Natty Roots, Natty Congo | 1. Cry Tough | **Label:** V7 |
| 2. Wrath Of Jah | 2. Crazy Baldhead | **Rel:** Feb 1977[5] |
| 3. Legalize It | 3. Simmer Down | **RRP:** £3.49[5] |
| 4. I Am Still Waiting | 4. Jah Jah See Them Come | |
| 5. Let Go Violence | 5. Give Up The Badness | |
| 6. Academy Award Version | 6. Freedom Blues | |

Mono.

---

**_V 2077_ _MALLARD: In A Different Climate_**

| Side 1 | Side 2 | |
|---|---|---|
| 1. Green Coyote | 1. Heartstrings | **Label:** V7 |
| 2. Your Face On Someone Else | 2. Old Man Grey | **Rel:** Feb[5]/Apr '77[1] |
| 3. Harvest | 3. Texas Weather | **RRP:** £2.99[1]/ |
| 4. Mama Squeeze | 4. Big Foot | £3.49[5] |

---

**_V 2078_ _THE MIGHTY DIAMONDS: Ice on Fire_**

| Side 1 | Side 2 | |
|---|---|---|
| 1. Country Living | 1. Sneakin Sally Through The Alley | **Label:** V7 |
| 2. You Are Just a Song | 2. Little Angel | **Rel:** Mar[5]/Apr '77[1] |
| 3. If I Should Leave You | 3. Cat–O–Nine | **RRP:** £2.99[1]/ |
| 4. Tonight | 4. Back Weh Mafia | £3.49[5] |
| 5. Comin Through | 5. Whole Wide World | |
| 6. Get Out Of My Life Woman | 6. Tracks Of My Tears | |

No cassette version issued according to the *Half Pounder* promotional compilation (RM BURG 1).

---

**_V 2079_ _CAN: Saw Delight_**

| Side 1 | Side 2 | |
|---|---|---|
| 1. Don't Say No | 1. Animal Waves | **Label:** V7 |
| 2. Sunshine Day And Night | 2. Fly By Night | **Rel:** Mar[5]/Apr '77[1] |
| 3. Call Me | | **RRP:** £2.99[1]/ |
| | | £3.49[5] |

Insert.

***V 2080*** ***ASHRA: New Age Of Earth***

| Side 1 | Side 2 | |
|---|---|---|
| 1. Sunrain | 1. Nightdust | **Label:** V7 |
| 2. Ocean Of Tenderness | | **Rel:** Jun 1977[5] |
| 3. Deep Distance | | **RRP:** £3.49[5] |

---

***V 2081*** ***PETER TOSH WITH WORDS SOUND AND POWER: Equal Rights***

| Side 1 | Side 2 | |
|---|---|---|
| 1. Get Up, Stand Up | 1. Equal Rights | **Label:** V6 |
| 2. Downpressor Man | 2. African | **Rel:** Apr[5]/May '77[1] |
| 3. I Am That I Am | 3. Jah Guide | **RRP:** £2.99[1]/ |
| 4. Stepping Razor | 4. Apartheid | £3.49[5] |

**Cassette:** TCV 2081 **Rel:** Apr 1977[6] **RRP:** not advised

First listed in *The New Records* as "Peter Tosh with Words, Sound & Power" and relisted in the June 1977 edition as "Peter Tosh with Words Sound & Power" (without the comma). The record has even more variations: the sleeve front and spine both credit "Peter Tosh", but the sleeve notes credit "Word Sound & Power" (without an "s"); whilst the labels credit "Peter Tosh with Words Sound & Power" (with an "s"). The record is published by and copyright CBS with the following sleeve credit, "... licensed through Island Records from CBS Records a division of CBS Inc."

---

***V 2082*** ***JOHN GREAVES/PETER BLEGVAD: Kew. Rhone.***

| Side 1 | Side 2 | |
|---|---|---|
| 1. Good Evening | 1. One Footnote (To Kew. Rhone.) | **Label:** V7 |
| 2. Twenty–Two Proverbs | 2. Three Tenses Onanism | **Rel:** Mar[5]/Apr '77[1] |
| 3. Seven Scenes From The Painting "Exhuming The First American Mastadon" By C.W. Peale | 3. Nine Mineral Emblems | **RRP:** £2.99[1]/ |
| 4. Kew. Rhone. | 4. Apricot | £3.49[5] |
| 5. Pipeline | 5. gegenstand | |
| 6. Catalogue Of Fifteen Objects And Their Titles | | |

Insert. The track "gegenstand" is credited with lower case "g", so who am I to argue?

---

***V 2083*** ***YELLOW DOG: Yellow Dog***

| Side 1 | Side 2 | |
|---|---|---|
| 1. Stood Up | 1. Indian Summer Rain | **Label:** V7 |
| 2. Gypsy Soul | 2. My Lady | **Rel:** Apr[5]/Jun '77[1] |
| 3. The Green Lizard | 3. City Bird | **RRP:** £2.99[1]/ |
| 4. Flash Gordon | 4. Nobody Got So Much Soul | £3.49[5] |
| | 5. For Whatever It's Worth | |

Insert. Promotional copies included a special information sheet. No cassette version issued according to the *Half Pounder* promotional compilation (RM BURG 1).

---

***V 2084*** ***PEKKA: The Mathematician's Air Display***

| Side 1 | Side 2 | |
|---|---|---|
| 1. The Percieved Journey–Lantern | 1. The Consequences Of Head Bending | **Label:** V7 |
| 2. Hands Straighten The Water | i. Part One: The Pain Left Melting | **Rel:** May[5]/Jun '77[1] |
| 3. The Mathematician's Air Display | ii. Part Two: The Plot Thickens | **RRP:** £2.99[1]/ |
| | 2. False Start Of The Shadows | £3.49[5] |

For this LP, Pohjola's surname was dropped. Two one–sided Utopia acetates known to exist. This later turned up in various countries credited to Mike (and Sally) Oldfield, some without Pohjola credit.

---

***V 2085*** ***PHILIP GLASS: North Star***

| Side 1 | Side 2 | |
|---|---|---|
| 1. Etoile Polaire (North Star) | 1. Lady Day | **Label:** V7 |
| 2. Victor's Lament | 2. Ange Des Oranges | **Rel:** Apr[5]/May '77[1] |
| 3. River Run | 3. Ave | **RRP:** £2.99[1]/ |
| 4. Mon Père, Mon Père | 4. Ik–ook | £3.49[5] |
| 5. Are Years What? (For Marianne Moore | 5. Montage | |

### *V 2086* — *SEX PISTOLS: Never Mind The Bollocks, Here's The Sex Pistols*

1. Holidays In The Sun
2. Liar
3. No Feelings
4. God Save The Queen
5. Problems

1. Seventeen
2. Anarchy In The UK
3. Bodies
4. Pretty Vacant
5. New York
6. EMI

**Label:** V9
**Rel:** Sep[5]/Oct '77[5]
**RRP:** £3.89[5]

**Cassette:** TCV 2086 **Rel:** Oct 1977[5] **RRP:** £3.99[5]

Some early copies issued without track listing on the rear of the sleeve. Export copies included a sleeve sticker with the "SPOTS 001" export catalogue number. These copies were shrinkwrapped with a poster and a one–sided single, *Submission* (VDJ 24). The sticker said, "UK Pressing includes one–sided single & Pistols poster". So there you go. *Music Master 1979* includes two release dates: October seems more likely judging by UK chart action.

---

### *V 2087* — *GLENN PHILLIPS: Swim In The Wind*

1. Sex Is So Strange
2. Vanity
3. Druid Hill
4. Sleeper
5. Lies

1. Sunspoon
2. Creeper
3. Xmas Song
4. Josh
5. My Name Is Time
6. Lenore

**Label:** V7
**Rel:** Sep[5]/Oct '77[1]
**RRP:** £3.89[1]

---

### *V 2088* — *DELROY WASHINGTON: Rasta*

1. Chant
2. Ratsa
3. Mystic Revelation
4. Brothers In Trouble
5. Wake Up Jamaica

1. Zion
2. There Must Be A Way
3. Dress Back
4. You Know I Want To Be
5. Chant 2

**Label:** V7
**Rel:** Aug[1]/Sep[5]/Oct 1977[1]
**RRP:** £3.89[1]

---

### *V 2089* — *THE MOTORS: 1*

1. Dancing The Night Away
2. Freeze
3. Cold Love
4. Phoney Heaven

1. Bring In The Morning Light
2. Emergency
3. Whiskey And Wine
4. Summertime (Is Calling)

**Label:** see below
**Rel:** Sep[5]/Oct '77[1]
**RRP:** £3.89[1]

**Cassette:** TCV 2089 **Rel:** 1979[6] (del 1980[6]) **RRP:** £5.30[6]

The blue 'neon' label includes the Motors logo in place of the Virgin logo. By the look of things the cassette version wasn't issued until 1979.

---

### *V 2090/Matrix H Quad* — *DAVID BEDFORD: Instructions For Angels*

1. Theme
2. Variation 1: "Wanderers Of The Pale Wood. Part 1"
3. Variation 2: "Wanderers Of The Pale Wood. Part 2"
4. Variation 3: "The Dazzling Burdon"
5. Variation 4: "Be Music Night"

1. Variation 5: "First Came The Lion–Rider"
2. Variation 6: "Instructions For Angels"
3. Finale: "The Valley–Sleeper, The Children, The Snakes And The Giant"

**Label:** V7
**Rel:** Sep[5]/Oct[1]/Dec 1977[1]
**RRP:** £3.89[1]

Inner sleeve. Matrix H Quad compatible. Sleeve includes the catalogue number as shown above though inner sleeve and labels only include "V 2090".

---

### *V 2091* — *ASHRA: Blackouts*

1. 77 Slightly Delayed
2. Midnight On Mars
3. Don't Trust The Kids
4. Blackouts

1. Shuttle Cock
2. Lotus 0 Part I – IV

**Label:** V7
**Rel:** Jan 1978[5]
**RRP:** £3.89[5]

### *V 2092* *U ROY: Rasta Ambassador*

| Side 1 | Side 2 | |
|---|---|---|
| 1. Control Tower | 1. Come Home Little Girl | **Label:** V7 |
| 2. Wear You To The Ball | 2. Say You | **Rel:** Dec 1977[5] |
| 3. Evil Doers | 3. No More War | **RRP:** £3.89[5] |
| 4. Mr. Slave Driver | 4. Tide Is High | **Del** 1980[6] |
| 5. Small Axe | 5. Jah Jah | |

Two–sided Master Room acetate known to exist.

---

### *V 2093* *COLIN TOWNS: Full Circle*

| Side 1 | Side 2 | |
|---|---|---|
| 1. Full Circle (Main Theme) | 1. Olivia | **Label:** V7 |
| 2. Park | 2. Love Scene | **Rel:** Feb 1978[5] |
| 3. Have YOU Got A Magnificent Problem? | 3. 'Magnus' – The Unwelcome Intrusion | **RRP:** £4.10[5] |
| 4. 'Pretty Men Are Very Receptive' (The Seance) | 4. Full Circle (Everything's Right Now) | |
| 5. Kate (Opening Sequence) | | |

Subtitled, "Music from the film 'Full Circle', written and performed by Colin Towns." The track subtitles are as they appear on the label credits. However, the sleeve includes further subtitles. *Full Circle (Main Theme)* is also subtitled "(Julia Steps Into Her New House)" and *Have YOU Got a Magnificent Problem?* is subtitled "(Inside the Mental Home)". Original UK copies exported from – and re–imported to – the UK (and sold in Virgin shops at 49p) are shrinkwrapped with a sticker that says, "now featured in the GILLAN band". No cassette version issued according to the *Half Pounder* promotional compilation (RM BURG 1).

---

### *V 2094* *DEREK AND CLIVE: Come Again*

| Side 1 | Side 2 | |
|---|---|---|
| 1. Coughing Contest | 1. In The Cubicles | **Label:** V7 |
| 2. Cancer | 2. Ross McPharter | **Rel:** Dec 1977[5] |
| 3. Non–Stop Dancer/My Mum Song | 3. Hello Colin | **RRP:** £3.89[5] |
| 4. Joan Crawford | 4. Having A Wank | |
| 5. Norman The Carpet | 5. I Saw This Bloke | |
| 6. How's Your Mother | 6. Parking Offence | |
| 7. Back Of The Cab | 7. Members Only | |
| 8. Alfie Noakes | | |
| 9. Nurse | | |

**Cassette:** TCV 2094 **Rel:** Dec 1977[5]/Jan 1978[2] **RRP:** £3.99[3]
Sleeve track credits do not match the actual tracks as listed on the labels, and are quite rude once you work them out. Not funny, just rude, as is much of the album – oh how the once mighty had fallen. On the other hand, they had obviously correctly identified what the post–punk, Great British Public wanted, because it reached number 18 in UK charts.

---

### *V 2095* *XTC: White Music*

| Side 1 | Side 2 | |
|---|---|---|
| 1. Radios In Motion | 1. Atom Age | **Label:** V9 |
| 2. X Wires | 2. Set Myself On Fire | **Rel:** Jan[5]/Mar '78[1] |
| 3. This Is Pop | 3. I'm Bugged | **RRP:** £3.89[5]/ £4.10[1] |
| 4. Do What You Do | 4. New Town Animal | |
| 5. Statue Of Liberty | 5. Spinning Top | |
| 6. All Along The Watch Tower | 6. Neon Shuffle | |

**Cassette:** TCV 2095 **Rel:** Sep 1979[6] (del 1981[6]) **RRP:** not advised
Inner sleeve. Another album that seems to have had a cassette release delayed.

### *V 2096* *KEVIN COYNE: Dynamite Daze*

| | | |
|---|---|---|
| 1. Dynamite Days | 1. Amsterdam | **Label:** V7 |
| 2. Brothers Of Mine | 2. I Only Want To See You Smile | **Rel:** Feb[5]/Mar '78[1] |
| 3. Lunatic | 3. Juliet And Mark | **RRP:** £4.10[1] |
| 4. Are We Dreaming? | 4. Woman, Woman, Woman | |
| 5. (Take Me Back To) Dear Old Blighty | 5. Cry | |
| 6. I Really Live Round Here | 6. Dance Of Bourgeoisie | |
| 7. I Am | | |

No cassette version issued according to the *Half Pounder* promotional compilation (RM BURG 1).

---

### *V 2097* *TANGERINE DREAM: Cyclone*

| | | |
|---|---|---|
| 1. Bent Cold Sidewalk | 1. Madrigal Meridian | **Label:** V7 |
| 2. Rising Runner Missed By Endless Sender | | **Rel:** Mar 1978[5] |
| | | **RRP:** £4.10[5] |

**Cassette:** TCV 2097 **Rel:** Mar 1978[5] **RRP:** £4.29[5]

---

### *V 2098* *STEVE HILLAGE: Green*

| | | |
|---|---|---|
| 1. Sea–Nature | 1. Unidentified (Flying Being) | **Label:** V7 |
| 2. Ether Ships | 2. U.F.O. Over Paris | **Rel:** May 1978[5] |
| 3. Musick Of The Trees | 3. Leylines To Glassdom | **RRP:** £4.10[5] |
| 4. Palm Trees (Love Guitar) | 4. Activation Meditation | |
| | 5. The Glorious Om Riff | |

**Cassette:** TCV 2098 **Rel:** May 1978[5] **RRP:** £4.29[5]

Initial pressing on green vinyl with poster and insert. Later black vinyl copies include only the insert.

---

### *V 2099* *GONG: Expresso II*

| | | |
|---|---|---|
| 1. Heavy Tune | 1. Soli | **Label:** V9 |
| 2. Golden Dilemma | 2. Boring | **Rel:** Feb[5]/Mar '78[1] |
| 3. Sleepy | 3. Three Blind Mice | **RRP:** £4.10[1] |

Insert or inner sleeve? Cut–price US imports on Arista were very common in the UK in the late 1970s.

---

### *V 2100* *MAGAZINE: Real Life*

| | | |
|---|---|---|
| 1. Definitive Gaze | 1. Motorcade | **Label:** V9 |
| 2. My Tulpa | 2. The Great Beautician In The Sky | **Rel:** Jun 1978[5] |
| 3. Shot By Both Sides | 3. The Light Pours Out Of Me | **RRP:** £4.10[5] |
| 4. Recoil | 4. Parade | |
| 5. Burst | | |

**Cassette:** TCV 2100 **Rel:** 1979[6] (del 1981[6]) **RRP:** not advised

---

### *V 2101* *THE MOTORS: Approved By The Motors*

| | | |
|---|---|---|
| 1. Airport | 1. Breathless | **Label:** V9 |
| 2. Mamma Rock 'N' Roller | 2. Soul Redeemer | **Rel:** May 1978[5] |
| 3. Forget About You | 3. Dreaming Your Life Away | **RRP:** £4.10[5] |
| 4. Do You Mind | 4. Sensation | |
| 5. You Beat the Hell Outta Me | 5. Today | |

**Cassette:** TCV 2101 **Rel:** May 1978[5] **RRP:** £4.29[5]

Original release on black vinyl with group photo and inner sleeve withdrawn. Reissued on red vinyl in different sleeve with two sleeve stickers: one says, "Red Vinyl Collectors Edition At No Extra Cost"; the other lists *Airport*, *Forget About You* and *Today*. Blue 'neon' label design with fake ink stamp, "Approved By The Motors", added.

### *V 2102* *THE DIAMONDS: Planet Earth*

1. Where Is Garvey?
2. Let The Answer
3. Struggling
4. Carefree World
5. Got To Get Away

1. Sweet Lady
2. Only Brothers
3. Just Can't Figure Out
4. Come Me Brethren
5. Planet Called Earth

**Label:** V9
**Rel:** 1978
**RRP:** pres. £4.10

**Cassette:** TCV 2102 **Rel:** not advised **RRP:** not advised
Cassette version listed on the *Half Pounder* promotional compilation (RM BURG 1).

---

### *V 2103* *NO RELEASE (SOME LISTINGS CLAIM V 2104 ON THIS CAT. NO.)*

---

### *V 2104* *YELLOW DOG: Beware Of The Dog*

1. Gee, Officer Krupke
2. Up In The Balcony
3. So This Is Love
4. Flying Saucers
5. Beware Of The Dog

1. Wait Until Midnight
2. Just One More Night
3. I Got Carried Away
4. Masters Of The Night

**Label:** V9
**Rel:** Jun 1978[5]
**RRP:** £4.10[5]

Embossed sleeve. Inner sleeve. No cassette version issued according to the *Half Pounder* promotional compilation (RM BURG 1), which credits the intended release date as 16 June 1978.

---

### *V 2105* *SOLID SENDERS: Solid Senders*

1. Blazing Fountains
2. You're In My Way
3. Dr. Dupree
4. Too Bad
5. First Thing In The Morning
6. Everybody's Carrying A Gun

1. Signboard
2. Keep Both Eyes On The Road
3. Shop Around
4. Burning Down
5. I've Seen The Signs

**Label:** V10
**Rel:** 1978
**RRP:** £4.69[5]

*Free Live LP – Side 1*

1. Walking On The Edge
2. Paradise
3. All Abroad

*Free Live LP –Side 2*

1. Highway 81
2. Neighbour Neighbour
3. Rock Me Baby

Initially included a free LP, Live (VDJ 26) with a sticker on the sleeve to this effect and another sticker saying "Sales Point Wilco". Export copies for the US market included the "Sales Point Wilco" sticker plus another saying, "This is a British Double Slice" and pointing out that the album included one studio and one live album with free poster.

---

### *V 2106* *DEVO: Q: Are We Not Men? A: No, We Are Devo*

1. Uncontrollable Urge
2. (I Can't Get No) Satisfaction
3. Praying Hands
4. Space Junk
5. Mongoloid
6. Jocko Homo

1. Too Much Paranoias
2. Gut Feeling/(Slap Your Mammy)
3. Come Back Jonee
4. Sloppy (I Saw My Baby Gettin')
5. Shrivel Up

**Label:** V10
**Rel:** Sep 1978[5]
**RRP:** £4.69[5]

**Cassette:** TCV 2106 **Rel:** Sep 1978[5] (del 1981[6]) **RRP:** £4.99[5]
Inner sleeve and insert. Issued on coloured vinyl – green, yellow, red and blue versions all exist. Later issued as a picture disc (VP 2106) with free flexi (VDJ 27). Did normal copies include the free flexi?

---

### *V 2107* *JULIE COVINGTON: Julie Covington*

1. (I Want To See The) Bright Lights
2. By The Time It Gets Dark
3. Sip The Wine
4. How
5. Barbara's Song

1. A Little Bit More
2. Let Me Make Something In Your Life
3. I Can't Dance
4. The Kick Inside
5. Dead Weight
6. Dancing In The Dark

**Label:** V10
**Rel:** 1978
**RRP:** £4.69[5]

**Cassette:** TCV 2017 **Rel:** 1978 **RRP:** £4.99[5]
Listed in *Music Master 1979* as also issued as a picture disc (VP 2107). Has anyone ever seen one?

---

***V 2108*** ***XTC: Go 2***

1. Meccanik Dancing (Oh We Go!)
2. Battery Brides (Andy Paints Brian)
3. Buzzcity Talking
4. Crowded Room
5. The Rhythm
6. Red

1. Beatown
2. Life Is Good In The Greenhouse
3. Jumping In Gomorrah
4. My Weapon
5. Super–Tuff
6. I Am The Audience

**Label:** V10
**Rel:** 1978
**RRP:** £4.69[5]

*Free 12" EP, side 1*
1. Dance With Me, Germany
2. Beat The Bible

*Free 12" EP, side 2*
1. A Dictionary Of Modern Marriage
2. Clap Clap Clap
3. We Kill The Beast

Inner sleeve. First 15,000 included the free 12" EP, 'Go Plus' (VS 233–12) and a poster.

---

***V 2109*** ***PENETRATION: Moving Targets***

1. Future Daze
2. Life's A Gamble
3. Lovers Of Outrage
4. Vision
5. Silent Community
6. Stone Heroes

1. Movement
2. Too Many Friends
3. Reunion
4. Nostalgia
5. Freemoney

**Label:** V10
**Rel:** 1978
**RRP:** £4.69[5]

**Cassette:** TCV 2109 **Rel:** 1979[6] (del 1981[6]) **RRP:** not advised
Initially on luminous vinyl.

---

***V 2110*** ***KEVIN COYNE: Millionaires And Teddy Bears***

1. People
2. Having A Party
3. I'll Go Too
4. I'm Just A Man
5. Pretty Park

1. Let Me Be With You
2. Marigold
3. Don't Blame Mandy
4. Little Miss Portabello
5. Wendy's Dream
6. The World Is Full Of Fools

**Label:** V10
**Rel:** not advised
**RRP:** pres. £4.69

Insert.

---

***V 2111*** ***TANGERINE DREAM: Force Majeure***

1. Force Majeure

1. Cloudburst Flight
2. Thru Metamorphic Rocks

**Label:** CUS
**Rel:** Jun 1979[9]
**RRP:** pres. £4.69

**Cassette:** TCV 2111 **Rel:** Jun 1979[6] **RRP:** not advised
Initially on clear vinyl with stickered, textured sleeve. Later black vinyl copies in non–textured sleeves.

---

***V 2112*** ***DEREK AND CLIVE: Ad Nauseum***

1. Endangered Species
2. Racing
3. T.V.
4. Bruce
5. Records
6. Soul Time
7. Russia
8. Sir
9. Celebrity Suicide
10. Politics
11. Labels
12. Street Music

1. The Horn
2. Mona
3. The Critics

**Label:** V10
**Rel:** 1978
**RRP:** £4.69[5]

**Cassette:** TCV 2112 **Rel:** 1978 **RRP:** £4.99[5]
Included stickered PVC outer sick bag.

---

***V 2113*** ***VARIOUS ARTISTS: Rhythm Of Resistance – Music of Black South Africa***

1. U Mama Uyajabula (Babsy Mlangeni)
2. Ka Ya Le leboha (Babsy Mlangeni)
3. Perefere (Malombo)
4. Pampa Madiba (Malombo)
5. Jesu Otsohile (Mparanyana And The Cannibals)

1. Umthombowase Golgota (Ladysmith Black Mambazo)
2. Yinhleleni (Ladysmith Black Mambazo)
3. Inkunzi Ayi Hlabi Ngokusima (Jonny And Sipho)
4. Igula Lamasi (Mahotella Queens)
5. Ubu Gowele (Abafana Baseqhudeni)

**Label:** pres. V10
**Rel:** Jan 1979[6]
**RRP:** £4.69[6]

---

***V 2114*** ***PUBLIC IMAGE LIMITED: First Issue***

1. Theme
2. Religion I
3. Religion II
4. Annalisa

1. Public Image
2. Low Life
3. Attack
4. Fodderstompf

**Label:** CUS
**Rel:** Sep 1978[9]
**RRP:** £4.69[5]

**Cassette:** TCV 2114 **Rel:** 1978 **RRP:** £4.99[5]
Inner sleeve. Copies evidently exist with the large PIL labels on both sides.

---

***V 2115*** ***SPARKS: No 1 In Heaven***

1. Tryouts For The Human Race
2. Academy Award Performance
3. La Dolce Vita

1. Beat The Clock
2. My Other Voice
3. The Number One Song In Heaven

**Label:** V10
**Rel:** Mar 1979[6]
**RRP:** pres. £4.69

**Cassette:** TCV 2115 **Rel:** not advised **RRP:** not advised
Initially on yellow vinyl. Inner sleeve. Almost certainly issued on cassette, bearing in mind that the record charted, but no confirmation as yet.

---

***V 2116*** ***SKIDS: Scared To Dance***

1. Into The Valley
2. Scared To Dance
3. Of One Skin
4. Dossier (Of Fallibility)
5. Melancholy Soldiers
6. Hope And Glory

1. The Saints Are Coming
2. Six Times
3. Calling The Tune
4. Integral Plot
5. Charles
6. Scale

**Label:** V12
**Rel:** not advised
**RRP:** not advised

**Cassette:** TCV 2116 **Rel:** not advised (del 1981[6]) **RRP:** not advised
Initial pressing on blue vinyl supposedly withdrawn.

---

***V 2117*** ***ASHRA: Correlations***

1. Ice Train
2. Club Cannibal
3. Oasis
4. Bamboo Sands

1. Morgana Da Capo
2. Pas De Trois
3. Phantasus

**Label:** V10
**Rel:** Mar 1979[9]
**RRP:** £4.69[6]

---

***V 2118*** ***SUPERCHARGE: Body Rhythm***

1. I Can See Right Thru' You
2. We Both Believe In Love
3. Four To The Floor
4. Don't Stop

1. I Think I'm Gonna Fall (In Love)
2. Taxi
3. Show Me How Real Your Love Is

**Label:** V10
**Rel:** May[6]/Jul '79[1]
**RRP:** £4.69[1]
**Del** 1981[6]

Listed in *The New Records* as "Body Rhythms". No cassette version issued according to the *Oversell* promotional compilation (RMOS 1).

***V 2119*** ***FINGERPRINTZ: The Very Dab***

1. Close Circuit Connection
2. Fingerprince
3. Wet Job
4. Punchy Judy
5. Temperamental
6. 2AT

1. Hey Mr. Smith
2. Tough Luck
3. Invisible Seams
4. On The Hop
5. Beam Me Up Scotty

**Label:** V10
**Rel:** Oct 1979[9]
**RRP:** £3.99[6]

Perforated sleeve.

---

***V 2120*** ***THE MEMBERS, At The Chelsea Nightclub***

1. Electricity
2. Sally
3. Soho A Go Go
4. Don't Push
5. Solitary Confinement

1. Frustrated Bagshot
2. Stand Up And Spit
3. Sound Of the Suburbs
4. Phone In Show
5. Love In A Lift
6. Chelsea Nightclub

**Label:** CUS
**Rel:** May 1979[6]
**RRP:** £4.69[6]

---

***V 2121*** ***MAGAZINE: Secondhand Daylight***

1. Feed the Enemy
2. Rhythm Of Cruelty
3. Cut–Out Shapes
4. Talk To The Body
5. I Wanted Your Heart

1. The Thin Air
2. Back To Nature
3. Believe That I Understand
4. Permafrost

**Label:** CUS
**Rel:** Mar 1979[6]
**RRP:** £4.69[6]

**Cassette:** TCV 2121 **Rel:** Mar 1979[6] (del 1981[6]) **RRP:** not advised

---

***V 2122*** ***THE RECORDS: Shades In Bed***

1. Girl
2. Teenarama
3. Girls That Don't Exist
4. Starry Eyes
5. Up All Night

1. All Messed Up And Ready To Go
2. Insomnia
3. Affection Rejected
4. The Phone
5. Another Star

**Label:** CUS
**Rel:** 1979
**RRP:** pres. £4.69

*Free 12" EP, side 1*

1. Abracadabra (Have You Ever Seen Her)
2. See My Friends

*Free 12" EP, side 2*

1. 1984
2. Have You Seen Your Mother, Baby, Standing In the Shadows

**Cassette:** TCV 2122 **Rel:** not advised (del 1981[6]) **RRP:** £5.30[6]
Initially included free 12" EP, *High Heels* (VDJ 29). Custom labels of free 12" say "Not for resale".

---

***V 2123*** ***INTERVIEW: Big Oceans***

1. You Didn't Have To Lie To Me
2. Here Come The Cavalry
3. Feet Start Walking
4. Love Fallout
5. Fire Island

1. Academies
2. Blow Wind From Alesund
3. St. Jean Wires
4. Hart Crane In Mexico
5. Shipyards

**Label:** CUS
**Rel:** Jul 1979[1]
**RRP:** £4.69[1]
**Del** 1981[6]

**Cassette:** TCV 2133 **Rel:** 1979[6] (del 1981[6]) **RRP:** not advised
Inner sleeve. Included a sticker with special introductory price of £2.99.

---

***V 2124*** ***PETER BAUMANN: Trans Harmonic Nights***

1. This Day
2. White Bench And Black Beach
3. Chasing The Dream
4. Biking Up The Strand

1. Phaseday
2. Meridian Moorland
3. The Third Site
4. Dance At Dawn

**Label:** V10
**Rel:** Jul 1979[1]
**RRP:** £4.69[1]

***V 2125 DEVO: Duty Now For The Future***

1. Devo Corporate Anthem
2. Clockout
3. Timing X
4. Wiggly World
5. Blockhead
6. Strange Pursuit
7. S.I.B. (Swelling Itching Brain)

1. Triumph Of The Will
2. The Day My Baby Gave Me A Surprise
3. Pink Pussycat
4. Secret Agent Man
5. Smart Patrol/Mr. DNA
6. Red Eye

**Label:** V10
**Rel:** Jul 1979[6]
**RRP:** £4.69[6]

Large postcard insert. Released in the UK with two different sleeves, one blue, one pink.

---

***V 2126 NOEL: Is There More To Life Than Dancing (picture disc)***

1. Dancing Is Dangerous
2. Is There More To Life Than Dancing?

1. The Night They Invented Love
2. Au Revoir
3. I Want A Man

**Label:** no labels
**Rel:** Jul 1979[1]
**RRP:** £4.69[1]

PIcture disc in die–cut sleeve. The question is, are there any black vinyl copies?

---

***V 2127 NO RELEASE***

---

***V 2128 KEVIN COYNE AND DAGMAR KRAUSE: Babble***

1. Are You Deceiving Me
2. Come Down Here
3. Dead Dying Gone
4. Stand Up
5. Lonely Man
6. I Really Love You
7. Sun Shines Down On Me

1. I Confess
2. Sweetheart
3. Shaking Hands With The Sun
4. My Mind's Joined Forces
5. It's My Mind
6. Love Together
7. Happy Homes
8. It Really Doesn't Matter
9. We Know Who We Are

**Label:** CUS
**Rel:** Jul[1]/Aug '79[6]
**RRP:** £4.69[1]/ £4.99[6]

Insert. Subcredited "Songs for Lonely Lovers". The last two tracks on side 2 have no track band and are bracketed together on the label.

---

***V 2129 XTC: Drums And Wires***

1. Making Plans For Nigel
2. Helicopter
3. Day In Day Out
4. When You're Near Me I Have Difficulty
5. Ten Feet Tall
6. Roads Girdle The Globe

1. Real by Reel
2. Millions
3. That Is The Way
4. Outside World
5. Scissor Man
6. Complicated Game

**Label:** V10
**Rel:** 1979
**RRP:** not advised

Insert. First 15,000 included free 7", *Chain of Command / Limelight* (VDJ 30).

---

***V 2130 SHOOTING STAR: Shooting Star***

1. You Got What I Need
2. Don't Stop Now
3. Higher
4. Just Friends
5. Bring It On

1. Tonight
2. Rainfall
3. Midnight Man
4. Stranger
5. Last Chance

**Label:** V10
**Rel:** see below
**RRP:** not advised
**Del** 1980[6]

**Cassette:** TCV 2130 **Rel:** Oct 1979[6] **RRP:** not advised

Oddly, *Music Master 1984* gives a 1979 release date for the cassette but 1980 for the LP. The October 1979 date seems most likely what with a 1980 deletion date for both in the same source. Certainly the album and cassette were both listed in an advert in the 22 September edition of *Music Week.*

### *V 2131* PENETRATION: *Coming Up For Air*

| | | |
|---|---|---|
| 1. Shout Above The Noise | 1. Come Into the Open | **Label:** CUS |
| 2. She Is The Slave | 2. What's Going On? | **Rel:** Sep 1979[6] |
| 3. Last Saving Grace | 3. Party's Over | **RRP:** £4.99[6] |
| 4. Killed In The Rush | 4. On Reflection | |
| 5. Challenge | 5. Lifeline | |
| | 6. New Recruit | |

| | | |
|---|---|---|
| **Cassette:** TCV 2131 | **Rel:** Sep 1979[6] (del 1980[6].) | **RRP:** £5.30[6] |

An advert in the 22 September edition of *Music Week* states a limited, introductory RRP of £3.99.

---

### *V 2132* THE RUTS: *The Crack*

| | | |
|---|---|---|
| 1. Babylon's Burning | 1. Savage Circle | **Label:** CUS |
| 2. Dope For Guns | 2. Jah War | **Rel:** Sep 1979[6] |
| 3. S U S | 3. Criminal Mind | **RRP:** £4.99[6] |
| 4. Something That I Said | 4. Back Biter | |
| 5. You're Just A | 5. Out Of Order | |
| 6. It Was Cold | 6. Human Punk | |

| | | |
|---|---|---|
| **Cassette:** TCV 2132 | **Rel:** Oct 1979[6] (del 1981[6].) | **RRP:** £5.30[6] |

Initially with stckered sleeve.

---

### *V 2133* THE HUMAN LEAGUE: *Reproduction*

| | | |
|---|---|---|
| 1. Almost Medieval | 1. Morale... | **Label:** CUS |
| 2. Circus Of Death | 2. You've Lost That Loving Feeling | **Rel:** Sep 1979[6] |
| 3. The Path Of Least Resistance | 3. Austerity/Girl One (Medley) | **RRP:** £4.99[6] |
| 4. Blind Youth | 4. Zero As A Limit | |
| 5. The Word Before Last | | |
| 6. Empire State Human | | |

| | | |
|---|---|---|
| **Cassette:** TCV 2133 | **Rel:** Oct 1979[6] | **RRP:** not advised |

Inner sleeve. "Morale..." and "You've Lost That Loving Feeling" are listed on sleeve and labels as two tracks but the label track timing is given for both tracks combined.

---

### *V 2134* JANE AIRE AND THE BELVEDERES: *Jane Aire And The Belvederes*

| | | |
|---|---|---|
| 1. Breaking Down The Walls Of Heartache | 1. Duke Of Love | **Label:** V10 |
| | 2. Come See About Me | **Rel:** pres. Sep '79 |
| 2. No More Cherry Icing | 3. Life After You | **RRP:** not advised |
| 3. Driviing | 4. Wind Up | |
| 4. When You Can't Be Loved | 5. Love Is A Fire | |
| 5. Take It To The Next Wave | | |

| | | |
|---|---|---|
| **Cassette:** TCV 2134 | **Rel:** Oct 1979[6] | **RRP:** not advised |

The sleeve misses the apostrophe on track 4, side 1. Labels credit "Jane Aire + The Belvederes".

---

### *V 2135* STEVE HILLAGE: *Open*

| | | |
|---|---|---|
| 1. Day After Day | 1. Don't Dither Do It | **Label:** V10 |
| 2. Getting Tune | 2. The Fire Inside | **Rel:** Sep1979[6] |
| 3. Open | 3. Earthrise | **RRP:** not advised |
| 4. Definite Activity | | |

| | | |
|---|---|---|
| **Cassette:** TCV 2135 | **Rel:** Sep 1979[11] | **RRP:** not advised |

Die–cut sleeve. Inner sleeve. Although a cassette issue is not mentioned in trade releases, it is listed as having been issued on cassette in an advert in the 22 September 1979 edition of *Music Week*.

***V 2136*** ***COWBOYS INTERNATIONAL: The Original Sin***

| | | |
|---|---|---|
| 1. Pointy Shoes | 1. Aftermath | **Label:** CUS |
| 2. Thrash | 2. Hands | **Rel:** Oct 1979[9] |
| 3. Part Of Steel | 3. M(emorie) 62 | **RRP:** £3.99[1] |
| 4. Here Comes A Saturday | 4. Lonely Boy | |
| 5. Original Sin | 5. The 'No' Tune | |
| | 6. Wish | |

Stickered PVC outer sleeve with inner sleeve.

---

*V 2137* *SPARKS: Terminal Jive (1980 RELEASE)*

*Insert. Issued January 1980 despite several sources claiming a September 1979 release – probably because its release (both cassette and LP versions) was originally listed in an advert in Music Week (22 September 1979). Cassette subsequently listed as both a February and March 1980 release[2].*

---

***V 2138*** ***SKIDS: Days In Europa***

*Original track listing*

| | | |
|---|---|---|
| 1. Animation | 1. Working For The Yankee Dollar | **Label:** CUS |
| 2. Charade | 2. The Olympian | **Rel:** Oct 1979[6] |
| 3. Dulce Et Decorum Est (Pro Patria Mori) | 3. Thanatos | **RRP:** not advised |
| 4. Pros And Cons | 4. A Day In Europa | |
| 5. Home Of The Saved | 5. Peaceful Times | |

*Amended version track listing*

| | |
|---|---|
| 1. Animation | 1. Working For The Yankee Dollar |
| 2. Charade | 2. Thanatos |
| 3. Dulce Et Decorum Est (Pro Patria Mori) | 3. Masquerade |
| 4. The Olympian | 4. A Day In Europa |
| 5. Home Of The Saved | 5. Peaceful Times |

**Cassette:** TCV 2138 **Rel:** Oct 1979[6] (del 1980[6].) **RRP:** not advised

Gatefold insert. Original sleeve with German 'gothic' lettering and 1936 Olympics picture withdrawn and the album reissued with different sleeve, altered track listing, remixed tracks (*Working For The Yankee Dollar* is a re–recording) and a sticker on the sleeve. An advert in the 22 September 1979 issue of *Music Week* lists the title for both LP and cassette issues as "War Games", which would have fitted well with the original sleeve design.

---

***V 2139*** ***EDGAR FROESE: Stuntman***

| | | |
|---|---|---|
| 1. Stuntman | 1. Drunken Mozart In The Desert | **Label:** V10 |
| 2. It Would Be Like Samoa | 2. A Dali–esque Sleep Fuse | **Rel:** Sep 1979[6] |
| 3. Detroit Snackbar Dreamer | 3. Scarlet Score For Mescalero | **RRP:** not advised |

Inner sleeve. Run–off has "V 1239" matrix numers crossed out and replaced by the correct number. An advert in the 22 September edition of *Music Week* confirms that no cassette version was issued.

---

***V 2140*** ***SNAKEFINGER: Chewing Hides The Sound***

| | | |
|---|---|---|
| 1. The Model | 1. Who Is The Culprit And Who Is The Victim? | **Label:** pres. V10 |
| 2. Kill the Great Raven | 2. What Wilbur? | **Rel:** 1979 |
| 3. Jesus Was A Leprechaun | 3. Picnic In The Jungle | **RRP:** not advised |
| 4. Here Comes The Burns | 4. Friendly Warning | |
| 5. The Vivian Girls | 5. I Love Mary | |
| 6. Magic And Ecstasy | 6. The Vultures Of Bombay | |

***V 2141*** ***MIKE OLDFIELD: Platinum***

| | | |
|---|---|---|
| 1. Part 1: Airborne | 1. Woodhenge | **Label:** CUS |
| 2. Part 2: Platinum | 2. Sally (see below) | **Rel:** 23 Nov '79[12] |
| 3. Part 3: Charleston | 3. Punkadiddle | **RRP:** pres. £4.99 |
| 4. Part 4: North Star/Platinum Finale | 4. I Got Rhythm | |

**Cassette:** TCV 2141 **Rel:** Dec 1979[6]/Feb 1980[2] **RRP:** £5.49[3]

Inner sleeve. Side 1 track titles taken from label: sleeve credits "Platinum (with extract from North Star by Philip Glass Arr. Mike Oldfield)". The first pressing was withdrawn with the track *Sally* replaced by *Into Wonderland* on subsequent pressings, though all labels and sleeves still credited the track as "Sally". Original pressings include 'B1' or 'B2' matrix suffixes. Still, waste not, want not – the withdrawn pressing was quietly pushed out cheaply in Woolworths stores in late 1982 (the shop in Bristol, at that point disasterously rebranded as "21st Century Shopping", had around 200 copies for sale at £1.99 each). Original cassette copies were not withdrawn and even later cassette issues (with credits printed directly onto the plastic casing) still played *Sally*.

---

***V 2142*** ***SEX PISTOLS: Flogging A Dead Horse (1980 RELEASE)***

*Despite a 1979 publishing credit, this was released in February 1980.*

---

***V 2143*** ***THE MEKONS: The Quality Of Mercy Is Not Strnen***

| | | |
|---|---|---|
| 1. Like Spoons No More | 1. What | **Label:** V10 |
| 2. Join Us In The Countryside | 2. Watch The Film | **Rel:** Nov 1979[6] |
| 3. Rosanne | 3. Beetroot | **RRP:** £4.99[6] |
| 4. Trevira Trousers | 4. I Saw You Dance | |
| 5. After 6 | 5. Lonely And Wet | |
| 6. What Are We Going To Do Tonight | 6. Dan Dare | |

Insert.

---

***V 2144*** ***SID VICIOUS: Sid Sings***

| | | |
|---|---|---|
| 1. Born To Lose | 1. Belsen | **Label:** CUS |
| 2. I Wanna Be Your Dog | 2. Something Else | **Rel:** Nov 1979[6] |
| 3. Take A Chance On Me | 3. Chatterbox | **RRP:** £4.99[6] |
| 4. Stepping Stone | 4. Search And Destroy | |
| 5. My Way | 5. Chinese Rocks | |
| | 6. I Killed The Cat | |

**Cassette:** TCV 2144 **Rel:** Jan 1980[2] **RRP:** £5.31[3]

Poster and inner sleeve.

---

**Note:** Before anyone pulls me up over this, Captain Beefheart's *Shiny Beast (Bat Chain Puller)*, which is a few catalogue numbers on (V 2149) has a publication date of 1979 on sleeve and labels but was issued in 1980.

## VC 500 series LPs

This series was started as something of a marketing gimmick, with the price of LPs pegged to that of 7" singles. In a publicity handout intended for retailers, the first LP was introduced thus, "The ... Faust Tapes by Faust VC501, will be selling for 48p ..." The marketing ploy worked in that a large amount of positive publicity was created and very healthy sales were enjoyed. Richard Branson, in his autobiography, said:

> We offered their album at the price of a single, which immediately fired sales, and it went straight into the charts at number 28. This marketing ploy also won attention for the new Virgin Music label, although probably more on the grounds of foolhardiness than judgement ... At 48 pence ... Faust sold 40,000 copies in the first week, and 100,000 copies after a month.

The last two releases were also pegged to the current price of a single and, like the first, were issued on the, by that time, old black and white label design. Perhaps it was cheaper! Although *The Faust Tapes* was deleted for good very quickly (because every copy sold reputedly lost Virgin 2p), the other two LPs were later reissued on the budget Caroline label, though by the look of things *Camembert Electrique* was originally planned as a Caroline issue in the first place based on the fact that the Caroline catalogue number appears in the run–off. Oddly, it was later issued twice on Caroline on different catalogue numbers. More of which later.

---

### *VC 501* *FAUST: The Faust Tapes*

| Side One | Side Two | |
|---|---|---|
| 1. Side One | 1. Side Two | **Label:** V1<br>**Rel:** 25 May 73[16]<br>**RRP:** 48p[1/4]<br>**Del** 1974[4] |

Listed in 5 May 1973 edition of *Music Week* as "Fast Tape". No track listing on either labels or sleeve. Deletion date above is curious (and wrong) because almost every music paper ran a story about the fact that the LP was going to be prematurely deleted on 20 July 1973.

---

### *VC 502* *GONG: Camembert Electrique*

| Side One | Side Two | |
|---|---|---|
| 1. Radio Gnome | 1. Squeezing Sponges Over Policemens Heads | **Label:** V1 |
| 2. You Can't Kill Me | 2. Fohat Digs Holes In Space | **Rel:** May[11]/Jun[4]/Jul 1974[1] |
| 3. I've Bin Stone Before | 3. Tried So Hard | **RRP:** 59p[4]/95p[1]/58p[12] |
| 4. Mister Long Shanks/O Mother I Am Your Fantasy | 4. Tropical Fish/Selene | |
| 5. Dynamite/I Am Your Animal | 5. Gnome the Second | |
| 6. Wet Cheese Delirium | | |

The price was incorrectly listed in the July edition of *The New Records* at 95p – perhaps they looked at the 59p price and decided that Virgin must have got the figures the wrong way around. Adverts in the music press point out that 59p is what you would otherwise pay for a Wombles single. The album was simultaneously issued for export on the Caroline imprint as C 1505, priced at £1.49 (or foreign equivalent). The VC 502 issue has the "C 1505" matrix in the run–off but with the "1505 " scratched out and a "V" added in front of the "C". "502" is added below the crossed out "1505" stamp. The LP ended up getting a second release on Caroline as C 1520 at £1.99. According to an article in the 29 June 1974 edition of *Music Week*, titled *Virgin hits Gong with 59p album* (no author attributed), "British Market Reseach Bureau's listing of top selling records at all prices shows Camembert Electrique as the country's fourth most popular album ... Virgin reports that total sales, two weeks after release, are now in the region of 57,000. It is not planned to keep the album available indefinitely and deletion is planned at a 150,000 ceiling."

***VC 503*** ***VARIOUS ARTISTS: The Front Line***

1. Right Time (The Mighty Diamonds)
2. Natty Rebel (U–Roy)
3. Declaration Of Rights (Johnny Clarke)
4. Don't Touch I Man Locks (I–Roy)
5. Looks Is Deceiving (The Gladiators)

1. Freedom Fighters (Delroy Washington)
2. The Great Psalms (U–Roy)
3. Civilisation (Keith Hudson)
4. Know Yourself Mankind (The Gladiators)
5. Africa (The Mighty Diamonds)

**Label:** V1
**Rel:** Sep 1976[1]
**RRP:** 69p[1]

## QV/QVQS 2000 series quadraphonic LPs

The accepted spelling for this format is now "quadraphonic" but all instances of the word on Virgin releases are spelled "quadrophonic". More records were issued in this format, but these appeared on normal catalogue sequences, all bar one (V 2090/Matrix H Quad) without any specific addition to the catalogue number. The appendices include a summary listing of all quadraphonic releases.

---

***QV 2001*** ***MIKE OLDFIELD: Tubular Bells***

Track listing as per V 2001

**Label:** V2
**Rel:** Jul[4/11]/ Sep 1974[1]
**RRP:** £2.45[4]/ £2.50[1]

The sleeve sticker says, "For people with four ears. A quadrophonic recording at no extra cost". Includes model aeroplane engine noise at end of side 2. Not the same quadraphonic mix as later included in *Boxed* (VBOX 1). Copies with stickered sleeve also confirmed on the short–lived beige mirrored girl label. A very rare 'variation' exists on the white–rimmed green mirrored girl label design – these are normal stereo copies in normal V 2001 sleeves (matrix numbers end "A–16U" and "B–15U") but they have quadraphonic credits printed on the labels. These are pointlessly rare and will set you back a silly amount of money if you are lucky enough to find one.

---

***QV 2043*** ***MIKE OLDFIELD: Ommadawn***

Track listing as per V 2043

**Label:** V2
**Rel:** Jan[5]/Mar '76[1]
**RRP:** £2.99[1]

Included a sticker on the sleeve. Listed in *The New Records* as "Quadrophonic Ommadawn (SQ)".

---

***QVQS 2043*** ***MIKE OLDFIELD: The QS Quadrophonic Ommadawn***

Track listing as per V 2043

**Label:** V2
**Rel:** Mar 1976[1]
**RRP:** £2.99[1]

Sleeve titled "Ommadawn" but the sleeve sticker and labels credit the title as "QS Quadrophonic Ommadawn". It is also listed *The New Records* as "QS Quadrophonic Ommadawn". Promotional labels include red "Promotion Copy Only" text. Side 2 has the credit, "Featuring Paddy Maloney on uilleann pipes". Despite being listed for release in trade publications it is possible that this LP was not issued – the only copies to hit the collectors' market seem to be promotional copies.

## VCL 5000 series 10" LPs

This series was on the rather interesting 10" LP format. A confusing gap in this sequence is explained by VCL 5002 being released on Front Line instead.

---

***VCL 5001*** ***VARIOUS ARTISTS: Guillotine***

1. You Beat The Hell Outta Me (The Motors)
2. Don't Dictate (Penetration)
3. Do The Standing Still (Classics Illustrated) (The Table)
4. Strange Gurl In Clothes (Avant Gardener)

1. Traffic Light Rock (XTC)
2. Bermuda (Roky Erickson)
3. All Wi Doin' Is Defendin' (Poet And The Roots)
4. Oh Bondage, Up Yours (X–Ray Spex)

**Label:** V9
**Rel:** Feb[5]/Mar '78[1]
**RRP:** £2.99[1]

Inner sleeve and poster.

---

***VCL 5002*** ***TWINKLE BROTHERS: Love (NOT RELEASED)***

Issued instead on the Front Line label with the one–off catalogue number FCL 5001

---

***VCL 5003*** ***VARIOUS ARTISTS: Short Circuit Live At The Electric Circus***

1. Stepping Out (The Fall)
2. (You Never See A Nipple In The) Daily Express (John Cooper Clarke)
3. At A Later Date (Joy Division)
4. Persecution Complex (The Drones)

1. Makka Spliff (Steel Pulse)
2. I Married A Monster From Outer Space (John Cooper Clarke)
3. Last Orders (The Fall)
4. Time's Up (The Buzzcocks)

**Label:** V9
**Rel:** Jun 1978[5]
**RRP:** £2.99[5]

Inner sleeve. Early copies may have included a poster. On electric blue vinyl with free pink vinyl John Dowie EP, *Another Close Shave* (VEP 1004). Stickers on sleeve state, "Limited Edition on Electric Blue Vinyl" and "including chart topping E.P "I Hate the Dutch" on Pink Vinyl". Also on orange vinyl. Later on black vinyl. Not one of these was a Virgin artist.

## VP 2000 series picture disc LPs

All issued in die–cut sleeves with the record housed in a clear, floppy PVC inner.

---

***VP 2001*** ***MIKE OLDFIELD: Tubular Bells***

Track listing as per V 2001

**Rel:** 1 Dec 1978[11]
**RRP:** £6.99[5]

Two versions available: one is a stereo remix of the *Boxed* quadraphonic mix, but with model plane noise at the end of side 2 after the original LP version of *Sailor's Hornpipe*. The other does not include the model plane noise. Release date as documented in the 11 November edition of *Music Week*, which went on to say that it was to be a limited edition of 25,000 copies. I remember a huge, bright display of these picture discs in Debenhams' windows, Gloucester, on an otherwise dark evening.

---

***VP 2086*** ***SEX PISTOLS: Never Mind The Bollocks, Here's The Sex Pistols***

Track listing as per V 2086

**Rel:** 1978
**RRP:** pres. £6.99

---

***VP 2106*** ***DEVO: Q: Are We Not Men? A: We Are Devo***

Track listing as per V 2106

**Rel:** 1978
**RRP:** pres. £6.99

Insert. Also included flexidisc, *Flimsy Wrap* (VDJ 27).

---

***VP 2107*** ***JULIE COVINGTON: Julie Covington (NOT RELEASED?)***

If it exists, track listing as per V 2107

**Rel:** 1978[5]
**RRP:** pres. £6.99

Listed in *Music Master 1979* but may not have been issued.

## VR series LPs

***VR 1*** ***STEVE HILLAGE: Rainbow Dome Musick***

| | | |
|---|---|---|
| 1. Garden Of Paradise | 1. Four Ever Rainbow | **Label:** V10 |
| | | **Rel:** May 1979[9] |
| | | **RRP:** £2.99[1] |

Original issue on clear vinyl. Clear and black vinyl copies had stickered sleeve showing RRP.

***VR 2*** ***SEX PISTOLS: Some Product Carri On Sex Pistols***

| | | |
|---|---|---|
| 1. The Very Name 'Sex Pistols' | 1. The Complex World Of John Rotten | **Label:** V10 |
| 2. From Beyond The Grave | 2. Sex Pistols Will Play | **Rel:** Jul[9]/Aug '79[1] |
| 3. Big Tits Across America | 3. Is The Queen A Moron? | **RRP:** £2.99[1] |
| | 4. The Fucking Rotter | |

***VR 3*** ***THE RESIDENTS: Nibbles***

| | | |
|---|---|---|
| 1. You Yesyesyes | 1. Laughing Song | **Label:** prob. V10 |
| 2. Santa Dog '78 | 2. (Excerpt From) The Making Of A Soul | **Rel:** Aug 1979[1/9] |
| 3. Gloria | | **RRP:** £2.99[1] |
| 4. (Excerpt From) Rest Aria | 3. Skratz | |
| 5. Semolina | 4. Good Lovin' | |
| 6. The Spot * | 5. Blue Rosebuds | |
| 7. (Excerpt From) Never Known Questions | 6. (Excerpt From) Six Things To A Cycle | |
| | 7. The Electrocutioner | |
| 8. Constantinople | | |

* credited to Snakefinger. Copy viewed includes sticker with RRP of £3.20 – perhaps a later copy?

***VR 4*** ***PETER COOK: Here Comes The Judge Live In Concert***

| | | |
|---|---|---|
| 1. Entirely A Matter For The Jury | 1. Well–Hung Jury | **Label:** prob. V10 |
| | 2. Thanksgiving | **Rel:** Aug 1979[6] |
| | 3. Rad Job | **RRP:** £2.99[15] |

Printed corner band on sleeve with the text, "You should not pay more than £2.99 for this record."

## VD 2500 series 2–LPs

***VD 2501*** ***KEVIN COYNE: Marjory Razorblade***

| | | |
|---|---|---|
| *Side 1* | *Side 2* | **Label:** V1 |
| 1. Marjorie Razor Blade | 1. I Want My Crown | **Rel:** Oct 1973[1] |
| 2. Marlene | 2. Nasty | **RRP:** £2.99[4] |
| 3. Talking To No One | 3. Lonesome Valley | |
| 4. Eastbourne Ladies | 4. House On The Hill | |
| 5. Old Soldier | 5. Cheat Me | |
| *Side 3* | *Side 4* | |
| 1. Jackie And Edna | 1. Dog Latin | |
| 2. Everybody Says | 2. This Is Spain | |
| 3. Mummy | 3. Chairman's Ball | |
| 4. Heaven In My View | 4. Good Boy | |
| 5. Karate King | 5. Chicken Wing | |

| | | |
|---|---|---|
| **Cassette:** TCVD 2501 | **Rel:** Jul 1974[17] | **RRP:** not advised |
| **8–track:** 8XVD 2501 | **Rel:** Jul 1974[17] | **RRP:** not advised |

Original sleeve has "130 Notting Hill Gate" credit. No cassette version available as at 1978 according to the *Half Pounder* promotional compilation (RM BURG 1). Original 8–track in clear hard plastic cover with wraparound inlay. Tape issue date is probably a relisting on issue of *Blame It On The Night.*

### *VD 2502* *VARIOUS ARTISTS: V*

*Side 1*
1. Yesterday Man (Robert Wyatt)
2. Don Alphonso (Mike Oldfield)
3. Go And Sit Upon The Grass (Ivor Cutler)
4. Overture (Tangerine Dream)

*Side 2*
1. Marjory Razorblade (Kevin Coyne)
2. Looking For The River (Kevin Coyne)
3. Mirror Man (Captain Beefheart And The Magic Band)
4. Upon The My–Oh–My (Captain Beefheart And The Magic Band)

**Label:** V2
**Rel:** Jan[4]/Mar '75[1]
**RRP:** £2.94[1]

*Side 3*
1. Extract From The Messiah (Slapp Happy)
2. A Worm Is At Work (Henry Cow)
3. Sad Sing (Tom Newman)
4. Super Man (Tom Newman)
5. Semba (Chilli Charles)
6. Baille – (They Are Gone) (Jabula)

Side 4
1. Extract From Part 1 (Clearlight Symphony)
2. Your Majesty Is Like A Cream Donut Incorporating Oh What A Lonely Lifetime (Hatfield And The North)
3. White Noise II (White Noise II)
4. Pentagramaspin (Steve Hillage)

**Cassette:** TCVD 2502 **Rel:** Mar 1975[2] **RRP:** £2.94

Red, poly–lined company inner sleeves. Sleeve sticker says, "'V' Has vays of making you listen" and the RRP (£2.94). The Clearlight Symphony track is actually an extract from *Part 2* – perhaps the sides were originally intended to be the other way around. The Robert Wyatt track had been intended for release as a single the previous year but wasn't issued in that format until 1977 (though with the originally assigned VS 115 catalogue number). The Mike Oldfield track is an otherwise unreleased long version of the track issued on single as VS 117. The Tangerine Dream track was otherwise unreleased, as were the Steve Hillage, Kevin Coyne and Captain Beefheart tracks (all tracks on side 2 are live recordings). The Clearlight Symphony and White Noise tracks were otherwise unavailable edits and the Hatfield and the North track included an otherwise unreleased alternative ending. In fact, the Hatfield track might be a completely different recording to that on *The Rotter's Club*.

---

### *VD 2503* *TANGERINE DREAM: Zeit*

*Side 1*
1. Birth Of Liquid Plejades

*Side 2*
1. Nebulous Dawn

**Label:** V5
**Rel:** Jun 1976[5]
**RRP:** £3.49[1]

*Side 3*
1. Origin Of Supernatural Probabilities

*Side 4*
1. Zeit

---

### *VD 2504* *TANGERINE DREAM: Alpha Centauri/Atem*

*Side 1*
1. Sunrise In The Third System
2. Fly Collision Of Comas Sola

*Side 2*
1. Alpha Centauri

**Label:** V4/V5
**Rel:** Jul[5]/Aug '76[1]
**RRP:** £3.49[1]

*Side 3*
1. Atem

*Side 4*
1. Fauni–Gena
2. Circulation Of Events
3. Wahn

Stickered sleeve. Sleeve says "Quadrophonische Produktion" but sleeve (again) and labels say "Stereo". Record one labelled "Alpha Centauri" on white–rimmed red labels. Record two labelled "Atem" on white–rimmed green labels. Set parts are VD 257 and VD 258. These appear as matrix numbers in the run–off and on labels under the VD 2504 set numbers. Not issued on cassette[6].

**_VD 2505_ _KEVIN COYNE: In Living Black And White_**

*Side 1*
1. Case History No. 2
2. Fat Girl
3. Talking To No One
4. My Mother's Eyes
5. Ol' Man River
6. Eastbourne Ladies

*Side 2*
1. Sunday Morning Sunrise
2. One Fine Day
3. Marjory Razorblade

**Label:** V7
**Rel:** Jan 1977[5]
**RRP:** £4.49[5]

*Side 3*
1. Coconut Island
2. Turpentine
3. House On The Hill
4. Knocking On Heaven's Door

*Side 4*
1. Saviour
2. Mummy
3. Big White Bird
4. America

Stereo/SQ Quad format only. No cassette version according to the *Half Pounder* promotional compilation (RM BURG 1).

---

**_VD 2506_ _TANGERINE DREAM: Encore_**

*Side 1*
1. Cherokee Lane

*Side 2*
1. Monolight

**Label:** V7
**Rel:** Oct[5]/Dec '77[1]
**RRP:** £4.99[1]

*Side 3*
1. Coldwater Canyon

*Side 4*
1. Desert Dream

**Cassette:** TCVD 2506 **Rel:** Oct[5]/Nov 1977[2] **RRP:** £4.99[3]

---

**_VD 2507_ _EDGAR FROESE: Ages_**

*Side 1*
1. Metropolis (Inspired By Fritz Lang's Movie)
2. Era of the Slaves

*Side 2*
1. Tropic Of Capricorn

**Label:** V7
**Rel:** Jan 1978[5]
**RRP:** £4.99[5]

*Side 3*
1. Nights Of Automatic Women
2. Icarus
3. Childrens Deeper Study

*Side 4*
1. Ode To Granny A.
2. Pizarro And Atahuallpa
3. Golgotha And The Circle Closes

---

**_VD 2508_ _VARIOUS ARTISTS: Dead On Arrival_**

*Side 1*
1. Dancing The Night Away (The Motors)
2. Oh Bondage (X Ray Spex)
3. Radios In Motion (XTC)
4. Firing Squad (Penetration)
5. Walking On The Edge (Wilko Johnson's Solid Senders)

*Side 2*
1. New Electric Ride (Captain Beefheart)
2. Hurdy Gurdy Man (Steve Hillage)
3. Full Moon On The Highway (Can)
4. 77 Slightly Delayed (Ashra)

**Label:** V10
**Rel:** 1978
**RRP:** not advised

*Side 3*
1. Babylon's Burning (U–Roy)
2. Let's Give Jah Praise (Johnny Clark)
3. Them Never Love Poor Marcus (The Mighty Diamonds)
4. Satta (I–Roy)
5. Freedom Fighters (Delroy Washington)
6. Fire In A Trenchtown (U–Roy)

*Side 4*
1. Love And The Single Girl (Roogalator)
2. I'm So Glad I'm So Proud (Link Wray)
3. Casablanca Moon (Slapp Happy)
4. Women's Lib Song (Elkie Brooks)
5. Desperados Waiting For A Train (Mallard)
6. Good Boy (Kevin Coyne)
7. Members Only (Derek And Clive)

Luminous vinyl. Poster. The Caroline Exports logo appears on the back sleeve, so this may have been produced specifically for export. Export copies to the US included a sticker on the sleeve with export catalogue number: "EXPACK 001" and the text, "This Limited Edition from BRITAIN is pressed in luminous vinyl which glows for an hour in the dark after exposure to a bright light for no more than three seconds. All the tracks are selected from recent releases as well as from the archives of VIRGIN RECORDS in LONDON. Suggested U.S. List price: $29.98". A sticker with "800 884 430" covered the UK catalogue number. *Women's Lib Song* credited to Elkie Brooks but is credited to Pete York's Camelo Pardalis on the original release (V 2003). The Link Wray track, credited as *I'm So Glad I'm So Proud*, is a segue of *Beans and Fatback* and *I'm So Glad* from V 2006.

---

***VD 2509 MIKE OLDFIELD: Space Movie (NOT RELEASED)***

Almost certainly assigned to the soundtrack for *Space Movie*, for which four one–sided acetates are documented as existing. See the Virgin Films section in the Appendices for (scanty) information on contents of the acetate. Dates would seem to match.

---

***VD 2510 SEX PISTOLS: The Great Rock 'N' Roll Swindle***

*Side 1*
1. God Save The Queen (Orchestral)
2. Rock Around The Clock
3. Johnny B Goode
4. Road Runner
5. Black Arabs
6. Watcha Gonna Do About It
7. Anarchy In The UK

*Side 2*
1. Silly Thing
2. Substitute
3. Don't Give Me No Lip Child
4. (I'm Not Your) Stepping Stone
5. Lonely Boy
6. Something Else

**Label:** CUS
**Rel:** Jun 1979[9]
**RRP:** not advised

*Side 3*
1. L'Anarchie Pour Le U.K.
2. Einmal Belsen War Vortrefflich (Live)
3. Einmal Belsen War Wirklich Vortrefflich
4. No One Is Innocent
5. My Way

*Side 4*
1. C'mon Everybody
2. E.M.I. (Orchestral)
3. The Great Rock 'N' Roll Swindle
4. You Need Hands
5. Friggin' In The Riggin'

**Cassette:** TCVD 2510 **Rel:** 1979[6] **RRP:** not advised

Insert and stickered sleeve – several stickers if memory serves. Original release includes *Whatcha Gonna Do About It* and a card insert. Later version has spoken overdubs on *God Save the Queen Symphony* and *Who Killed Bambi* replaces *Watcha Gonna Do About It*. Front sleeve sticker says "Sex Pistols Film Soundtrack featuring 21 new tracks".

---

***VD 2511 MIKE OLDFIELD: Exposed***

*Side 1*
1. Incantations, Parts One And Two

*Side 2*
1. Incantations, Parts Three And Four

**Label:** CUS
**Rel:** Aug 1979[1]
**RRP:** £4.99[1]

*Side 3*
1. Tubular Bells, Part One

*Side 4*
1. Tubular Bells, Part Two
2. Guilty

**Cassette:** TCVD 2511 **Rel:** 1979[11] **RRP:** not advised

Only issued in SQ Quad format. Original copies include a yellow sticker with red text stating limited edition of 100,000 at £4.99. However, as soon as this sold out it was immediately repressed, only without the sticker and, if I remember correctly, with higher RRP of £5.29 – so ultimately the only real limited edition item was the sticker (and the original cheaper price). Some early copies also included a second yellow sticker with red text that stated, "Includes live versions of 'Tubular Bells', 'Incantations' and 'Guilty'". Cassette version listed as to be released in the 28 July 1979 edition of *Music Week*.

## VGD 3500 series 2–LPs

### *VGD 3501 GONG: Gong Live Etc*

*Side 1*
1. You Can't Kill Me
2. Zero The Hero And The Witch's Spell
3. Flying Teapot

*Side 2*
1. Dynamite/I Am Your Animal
2. 6/8
3. Est–Ce Que Je Suis
4. Ooby–Scooby Doomsday Or The D–Day DJ's Got The D.D.T. Blues

**Label:** V7
**Rel:** Aug 1977[5]
**RRP:** £3.99[5]

*Side 3*
1. Radio Gnome Invisible
2. Oily Way
3. Outer Temple
4. Inner Temple
5. Where Have All The Flowers Gone?

*Side 4*
1. Isle Of Everywhere
2. Get It Inner
3. Master Builder
4. Flying Teapot

Die–cut single–sleeve with inner sleeves, later in non–die–cut single sleeve, still with inner sleeves.

---

### *VGD 3502 STEVE HILLAGE: Live Herald*

*Side 1*
1. Salmon Song
2. The Dervish Riff/Castle In The Clouds/Hurdy Gurdy Man

*Side 2*
1. Light in the Sky
2. Searching For The Spark
3. Elecrick Gypsies

**Label:** V10
**Rel:** 1979
**RRP:** not advised
**Del** 1981[6]

*Side 3*
1. Radiom/Lunar Musick Suite/ Meditation Of The Dragon
3. It's All Too Much/The Golden Vibe

*Side 4*
1. Talking To The Sun
2. 1988 Aktivator
3. New Age Synthesis (Unzipping The Zype)
4. Healing Feeling

Limited edition lyric sheet in English, French, or German available by mail–order. I've never seen a copy with lyric sheet in any language. Did anyone out there send off for one?

---

### *VGD 3503 WIGWAM: Rumours On The Rebound*

*Side 1*
1. Freddie Are You Ready
2. International Disaster
3. Nuclear Nightclub
4. Eddie And The Boys
5. June May Be Too Late
6. Wardance

*Side 2*
1. Tram Driver
2. Colussus
3. Lucky Golden Stripes And Starpose
4. Never Turn You In

**Label:** V10
**Rel:** Aug 1979[1]
**RRP:** £4.99[1]

*Side 3*
1. Bertha Come Back
2. Cheap Evening Return
3. A Better Hold (And A Little View)
4. The Big Farewell
5. Goddammadog

*Side 4*
1. Helsinki Nights
2. Horace's Aborted Ripoff Scheme
3. All Over Too Soon
4. Masquerade At The White Palace
5. The Item Is The Totem
6. Daemon Duncetan's Request

Single sleeve. Oddly, a sticker on sleeve stated a RRP of £5.30. Possibly a bit of a cynical issue by Virgin, containing, as it does, tracks from Jim Pembroke's solo LP, *Corporal Cauliflower's Mental Function* and the final Wigwam LP, *Dark Album*, both of which had been rejected for issue by Virgin. *Daemon Duncetan's Request* was previously unissued. *June May Be Too Late* credited as "June Maybe Too Late" on the original release on *The Lucky Golden Stripes and Starpose* (V 2051).

## Custom catalogue LPs (in order of release)

***VBOX 1*** ***MIKE OLDFIELD: Boxed (4–LP box)***

*Side 1*
1. Tubular Bells Part One

*Side 2*
1. Tubular Bells Part Two

**Label:** V7
**Rel:** Oct 1976[5]
**RRP:** £7.99[5]

*Side 3*
1. Hergest Ridge Part One

*Side 4*
1. Hergest Ridge Part Two

*Side 5*
1. Ommadawn Part One

*Side 6*
1. Ommadawn Part Two

*Side 7 – Collaborations*
1. The Phaeacian Games
2. Extract From Star's End
3. The Rio Grande

*Side 8 – Collaborations*
1. First Excursion
2. Argiers
3. Portsmouth
4. In Dulce Jubilo
5. Speak (Tho You Only Say Farewell)

**Cassette:** TCVX 1 **Rel:** Dec 1976[17] **RRP:** not advised

4–LP boxed set with booklet. Original release includes dark sticker: "FOUR ALBUMS for the price of two £7.99" (somewhat ingenuous in that two Virgin label LPs at this point would cost around £6.50 and even two LPs on mainstream labels would scrape in at around £7.00). Later copies on the original label design and copies on the green/red label design have different design stickers, though both include the text, "Including 4 LP's And 12 Page Booklet" along with LP titles in a circle around the sticker edge. (Original UK copies available in Italy with sticker added to the top, left–hand corner of the box: "4 LP + L.12000! IVA COMPRESA".) Original copies exist with "Factory Sample Not For Sale" stickers on labels whilst promotional copies exist with the circular "D.J. Copy. For promotional use only." text on labels. Copies (probably promotional) exist with ink stamp on the rear of the box stating, "MIKE OLDFIELD "Collaborations" Released with "Tubular Bells" "Hergest Ridge" and "Ommadawn" in the four record set "BOXED" (Virgin Records V BOX 1)" – this stamp is also included on the plain white inner sleeve that housed *Collaborations* in factory sample copies. Rare and highly–sought after copies exist on the blue 'neon' label design.

Comprised SQ Quad mixes of *Tubular Bells*, *Hergest Ridge*, *Ommadawn* and *Collaborations*, each in different coloured, poly–lined, company inner sleeve. *Tubular Bells* seems to be a different SQ Quad mix to QV 2001 and does not include the model aeroplane engine sound. It also includes a different version of *The Sailor's Hornpipe* with drunken monologue from Vivian Stanshall. Legend has it that this was intended as the original ending, but that the 'straight' version was used instead. Record 4, *Collaborations*, includes material previously issued on the David Bedford's LPs, *Star's End* (V 2020), *The Rime of the Ancient Mariner* (V 2038) and *The Odyssey* (V 2069), along with tracks from various Mike Oldfield singles. Only *First Excursion* was previously unreleased.

Stereo cassette version issued in a small box with two double–play cassettes (and miniature booklet?): the inlays of each cassette reproduced two sleeves each – or, at least, for the *Collaborations* album there was a photo of Mike Oldfield sitting with guitar collection. First cassette inlay states both sides had been remixed, though this is conspicuous by its absence on the second cassette inlay. Cassette issue rather more expensive than the LP version if memory serves.

---

***V 2777*** ***STEVE HILLAGE: Motivation Radio (LP)***

1. Hello Dawn
2. Motivation
3. Light In The Sky
4. Radio

1. Wait One Moment
2. Saucer Surfing
3. Searching For The Spark
4. Octave Doctors
5. Not Fade Away (Glid Forever)

**Label:** V7
**Rel:** Sep[5]/Oct[1]/ Dec 1977[1]
**RRP:** £3.89[1]

**Cassette:** TCV 2777 **Rel:** Sep[5]/Oct 1977[2] **RRP:** £3.99[3]

Inner sleeve. Steve Hillage has shown a certain fondness for the "777" motif – indeed it would appear that the glissando guitar tracks were recorded on 7 July 1977 (which gives us four sevens – 7/7/77).

***VDT 101*** ***MIKE OLDFIELD: Incantations (2–LP)***

| *Side 1* | *Side 2* | **Label:** CUS |
|---|---|---|
| 1. Incantations (Part One) | 1. Incantations (Part Two) | **Rel:** 1978 |
| | | **RRP:** £6.25[5] |
| *Side 3* | *Side 4* | |
| 1. Incantations (Part Three) | 1. Incantations (Part Four) | |

**Cassette:** TCVDT 101 **Rel:** 1978 **RRP:** £6.49[5]

One copy known to exist with record one on red vinyl and record two on blue vinyl. Originally intended for release in quadraphonic format. but remixed to stereo by Phil Newell. Rumours of copies with poster and red vinyl Julie Covington single are unsubstantiated.

---

***METAL 1*** ***PUBLIC IMAGE LIMITED: Metal Box (3 x 12" single)***

| *Side 1* | *Side 2* | **Label:** CUS |
|---|---|---|
| 1. Albatross | 1. Memories | **Rel:** 23 Nov '79[13] |
| | 2. Swanlake | **RRP:** £7.45[13] |
| *Side 3* | *Side 4* | |
| 1. Poptones | 1. No Birds | |
| 2. Careering | 2. Graveyard | |
| *Side 5* | *Side 6* | |
| 1. The Suit | 1. Socialist | |
| 2. Bad Baby | 2. Chant | |
| | 3. Radio 4 | |

**Cassette:** MBCAS 1 **Rel:** 1980 **RRP:** not advised

Insert and three circular, paper record dividers. Catalogue number sticker on tin rear. Three 45 rpm records in circular metal box. Strictly speaking not an LP, but listed as an LP release in trade publications probably for want of a section for triple 12" singles – same as here. Supposedly withdrawn on day of release (all 60,000 copies pre–sold) then reissued as a double LP in the new year. An advert in the 22 September edition of *Music Week* suggests that no cassette version was issued but a UK cassette exists (MBCAS 1). However, this was issued in 1980 along with the double LP reissue – even though supposedly this is the belated cassette version of the original release and not of the reissue – complicated, isn't it? Release date and RRP from the 24 November 1979 edition of the *NME*. Lyrics not included in the set but printed in adverts in the music press (p. 39 in above *NME*).

## VS 100 series 7" singles

The VS 100 sequence is fairly straightforward, at least to start with. Later on 12" singles were introduced with "12" added at the end of the catalogue number – these are documented in the following section. In a few cases only the 12" version of a record was issued, but there are several instances where 7" copies are rumoured to exist, these rumours helped by trade publications either having been advised of 7" releases – or perhaps just assuming that both 7" and 12" versions must have been issued.

Many 7" singles exist both with a block "A" on the label and were presumably intended as promotional records, but many were available in the shops. "A" copies are not documented unless there is good reason.

---

***VS 101*** ***MIKE OLDFIELD: Mike Oldfield's Single / Froggy Went A–Courting***

**Label:** V1 **Rel:** 19 Jul 1974[3] (del 1977[10]) **RRP:** 50p or 55p

First 20,000 copies in picture sleeve. A–side label subtitled "Theme from Mike Oldfield's album 'Tubular Bells'" whilst the sleeve was subtitled "Theme from Tubular Bells".

---

***VS 102*** ***KEVIN COYNE: Marlene / Everybody Says***

**Label:** V1 **Rel:** Apr 1974[8] **RRP:** 50p[18]

***VS 103*** **LINK WRAY: *I'm So Glad, I'm So Proud / Shawnee Tribe***
**Label:** V1 **Rel:** 23 Nov 1973[3] (del 1979[8]) **RRP:** 48p[18]

---

***VS 104*** **KEVIN COYNE: *Lovesick Fool / Sea of Love***
**Label:** V1 **Rel:** 23 Nov 1973[3] **RRP:** 48p[18]

---

***VS 105*** **SLAPP HAPPY: *Casablanca Moon / Slow Moon's Rose***
**Label:** V1 **Rel:** between Apr and Jun 1974[18] **RRP:** 50p[18]
Advertised in the 27 April 1974 edition of *Music Week*.

---

***VS 106*** **MAX: *Stephanie / All I Know***
**Label:** V1 **Rel:** pres. between Apr and Jun 1974 **RRP:** 50p[18]

---

***VS 107*** **KEVIN COYNE: *I Believe In Love / Queenie Queenie Caroline***
**Label:** V1 **Rel:** between Apr and Jun 1974[18] **RRP:** 50p[18]

---

***VS 108*** **CHILI CHARLES: *High School / Sunrise***
**Label:** V1 **Rel:** pres. between Apr and Jun 1974 **RRP:** 50p[18]

---

***VS 109*** **CAROL GRIMES: *You're The Only One / Southern Boogie***
**Label:** V1 **Rel:** between Apr and Jun 1974[18] **RRP:** 50p[18]

---

***VS 110*** **CAPTAIN BEEFHEART: *Upon The My–O My / Magic Be***
**Label:** V1 **Rel:** between Apr and Jun 1974[18] **RRP:** 50p[18]
Title as printed on the label (i.e. only one hyphen). No credit to the Magic Band.

---

***VS 111*** **B. B. SEATON: *Dancing Shoes / Moon River***
**Label:** V1 **Rel:** 19 Jul 1974[3] **RRP:** 50p or 55p

---

***VS 112*** **MIKE OLDFIELD: *Hergest Ridge / Spanish Tune (NOT RELEASED)***
White label copies known to exist. A–side label of copy viewed has "A Cut Running 3 mins 2 secs", "Hergest Ridge" and "M. Oldfield" written in biro (b–side label is blank).

---

***VS 113*** **ROGER WOOTTON: *Fiesta Fandango / New Ride***
**Label:** V1 **Rel:** 15 Nov 1974[3] **RRP:** 50p or 55p

---

***VS 114*** **ROBERT WYATT: *I'm A Believer / Memories***
**Label:** V1 **Rel:** 13 Sep 1974[3] (del 1977[10]) **RRP:** 50p or 55p

---

***VS 115*** **ROBERT WYATT: *Yesterday Man / Sonia***
**Label:** V9 **Rel:** 22 Apr 1977[3] **RRP:** 70p[18]
Recorded at same sessions as VS 114 and assigned next number in sequence but subsequently shelved for the best part of three years. A–side first appeared on *V* (VD 2502) in 1975.

---

***VS 116*** **HATFIELD AND THE NORTH: *Let's Eat (Real Soon) / Fitter Stoke Has A Bath***
**Label:** V1 **Rel:** 15 Nov 1974[3] **RRP:** 49p[12]
Not the same version of *Fitter Stoke Has A Bath* as that included on V 2008. Virgin's adverts for the single in the 16 November 1974 *Melody Maker* miscredit the a–side as "Let's Eat Again Real Soon".

---

***VS 117*** **MIKE OLDFIELD: *Don Alphonso / In Dulci Jubilo (For Maureen)***
**Label:** V1 **Rel:** 14 Feb 1975[3] **RRP:** 50p or 55p
Picture sleeve rumoured to exist. A–side includes subcredit "featuring David Bedford on vocals". The b–side is a different version to that later issued as the a–side of VS 131.

---

***VS 118*** **JABULA: *Jabula Happiness / Baile They Are Gone***
**Label:** V1 **Rel:** 21 Feb 1975[3] **RRP:** 50p or 55p

***VS 119*** ***KEVIN COYNE: Rock 'N' Roll Hymn / It's Not Me***
**Label:** V1 **Rel:** 25 Apr[3]/9 May 1975[3] **RRP:** 55p[18]

---

***VS 120*** ***TOM NEWMAN: Sad Sing / Ali's Got A Broken Bone***
**Label:** V1 **Rel:** 28 Feb 1975[3] **RRP:** 50p or 55p

---

***VS 121*** ***WIGWAM: Freddie Are You Ready / Kite***
**Label:** V1 **Rel:** 13 Jun 1975[3] (del 1979[8]) **RRP:** 55p[18]
Finnish issue released on Love Records (LRS 2082).

---

***VS 122*** ***TREVOR WILLIAMS: Lucy Brown / We Slowed Down***
**Label:** V1 **Rel:** 20 Jun[3]/4 Jul 1975[3] **RRP:** 55p[18]

---

***VS 123*** ***DAEVID ALLEN: It's The Time Of Your Life / Fred The Fish (And The Chip On His Shoulder)***
**Label:** V1 **Rel:** 1975
Promotional picture sleeve rumoured to exist. Despite being from the 1971 French Byg label LP, *Bananamoon*, labels have 1975 Virgin publication credits.

---

***VS 124*** ***SLAPP HAPPY FEATURING ANTHONY MOORE: Johnny's Dead / Mr. Rainbow***
**Label:** V1 **Rel:** 25 Jul 1975[3] **RRP:** 60p[18]
Picture sleeve. *Johnny's Dead* is not the same version as intended for Anthony Moore's unreleased Virgin LP, *Out*.

---

***VS 125*** ***RUAN: Another Street Gang / Suburban Disturbance***
**Label:** V1 **Rel:** 5 Sep 1975[3] **RRP:** 60p[18]
Picture sleeve. Also pressed as a 12" promotional record (VDJ 3).

---

***VS 126*** ***KEVIN COYNE: Lorna / Shangri La***
**Label:** V1 **Rel:** 31 Oct 1975[3] (del 1977[5]) **RRP:** 60p[18]

---

***VS 127*** ***MATAYA CLIFFORD: Star Fell From Heaven / Pound And Grind***
**Label:** V1 **Rel:** 10 Oct[3]/14 Nov 1975[3] (del 1977[5]) **RRP:** 60p[18]
Picture sleeve. Also pressed as a 12" promotional record (VDJ 7).

---

***VS 128*** ***WIGWAM: Tram Driver / Nuclear Nightclub***
**Label:** V1 **Rel:** 14 Nov 1975[3] **RRP:** 60p[18]

---

***VS 129*** ***ARCHIE LEGGET: Jamaican Jockey / Alberto***
**Label:** V1 **Rel:** 17 Oct 1975[3] **RRP:** 60p[18]
Picture sleeve. Also pressed as a 12" promotional record (VDJ 4).

---

***VS 130*** ***TOM NEWMAN: Don't Treat Your Woman Bad / Why Does Love Hurt So Bad***
**Label:** V1 **Rel:** 14 Nov 1975[3] **RRP:** 60p[18]

---

***VS 131*** ***MIKE OLDFIELD: In Dulci Jubilo / On Horseback***
**Label:** V1 **Rel:** 14 Nov 1975[3] (del 1979[8]) **RRP:** 60p[18]
Double a–side (*On Horseback* has the "B" matrix suffix). Most copies die–cut, some with solid centres.

---

***VS 132*** ***NO RELEASE***

---

***VS 133*** ***TOM NEWMAN: Sleep / Darling Corey***
**Label:** V1 **Rel:** 23 Jan[5]/6 Feb 1976[3] (del 1979[8]) **RRP:** 60p[18]

---

***VS 134*** ***SUPERCHARGE: Get Down Boogie / Don't Let Go***
**Label:** V1 **Rel:** 30 Jan[3]/5 Mar 1976[3] **RRP:** 60p[18]
Picture sleeve. *The New Records* for 30 January 1976 lists the a–side as "Who Needs The Black

Who Needs The White". The 5 March edition gets the title right. Also pressed as a 12" promotional record (VDJ 11).

---

***VS 135*** ***BOXER: All the Time In The World / Don't Wait***
**Label:** V1 **Rel:** 6 Feb 1976[3] **RRP:** 60p[18]
Promotional copy with large "A" has a–side track timing of 2.58, whilst stock copies have timing of 3.08. Also pressed as a 12" promotional record (VDJ 12).

---

***VS 136*** ***KEVIN COYNE: Don't Make Waves / Mona Where's My Trousers***
**Label:** V1 **Rel:** 20 Feb 1976[3] (del 1978[5]) **RRP:** 60p[18]
Picture sleeve.

---

***VS 137*** ***THE MIGHTY DIAMONDS: Have Mercy / Them Never Love Poor Marcus***
**Label:** V1 **Rel:** 27 Feb 1976[3] **RRP:** 60p[18]
Publication date is 1975, but issued in 1976. Also pressed as a 12" promotional record (VDJ 14).

---

***VS 138*** ***U ROY: Runaway Girl / Chalice In The Palace***
**Label:** V1 **Rel:** 27 Feb 1976[3] **RRP:** 60p[18]
Also pressed as a 12" promotional record (VDJ 13).

---

***VS 139*** ***NO RELEASE***

---

***VS 140*** ***PETER TOSH: Legalize It / Brand New Second Hand***
**Label:** V8 **Rel:** 5 Mar[3]/9 Jul[3]/Aug 1976[5] **RRP:** 60p[18]
No V1 copies seem to exist so either the July or August release date seems much more likely.

---

***VS 141*** ***TOM NEWMAN: Ebony Eyes / Draught Guinness***
**Label:** V1 (if record exists) **Rel:** 26 Mar[3]/Apr 1976[5] **RRP:** 60p[18]

---

***VS 142*** ***LINK WRAY: I Know You're Leaving Me Now / Quicksand***
**Label:** V1 **Rel:** 12 Mar[3]/9 Apr 1976[3] **RRP:** 60p[18]

---

***VS 143*** ***MATAYA CLIFFORD: Things Are Going My Way / Magic Ring***
**Label:** V1 **Rel:** 2 Apr 1976[3] (del 1979[8]) **RRP:** 60p[18]

---

***VS 144*** ***ANTHONY MOORE: Catch A Falling Star / Back to the Top***
**Label:** V1 **Rel:** 2 Apr 1976[3] (del 1979[8]) **RRP:** 60p[18]

---

***VS 145*** ***SUPERCHARGE: Lonely And In Love / Give It the Nasty***
**Label:** V1 **Rel:** 9 Apr 1976[3] **RRP:** 60p[18]

---

***VS 146*** ***B. B. SEATON: Moon River / No More Tribalism***
**Label:** V1 **Rel:** 23 Apr 1976[3] (del 1979[8]) **RRP:** 60p[18]

---

***VS 147*** ***ROY ST. JOHN: Way You Look Tonight / Cincinnati***
**Label:** V1 **Rel:** 7 May[3]/Jun 1976[5] **RRP:** 60p[18]

---

***VS 148*** ***KEVIN COYNE: Walk On By / Shangri–La***
**Label:** V8 **Rel:** 28 May[3]/Jun 1976[5] (del 1978[5]) **RRP:** 60p[18]

---

***VS 149*** ***LEA NICHOLSON: Lazy Afternoon / Sorry About The Phone Stephanie***
**Label:** V8 **Rel:** 4 Jun[3]/18 Jun 1976[3] **RRP:** 60p[18]

---

***VS 150*** ***GEOFF APPLEBY: Make Me Take Me / Live Wire***
**Label:** V8 **Rel:** 4 Jun 1976[3] (del 1978[5]) **RRP:** 60p[18]

***VS 151*** ***KEITH HUDSON: Thank You Baby / Too Expensive (Version)***
**Label:** V8 **Rel:** 25 Jun 1976[3] (del 1979[8]) **RRP:** 60p[18]

---

***VS 152*** ***JOHNNY CLARKE: I Wish It Would Go On Forever / I Wish It Would Go On Forever (version)***
**Label:** V8 **Rel:** 2 Jul[3]/16 Jul 1976[3] **RRP:** 70p[18]

---

***VS 153*** ***CAN: I Want More / More***
**Label:** V8 **Rel:** 23 Jul 1976[3] (del Aug 1979[10]) **RRP:** 70p[18]

---

***VS 154*** ***BASHERS: Womble Bashers / Womble Bashers Rock***
**Label:** V8 **Rel:** 11 Jun 1976[3] (del 1978[5]) **RRP:** 70p[18]
Bashers were Roger McGough and Mike McGear (Scaffold/Grimms). Grimms' version of the song, *The Womble Bashers of Walthamstow* was released by DJM the same month[5]. The Virgin release credits the writers as McGough and McGear, whist the DJM release credits McGough and Innes.

---

***VS 155*** ***THE MIGHTY DIAMONDS: Shame And Pride / Africa***
**Label:** V8 **Rel:** 25 Jun 1976[3] (del 1979[8]) **RRP:** 70p[18]

---

***VS 156*** ***DANDELION: What's The Matter Baby / Please Please***
**Label:** V8 **Rel:** 10 Sep 1976[3] (del 1978[5]) **RRP:** 70p[18]

---

***VS 157*** ***GEOFF APPLEBY: Hey Sadie / Move On Down The Road***
**Label:** prob. V8 **Rel:** 27 Aug[3]/Sep 1976[5] (del 1978[5]) **RRP:** 70p[18]

---

***VS 158*** ***SURVIVAL: Sweet Music / Fiesta***
**Label:** prob. V8 **Rel:** 10 Sep 1976[3]/Oct 1976[5] **RRP:** 70p[18]

---

***VS 159*** ***JOHNNY CLARKE: Crazy Bald Head / Crazy Bald Head (version)***
**Label:** V8 **Rel:** 15 Oct 1976[3] **RRP:** 70p[18]

---

***VS 160*** ***KEVIN COYNE: Fever / Daddy***
**Label:** V8 **Rel:** 8 Oct 1976[3] (del 1978[5]) **RRP:** 70p[18]

---

***VS 161*** ***STEVE HILLAGE: It's All Too Much / Shimmer***
**Label:** V8 **Rel:** 15 Oct 1976[3] **RRP:** 70p[18]

---

***VS 162*** ***NO RELEASE***

---

***VS 163*** ***MIKE OLDFIELD: Portsmouth / Speak (Tho' You Only Say Farewell)***
**Label:** V8 **Rel:** Oct[5]/12 Nov 1976[3] (del 1979[10]) **RRP:** 70p[18]
Initial copies on the blue mirrored girl label. Later copies on the blue 'neon' label. Some copies on the second label design have appeared in what appears to be a commemorative sleeve – the front includes a scroll that says, "HIGHEST POSITION", "No.3 Nov '76" and "12 Weeks in Charts": the rear credits the b–side as just "Speak".

---

***VS 164*** ***THE RAWTENSTALL CONCERTINA BAND CONDUCTED BY LEA NICHOLSON: The Dambusters March / Southampton***
**Label:** V8 **Rel:** 19 Nov 1976[3] **RRP:** 70p[18]

---

***VS 165*** ***THE MAN EZEKE GRAY AND TONY GRIEG: We're The Greatest / THE MAN EZEKE GRAY: 'Enoch' De Nook***
**Label:** V8 **Rel:** 19 Nov 1976[3] (del 1979[8]) **RRP:** 70p[18]
Copies sent with promotional information sheet (which was oddly dated "November 15th 1975" instead of 1976) had "AND TONY GRIEG" blocked out in what looks like felt tip pen on the b–side label.

---

***VS 166*** ***CAN: Silent Night / Cascade Waltz***
**Label:** V9 **Rel:** 19 Nov 1976[3] (del 1979[8]) **RRP:** 70p[18]

***VS 167*** ***MIKE OLDFIELD: William Tell Overture / Argiers***
**Label:** V9 **Rel:** 28 Jan[3]/Feb 1977[5] (del 1979[8]) **RRP:** 70p[18]

---

***VS 168*** ***MALLARD: Harvest / Green Coyote***
**Label:** V9 **Rel:** 11 Feb 1977[3] (del 1979[8]) **RRP:** 70p[18]

---

***VS 169*** ***THE MIGHTY DIAMONDS: Country Living / Coming Through***
**Label:** V9 **Rel:** 11 Mar 1977[3] **RRP:** 70p[18]
Picture sleeve.

---

***VS 170*** ***SUPERCHARGE: Get Up And Dance / Rip It Off***
**Label:** V9 **Rel:** 28 Jan[3]/Feb 1977[5] **RRP:** 70p[18]

---

***VS 171*** ***STEVE HILLAGE: Hurdy Gurdy Man / Om Nama Shivaya***
**Label:** V9 **Rel:** Feb[5]/25 Mar 1977[3] **RRP:** 70p[18]

---

***VS 172*** ***CAN: Don't Say No / Return***
**Label:** V9 **Rel:** 4 Mar[3]/Apr 1977[5] **RRP:** 70p[18]

---

***VS 173*** ***JOHNNY CLARKE: Roots, Natty Roots, Natty Congo / Roots, Natty Roots, Natty Congo (Version)***
**Label:** V9 **Rel:** 18 Mar 1977[3] (del 1979[8]) **RRP:** 70p[18]

---

***VS 174*** ***GLADIATORS: Chatty Chatty Mouth / Hearsay***
**Label:** V9 **Rel:** 18 Mar 1977[3] (del 1979[8]) **RRP:** 70p[18]

---

***VS 175*** ***KEVIN COYNE: Marlene / England is Dying***
**Label:** V9 **Rel:** 1 Apr 1977[3] **RRP:** 70p[18]
Picture sleeve.

---

***VS 176*** ***THE TABLE: Do The Standing Still (Classics Illustrated) / Magical Melon Of The Tropics***
**Label:** V9 **Rel:** 8 Apr[3]/9 Sep 1977[3] (del 1979[8]) **RRP:** 70p[18]
Picture sleeve.

---

***VS 177*** ***YELLOW DOG: For Whatever It's Worth / So Alive***
**Label:** V9 **Rel:** 15 Apr 1977[3] **RRP:** 70p[18]

---

***VS 178*** ***SUPERCHARGE: Limbo Love / Skid Markos (Live)***
**Label:** V9 **Rel:** 29 Apr[3]/May 1977[5] (del 1979[8]) **RRP:** 70p[18]

---

***VS 179*** ***PETER TOSH WITH WORDS SOUND AND POWER: African / Stepping Razor***
**Label:** V9 **Rel:** 22 Apr 1977[5] **RRP:** 70p[18]

---

***VS 180*** ***ROKY ERIKSON: Bermuda / The Interpreter***
**Label:** V9 **Rel:** May[5]/9 Sep 1977[3] (del 1979[8]) **RRP:** 70p[18]
Picture sleeve. Labels include a Rhino Records logo.

---

***VS 181*** ***SEX PISTOLS: God Save The Queen / Did You No Wrong***
**Label:** custom **Rel:** 27 May 1977[3] **RRP:** 70p[18]
Picture sleeve. Original copies have silver text on labels. Later ones have white text. There are also various differing shades of blue just to add to the fun. Three known copies in plain blue sleeve with no Queen's head.

---

***VS 182*** ***MIGHTY DIAMONDS: Sneakin Sally Through The Alley / She Put The Hurt On Me***
**Label:** V9 **Rel:** Jun 1977[5] (del 1979[8]) **RRP:** 70p[18]

***VS 183*** ***YELLOW DOG: Stood Up / California Here I Don't Come***
**Label:** V9 **Rel:** 8 Jul 1977[3] (del 1979[8]) **RRP:** 70p[18]

---

***VS 184*** ***SEX PISTOLS: Pretty Vacant / No Fun***
**Label:** V9 **Rel:** 1 Jul 1977[3] **RRP:** 70p[18]
Picture sleeve. Later available on the green/red label design.

---

***VS 185*** ***ROOGALATOR: Love And The Single Girl / I Feel Good (I Got You)***
**Label:** V9 **Rel:** Aug[5]/9 Sep 1977[3] **RRP:** 70p[18]
Picture sleeve.

---

***VS 186*** ***THE MOTORS: Dancing The Night Away / Whisky And Wine***
**Label:** V9 **Rel:** 9 Sep 1977[3] (del 1980[10]) **RRP:** 70p[18]
Picture sleeve. Also issued on 12" – see following section for details.

---

***VS 187*** ***NO RELEASE***
Only issued on 12" – see following section for details.

---

***VS 188*** ***XTC: Science Friction / She's So Square***
**Label:** V9 **Rel:** Oct 1977[5]
7" in picture sleeve quickly withdrawn – copies are super–rare (listed in *Music Master*[8] under the title "3D EP"). Much more common on 12" – see following section for details.

---

***VS 189*** ***X–RAY SPEX: Oh Bondage, Up Yours! / I Am A Cliché***
**Label:** V9 **Rel:** Oct[5]/4 Nov 1977[3]
Picture sleeve. Two variations of the green/red label design – first includes the tiny twin girl logo (some rumoured in the picture sleeve); later (probably 1980) copies do not include the girl logo. Also issued on 12" – see following section for details.

---

***VS 190*** ***NO RELEASE***
Issued on 12" – see following section for details. Although listed with both October[5] and December 1977[8] release dates it is unlikely that a 7" version was issued.

---

***VS 191*** ***SEX PISTOLS: Holidays In The Sun / Satellite***
**Label:** V9 **Rel:** Oct[5]/4 Nov 1977[3]
Picture sleeve withdrawn. Some copies with post card. Some with a–side label both sides.

---

***VS 192*** ***PENETRATION: Don't Dictate / Money Talks***
**Label:** V9 **Rel:** Nov[5]/30 Dec 1977[3]
Picture sleeve. Later copies on green/red label design.

---

***VS 193*** ***NO RELEASE***
Only issued on 12" – see following section for details. Although listed with a January 1978 release[5] it is unlikely that a 7" version was issued.

---

***VS 194*** ***THE MOTORS: Be What You Gotta Be / You Beat The Hell Outta Me***
**Label:** V9 **Rel:** 30 Dec 1977[3] (del 1979[8])
Picture sleeve.

---

***VS 195*** ***YELLOW DOG: Just One More Night / Up In The Balcony***
**Label:** V9 **Rel:** Jan[5]/10 Feb 1978[3] (del 1981[10])
Picture sleeve.

---

***VS 196*** ***JULIE COVINGTON: Only Women Bleed / Easy To Slip***
**Label:** V9 **Rel:** Nov[5]/30 Dec 1977[3] (del Dec 1980[10])
Picture sleeve. Orange vinyl. Orange and initial black vinyl pressings include full musician credits on the right–hand side of the labels. Later pressings on the same label design omit these credits.

***VS 197*** ***STEVE HILLAGE: Not Fade Away (Glid Forever) / Saucer Surfing***
**Label:** V9 **Rel:** 30 Dec 1977[3]

---

***VS 198*** ***MIKE OLDFIELD WITH LES PENNING: The Cuckoo Song / MIKE OLDFIELD: Pipe Tune***
**Label:** V9 **Rel:** 30 Dec 1977[3]

---

***VS 199*** ***TANGERINE DREAM: Encore / Hobo March***
**Label:** V9 **Rel:** 30 Dec[3]/Jan 1978[5]
Has "VDJ 25" scratched out in the runoff. Presumably initially intended as a promo–only pressing.

---

***VS 200*** ***MAGAZINE: Shot By Both Sides / My Mind Ain't So Open***
**Label:** V9 **Rel:** Jan[5]/3 Feb 1978[3] (del 1981[6])
Initially in card picture sleeve. Later copies in thinner paper picture sleeve.

---

***VS 201*** ***XTC: Statue Of Liberty / Hang On To The Night***
**Label:** V9 **Rel:** Jan 1978[5]/10 Feb 1977[3]
Picture sleeve. On catalogue long enough to appear on the green/red label.

---

***VS 202*** ***SUPERCHARGE: I Think I'm Gonna Fall (In Love) / I Think I'm Gonna Fall (In Love) Part 2***
**Label:** V9 **Rel:** Jan[5]/3 Feb 1978[3]
Picture sleeve. Labels have "In Love" in brackets on both sides, whilst sleeve does not: b–side, label credits "Part 2", whilst sleeve credits "Part II". Also issued on 12" – see following section for details.

---

***VS 203*** ***KEVIN COYNE: Amsterdam / I Really Love You***
**Label:** V9 **Rel:** Jan[5]/3 Feb 1978[3] (del 1979[8])
Picture sleeve.

---

***VS 204*** ***COLIN TOWNS: Full Circle (Main Theme) / Olivia***
**Label:** V9 **Rel:** Feb[5]/17 Mar 1978[3]
Picture sleeve.

---

***VS 205*** ***YOUNG ONES: Rock 'N' Roll Radio / Little Bit Of Loving***
**Label:** V9 **Rel:** 24 Feb[3]/Apr 1978[5] (del 1979[8])
Picture sleeve credits song as "Rock 'n' Roll Radio" whilst label credits "Rock and Roll Radio".

---

***VS 206*** ***THE MOTORS: Sensation / The Day I Found A Fiver***
**Label:** V9 **Rel:** Apr 1978[5] (del 1979[8])
Picture sleeve. Initially with £5 note offer. Some copies included an "Approved by The Motors" sticker.

---

***VS 207*** ***MAGAZINE: Touch And Go / Goldfinger***
**Label:** V9 **Rel:** Apr 1978[5]
Picture sleeve. Some copies include a tour date 'insert' – this wasn't issued with the single, but was left on the counter in Virgin shops. Looks like various people married the two up.

---

***VS 208*** ***THE DIAMONDS: Sweet Lady / Jah Will Work It Out***
**Label:** V9 **Rel:** Apr 1978[5]

---

***VS 209*** ***XTC: This Is Pop? / Heatwave***
**Label:** V9 **Rel:** 1978
Picture sleeve.

---

***VS 210*** ***NO RELEASE***

---

***VS 211*** ***YELLOW DOG: Gee, Officer Krupke / Fat Johnny***
**Label:** V9 **Rel:** May[5]/2 Jun 1978[3] (del 1979[8]) **RRP:** 80p[5]
Picture sleeve.

***VS 212*** ***STEVE HILLAGE: Getting Better / Palm Trees (Love Guitar)***
**Label:** V9 **Rel:** May 1978[5] **RRP:** 80p[5]
Picture sleeve.

---

***VS 213*** ***PENETRATION: Firing Squad / NEVERr***
**Label:** V9 **Rel:** May 1978[5] **RRP:** 80p[5]
Picture sleeve. On catalogue long enough to later appear on the green/red label design.

---

***VS 214*** ***WILKO JOHNSON'S SOLID SENDERS: Walking On The Edge / Dr. Dupree***
**Label:** V9 **Rel:** May 1978[5] **RRP:** 80p[5]
Picture sleeve. Double a–side: includes "A1"/"B1" matrix endings, hence the order of tracks above.

---

***VS 215*** ***ALAN CLAYSON AND ARGONAUTS: The Taster / Landwaster (Live)***
**Label:** V9 **Rel:** May[5]/2 Jun 1978[3] **RRP:** 80p[5]
Picture sleeve

---

***VS 216*** ***2 TIMERS: Now That I've Lost My Baby / Fast And Furious***
**Label:** V9 **Rel:** 16 Jun 1978[3] **RRP:** 80p[5]
Picture sleeve.

---

***VS 217*** ***YELLOW DOG: Wait Until Midnight / Down At The Vortex***
**Label:** V9 **Rel:** Jun 1978[5] (del 1979[8]/1981[10]) **RRP:** 80p[5]
Picture sleeve. Initially yellow vinyl (some on orange vinyl). Some coloured vinyl copies in plain white sleeve with sticker saying "A Very Limited Edition Yellow Dog so yellow record" with "Snap it up" upside down at the bottom.

---

***VS 218*** ***INTERVIEW: Birmingham / New Hearts In Action***
**Label:** V9 **Rel:** 30 Jun 1978[3]
Picture sleeve.

---

***VS 219*** ***THE MOTORS: Airport / Cold Love (live)***
**Label:** V9 **Rel:** 2 Jun 1978[3] (del 1979[8]/1981[10]) **RRP:** 80p[5]
Picture sleeve. Also issued on 12" – see following section for details.

---

***VS 220*** ***SEX PISTOLS: No One Is Innocent (A Punk Prayer By Ronald Biggs) / SID VICIOUS: My Way***
**Label:** CUS **Rel:** Jun[5]/7 Jul 1978[3]
Picture sleeve. Some evidently mispressed with a Motors track. Also listed as *My Way / God Save the Sex Pistols*. Also issued on 12" – see following section for details.

---

***VS 221*** ***THE MIGHTY DIAMONDS: Planet Called Earth / Lovely Lady***
**Label:** V9 **Rel:** Jul 1978[5] **RRP:** 80p[5]

---

***VS 222*** ***THE MOTORS: Forget About You / Picturama***
**Label:** V9 **Rel:** 18 Aug 1978[3] **RRP:** 80p[5]
Picture sleeve. On catalogue long enough to also appear on the green/red label design. Also issued on 12" – see following section for details.

---

***VS 223*** ***DEVO: Come Back Jonee / Social Fools***
**Label:** V11 **Rel:** Sep 1978[5] (del 1981[10]) **RRP:** 90p[5]
Picture sleeve. Initially on grey vinyl with sticker. Some with black artist credit on labels, some with dark grey.

---

***VS 224*** ***YELLOW DOG: Little Gods / Fat Johnny***
**Label:** V10 **Rel:** 22 Sep 1978[3] **RRP:** 90p[5]
Initially on luminous vinyl in printed PVC sleeve.

***VS 225*** ***JULIE COVINGTON: (I Want To See The) Bright Lights / A Little Bit More***
**Label:** V10 **Rel:** 27 Oct 1978[3] **RRP:** 90p[5]

---

***VS 226*** ***PENETRATION: Life's a Gamble / V.I.P.***
**Label:** V10 **Rel:** 13 Oct 1978[3] **RRP:** £1.05[8]
Picture sleeve. RRP most likely as at a later date.

---

***VS 227*** ***SKIDS: Sweet Suburbia / Open Sound***
**Label:** V10 **Rel:** 15 Sep 1978[3] **RRP:** 90p[5]
Picture sleeve. White vinyl. Sleeve sticker says, "This white vinyl record has a Weird Gimmick You'll Like It!"

---

***VS 228*** ***PUBLIC IMAGE LIMITED: Public Image / Cowboy Song***
**Label:** V10 **Rel:** Sep[9]//27 Oct 1978[3] **RRP:** 90p[5]
Foldout 'newspaper' picture sleeve. Price on newspaper says, "Still only 90p".

---

***VS 229*** ***NO RELEASE***

---

***VS 230*** ***FLYING LIZARDS: Summertime Blues / All Guitars***
**Label:** V10 **Rel:** 27 Oct 1978[3] (del1981[6]) **RRP:** £1.05[8]
Picture sleeve.

---

***VS 231*** ***XTC: Are You Receiving Me / Instant Tunes***
**Label:** V10 **Rel:** 29 Sep 1978[3] (del 1979[8]) **RRP:** 90p[5]
Picture sleeve. Both solid and 4–prong die–cut centre copies exist.

---

***VS 232*** ***SKIDS: Wide Open***

| | |
|---|---|
| 1. The Saints Are Coming | 1. Night And Day |
| 2. Of One Skin | 2. Contusion |

**Label:** V10 **Rel:** Nov 1978[10] (del 1981[6]) **RRP:** 90p[5]
Picture sleeve. Also issued on 12" – see following section for details.

---

***VS 233*** ***NO RELEASE***
Only issued on 12" – see following section for details.

---

***VS 234*** ***CRY: Sympathy / Policeman Blues***
**Label:** V10 **Rel:** 10 Nov 1978[3] **RRP:** 90p[5]
Picture sleeve.

---

***VS 235*** ***FINGERPRINTZ: Dancing With Myself / Sync Unit***
**Label:** V10 **Rel:** Jan 1979[6] (del 1980[6]) **RRP:** 90p[8]
Picture sleeve. Also issued on 12" – see following section for details.

---

***VS 236*** ***THE MOTORS: Today / Here Comes The Hustler***
**Label:** V10 **Rel:** 1978 **RRP:** 90p[5]
Picture sleeve.

---

***VS 237*** ***MAGAZINE: Give Me Everything / I Love You, You Big Dummy***
**Label:** V10 **Rel:** 24 Nov 1978[3] **RRP:** 90p[5]
Picture sleeve.

---

***VS 238*** ***MIKE OLDFIELD: Take 4***

| | |
|---|---|
| 1. Portsmouth | 1. Wreckorder Rondo |
| 2. In Dulce Jubilo | 2. Sailor's Hornpipe |

**Label:** V10 **Rel:** 8 Dec 1978[3] (del 1981[10]) **RRP:** 90p[5]
Picture sleeve. Also issued on 12" – see following section for details.

***VS 239*** ***DON LETTS, STRATETIME KEITH, STEEL LEG AND JAH WOBBLE: Steel Leg V. The Electric Dread***

1. Steel Leg
2. Strateman And The Wide Man

1. Haile Unlikely By The Electric Dread
2. Unlikely Pub

**Label:** V10 **Rel:** Dec 1978[8]

Picture sleeve. Also issued on 12" – see following section for details.

---

***VS 240*** ***SEX PISTOLS: Something Else / Friggin' In The Riggin'***

**Label:** CUS **Rel:** Feb[9]/9 Mar 1979[3] **RRP:** 90p[8]

Picture sleeve. Some mispressed and play 'Silly Thing'. Black and white labels also seem to exist.

---

***VS 241*** ***SKIDS: Into The Valley / TV Stars***

**Label:** V12 **Rel:** 16 Feb 1979[3] **RRP:** 90p[8]

Picture sleeve. White vinyl.

---

***VS 242*** ***THE MEMBERS: The Sound Of The Suburbs / Handling The Big Jets***

**Label:** V10 **Rel:** Feb 1979[10] (del 1982[10]) **RRP:** 90p[8]

Initially in 'window' picture sleeve on clear vinyl with credits etched into the vinyl. Later copies in normal picture sleeve on black vinyl. Supposedly copies exist mispressed with *In A Rut* by the Ruts.

---

***VS 243*** ***SUPERCHARGE: I Can See Right Thru You, Part 1 / I Can See Right Thru You, Part 2***

**Label:** V10 **Rel:** May[6]/15 Jun 1979[3] (del 1981[6]) **RRP:** 99p[8]

Picture sleeve. Also issued on 12" – see following section for details.

---

***VS 244*** ***SPARKS: No One Song In Heaven / No One Song In Heaven (Long Version)***

**Label:** V10 **Rel:** 23 Mar[3]/Apr 1979[10] (del Apr 1982[10]) **RRP:** 90p[8]

Green vinyl in picture sleeve. Also issued on 12" – see following section for details.

---

***VS 245*** ***MIKE OLDFIELD: Guilty / Excerpt From Incantations***

**Label:** V13 **Rel:** 30 Mar[3]/27 Apr 1979[3] **RRP:** 90p[8]

Picture sleeve. Also on green/red label. 7" and 12" versions have different b–sides. See following section for 12" details.

---

***VS 246*** ***PHIL CORDELL: Hearts On Fire / Ginny Was A Rock 'N' Roller***

**Label:** CUS **Rel:** 27 Apr[3]/May 1979[8] **RRP:** 99p[8]

Red vinyl in picture sleeve. Also issued on 12" – see following section for details.

---

***VS 247*** ***THE RECORDS: Rock And Roll Love Letter / Wives And Mothers Of Tomorrow***

**Label:** CUS **Rel:** 30 Mar[3]/Apr 1979[6] (del 1981[6]) **RRP:** 90p[8]

Picture sleeve. According to www.therecords.com/discography.htm, the a–side was produced by Robert John Lang but an alternative version produced by Mick Glossop, "was 'accidentally' pressed on a limited number of copies". Also issued on 12" – see following section for details.

---

***VS 248*** ***THE MEMBERS: Offshore Banking Business / Solitary Confinement***

**Label:** V10 **Rel:** 23 Mar[3]/Apr 1979[10] (del 1982[10]) **RRP:** 90p[8]

Picture sleeve. Also issued on 12" – see following section for details.

---

***VS 249*** ***INTERVIEW: You Didn't Have To Lie To Me / That Kind Of Boy***

**Label:** V10 **Rel:** 29 Jun 1979[3] (del 1980[6]) **RRP:** 99p[8]

Picture sleeve.

***VS 250*** ***THE RECORDS: Teenarama / Held Up High***
**Label:** custom **Rel:** 15 Jun 1979[3] (del 1980[6]) **RRP:** £1.05[8]
Picture sleeve. Radio edit version has "VS 250–A1–DJ" matrix.

---

***VS 251*** ***MAGAZINE: Rhythm Of Cruelty / T.V. Baby***
**Label:** CUS **Rel:** Feb[8]/9 Mar 1979[3] **RRP:** 90p[8]
Picture sleeve. The b–side run–off includes the message "On the blink".

---

***VS 252*** ***FINGERPRINTZ: Who's Your Friend?***
1. Who's Your Friend?
2. Secret

1. Nervz
2. Night Nurse

**Label:** V13 **Rel:** Mar 1979[6] (del 1980[6]) **RRP:** 90p[8]
Picture sleeve. Blue vinyl. Track 1 without "?" on label but with "?" on sleeve.

---

***VS 253*** ***COWBOYS INTERNATIONAL: Aftermath / Future Noise***
**Label:** V10 **Rel:** 30 Mar 1979[3] **RRP:** £1.05[8]
Picture sleeve. Orange vinyl. Promotional version black vinyl with labels and green/red company sleeve stamped with : "DJ COPY EDITED VERSION": Matrix number on these is "VS 253 A1 DJ".

---

***VS 254*** ***ADRIAN MUNSEY, HIS SHEEP, WIND, AND ORCHESTRA: The Lost Sheep / ADRIAN MUNSEY: Echoing***
**Label:** V10 **Rel:** 20 Apr[3]/ 4 May 1979[3] **RRP:** 90p[8]
Picture sleeve.

---

***VS 255*** ***KEVIN COYNE: I'll Go Too / Having A Party***
**Label:** V10 **Rel:** 23 Mar 1979[3]
Picture sleeve. Green vinyl. Black vinyl copies in green/red generic company sleeve much rarer than green press.

---

***VS 256*** ***SEX PISTOLS: Silly Thing / Who Killed Bambi***
**Label:** custom **Rel:** Mar 1979[9] **RRP:** 90p[8]
Picture sleeve.

---

***VS 257*** ***PENETRATION: Danger Signs / Stone Heroes (live)***
**Label:** V10 **Rel:** 27 Apr 1979[3] **RRP:** 95p[8]
Picture sleeve. Also issued on 12" – see following section for details.

---

***VS 258*** ***NOEL: Dancing is Dangerous (Part One) / Dancing is Dangerous (Part Two)***
**Label:** V10 **Rel:** May[8]/15 Jun 1979[3] **RRP:** 99p[8]
Picture sleeve. Also issued on 12" – see following section for details.

---

***VS 259*** ***XTC: Life Begins At The Hop / Homo Safari***
**Label:** custom **Rel:** 27 Apr 1979[3]/May 1979[6] (del '82[10]) **RRP:** 99p[8]
First 30,000 clear vinyl with PVC sleeve and gatefold insert. PVC outer overprinted to look like an autochanger record player. If single is placed to rear of the inner, then it looks as though the clear vinyl single is being played. However, if the clear vinyl single is placed to the front, then the back of the inner showed the label for the previous single (albeit with black and white label instead of green).

---

***VS 260*** ***BARRY ANDREWS: Town And Country***
1. Mousetrap
2. Sargasso Bar

1. Me And My Mate Can Sing
2. Bring On The Alligators

**Label:** V10 **Rel:** Jun 1979[6] (del 1980[6]) **RRP:** 99p[8]
Picture sleeve.

***VS 261*** ***ESSENTIAL LOGIC: Wake Up***

1. Wake Up
2. Eagle Bird

1. Quality Crayon Wax O.K.
2. Bod's Message

**Label:** pres. CUS **Rel:** 1979

Picture sleeve. Also issued on 12" – see following section for details.

---

***VS 262*** ***SKIDS: Masquerade (doublepack – see below)***

***VS 262*** ***SKIDS: Masquerade / Out Of Town***

*Record 1, side 1*
Masquerade

*Record 1, side 2*
Out Of Town

*Record 2, side 1*
Another Emotion

*Record 2, side 2*
Aftermath Dub

**Label:** V12 **Rel:** May[10]/15 Jun '79[3] (del '80[6]/May '82[10])**RRP:** 99p[15]

Limited edition doublepack in stickered, gatefold sleeve – both records include the VS 262 catalogue number. Also issued as a single record in normal picture sleeve with the same catalogue number, presumably at the same price. Both listed deletion dates are for the normal version. Odd copy with 'starburst' blue/black vinyl known to exist.

---

***VS 263*** ***THE MOTORS: Love And Lonliness / Time For Make Up (1980 RELEASE)***

Originally intended for late 1979 release with, reputedly, *Nightmare Zero* as the b–side. 10" version issued with 7" catalogue number.

---

***VS 264*** ***NO RELEASE***

---

***VS 265*** ***DEVO: The Day My Baby Gave Me A Surprise / Penetration In The Centrefold***

**Label:** V10 **Rel:** 1 Jun 1979[3] **RRP:** 99p[8]

Picture sleeve.

---

***VS 266*** ***ADRIAN MUNSEY: C'Est Sheep (Part 1) / C'Est Sheep (Part 2)***

**Label:** V10 **Rel:** 29 Jun 1979[3]

Picture sleeve. Also issued on 12" – see following section for details.

---

***VS 267*** ***COWBOYS INTERNATIONAL: Nothing Doing / 2 Millions***

**Label:** V10 **Rel:** 29 Jun 1979[3] **RRP:** £1.05[8]

Picture sleeve. Included blank, clear flexi, "Many Times".

---

***VS 268*** ***PENETRATION: Come Into The Open / Lifeline***

**Label:** CUS **Rel:** 24 Aug 1979[3] **RRP:** 90p[8]

Picture sleeve. Just to confuse, the edition of *The New Singles* has the wrong date and volume number – it says number 787 with the date 17 August, but is actually number 788 for a week later.

---

***VS 269*** ***THE MEN: I Don't Depend On You / Cruel***

**Label:** pres. V10 **Rel:** 1979

Picture sleeve. Also issued on 12" – see following section for details.

---

***VS 270*** ***SPARKS: Beat The Clock / Beat The Clock (Alternative Mix)***

**Label:** V10 **Rel:** 27 Jul 1979[3] (del Jul 1982[10]) **RRP:** £1.05[8]

Picture sleeve. Also issued on 12" – see following section for details.

---

***VS 271*** ***THE RUTS: Babylon's Burning / Society***

**Label:** CUS **Rel:** 22 Jun 1979[3] **RRP:** 99p[8]

Picture sleeve. Sold at HMV at £1.10 according to the original price sticker on the copy I'm currently looking at. It would have been cheaper at Virgin. Also issued on 12" – see following section for details.

***VS 272*** ***SEX PISTOLS: C'mon Everybody / God Save The Queen Symphony / Watcha Gonna Do About It***

**Label:** CUS **Rel:** 22 Jul 1979[3] **RRP:** £1.05[8]

Picture sleeve. B–side label exists with both yellow (probably original) and orange background colour.

---

***VS 273*** ***JANE AIRE AND THE BELVEDERES: Call Me Every Night / Lazy Boy (Picture disc)***

***VS 273*** ***JANE AIRE AND THE BELVEDERES: Call Me Every Night / Lazy Boy***

**Label:** **Rel:** 27 Jul 1979[3] (del 1980[6]) **RRP:** £1.05[8]

First 40,000 copies were picture discs. No wonder the normal version is so hard to find. Same catalogue number used for both picture disc and black vinyl issues. Picture disc includes a white sticker with red text on clear PVC sleeve: "You should not pay more than 99p for this record".

---

***VS 274*** ***PUBLIC IMAGE LIMITED: Death Disco / And No Bird Do Sing***

**Label:** CUS **Rel:** 29 Jun 1979[3] **RRP:** £1.05[8]

Picture sleeve. Also issued on 12" – see following section for details.

---

***VS 275*** ***DAN MACARTHUR: Dan MacArthur (Disco Dummy) / Dan MacArthur II***

**Label:** CUS (7") **Rel:** 1979

Picture sleeve. No track credits on sleeve/label. Also issued on 12" – see following section for details.

---

***VS 276*** ***FLYING LIZARDS: Money / Money B***

**Label:** CUS **Rel:** 27 Jul[3]/Aug 1979[6] (del '80[6]/'82[10]) **RRP:** £1.05[8]

Picture sleeve. Later copies on green/red label design.

---

***VS 277*** ***LOCAL OPERATORS: Pressure Zone / Untouchables***

**Label:** V10 **Rel:** 27 Jul[3]/Aug 1979[6] (del 1980[6]) **RRP:** £1.10[8]

Centre–opening picture sleeve.

---

***VS 278*** ***FINGERPRINTZ: Tough Luck / Detonator***

**Label:** V10 **Rel:** 24 Aug 1979[3] (del 1980[6]) **RRP:** £1.10[8]

Picture sleeve. *The New Singles* has the wrong date and volume number – see VS 268 above.

---

***VS 279*** ***NO RELEASE – POSSIBLY RELEASED ON DINDISC INSTEAD***

---

***VS 280*** ***DEVO: Secret Agent Man / Soo Bawlz***

**Label:** V10 **Rel:** 24 Aug 1979[3] **RRP:** £1.05[8]

Picture sleeve. Early copies seem to have included the *Flimsy Wrap* flexidisc (VDJ 27) as otherwise included with the picture disc of *Q. Are We Not Men? A. We Are Devo* (VP 2106). *The New Singles* has the wrong date and volume number – see VS 268 above.

---

***VS 281*** ***NO RELEASE – POSSIBLY RELEASED ON DINDISC INSTEAD***

---

***VS 282*** ***XTC: Making Plans For Nigel / Bushman President / Pulsing, Pulsing***

**Label:** V10 **Rel:** 28 Sep 1979[3] **RRP:** £1.05[8]

First 20,000 copies in PVC outer with foldout gameboard sleeve, insert and three playing pieces for cutting out (die, Nigel and Parents). Later in normal picture sleeve. Later copies on green/red label.

---

***VS 283*** ***ZIPPER: The Life Of Riley / Treat Me Right***

**Label:** V10 **Rel:** 24 Aug 1979[3] **RRP:** £1.10[8]

Picture sleeve. *The New Singles* has the wrong date and volume number – see VS 268 above.

---

***VS 284*** ***PHIL CORDELL: Movie Star / Lying Down By The River***

**Label:** V10 **Rel:** 28 Sep 1979[3] **RRP:** £1.05[8]

Picture sleeve.

***VS 285*** ***THE RUTS: Something That I Said / Give Youth A Chance***
**Label:** CUS **Rel:** 31 Aug 1979[3] (del 1980[6]/1982[10]) **RRP:** £1.05[8]
Picture sleeve. B–side listed erroneously as "Black Man's Pinch" in all *Music Master* publications.

---

***VS 286*** ***NOEL: The Night They Invented Love / Au Revoir***
**Label:** V10 **Rel:** 31 Aug 1979[3] **RRP:** £1.05[8]
Picture sleeve.

---

***VS 287*** ***NO RELEASE – POSSIBLY RELEASED ON DINDISC INSTEAD***

---

***VS 288*** ***SKIDS: Charade / Grey Parade***
**Label:** V12 **Rel:** 28 Sep 1979[3] (del '81[6]/Sep '82[10]) **RRP:** £1.05[8]
Picture sleeve.

---

***VS 289*** ***SPARKS: Tryouts For The Human Race / Tryouts For The Human Race (Long Version)***
**Label:** V10 **Rel:** 19 Oct 1979[3] (del Oct 1982[6])
Picture sleeve. Also issued on 12" – see following section for details.

---

***VS 290*** ***SEX PISTOLS: The Great Rock'N'Roll Swindle / Rock Around The Clock***
**Label:** custom **Rel:** Sep[9]/19 Oct 1979[3] **RRP:** £1.05[8]
American Express' picture sleeve withdrawn. Some mispressed with lawyer's telephone conversation – these seem to be on yellow, rather than normal purple b–side label design.

---

***VS 291*** ***SHOOTING STAR: You've Got What I Need / Wild In The Streets***
**Label:** **Rel:** 28 Sep 1979[3] **RRP:**
Generally documented as being a 1980 release, though listed as above for Septmebr 1979 release.

---

***VS 292*** ***THE MEMBERS: Killing Time / G.L.C.***
**Label:** custom **Rel:** 21 Sep 1979[3] **RRP:** £1.05[8]
Die–cut picture sleeve.

---

***VS 293*** ***COWBOYS INTERNATIONAL: Thrash / Many Times Revised***
**Label:** V10 **Rel:** 28 Sep[3]/19 Oct 1979[3] **RRP:** £1.05
Picture sleeve.

---

***VS 294*** ***THE HUMAN LEAGUE: Empire State Human / Introducing***
**Label:** CUS **Rel:** Sep[9]/19 Oct 1979[3] **RRP:** £1.05[8]
Picture sleeve. Reissued in 1980 as VS 351.

---

***VS 295*** ***NO RELEASE – POSSIBLY RELEASED ON DINDISC INSTEAD***

---

***VS 296*** ***JANE AIRE AND THE BELVEDERES: Breaking Down The Walls Of Heartache / Life After You***
**Label:** V10 **Rel:** Sep 1979[6] (del 1980[6]) **RRP:** prob £1.05
Picture sleeve.

---

***VS 297*** ***Z.E.R.O. PASS S.E.V.E.N.: Worry One / Worry Two***
**Label:** V10 **Rel:** Sep[6]/ 19 Oct 1979[3] (del 1980[6]) **RRP:** £1.05[8]
Picture sleeve. Sleeve credits group as "Z.E.R.O PASS S.E.V.E.N" (no full stop after "O" or "N") whilst labels credit "Z.E.R.O. PASS S.E.V.E.N." (with full stop after "O" and "N").

---

***VS 298*** ***THE RUTS: Jah War / I Ain't Sofisticated***
**Label:** custom **Rel:** 9 Nov 1979[3] (del 1980[6]) **RRP:** £1.05[8]
Picture sleeve.

***VS 299*** ***PUBLIC IMAGE LIMITED: Memories / Another***
**Label:** CUS **Rel:** Sep[8]/19 Oct 1979[3] **RRP:** £1.05[8]
Picture sleeve. Also issued on 12" – see following section for details.

---

***VS 300*** ***THE MEKONS: Work All Week / Unknown Wrecks***
**Label:** CUS **Rel:** Sep1979[6] **RRP:** £1.05[8]
Picture sleeve. Labels say "Meeks on Virgin" in the same style as the "Virgin" logo.

---

***VS 301*** ***HUDSON PEOPLE: Boogie On Downtown / Boogie On Downtown (Instrumental)***
**Label:** V10 **Rel:** 19 Oct[3]/9 Nov 1979[3] (del 1980[6]) **RRP:** £1.05[8]
Also issued on 12" – see following section for details.

---

***VS 302*** ***LOCAL OPERATORS: Law And Order / All We're Gonna Get***
**Label:** V10 **Rel:** Nov[6]/ 7 Dec 1979[3] (del 1980[6]) **RRP:** £1.05[8]
Picture sleeve.

---

***VS 303*** ***JOHN FOXX: A New Kind Of Man / Metal Beat (NOT RELEASED)***
A–side remixed version, but single never released. Sleeve design later used for *Underpass*. *Young Love* rumoured to have been the originally–planned a–side.

---

***VS 304*** ***PETER TOSH: Stepping Razor / Legalize It***
**Label:** V10 **Rel:** 26 Oct 1979[3] (del 1980[6]) **RRP:** £1.05[8]
Picture sleeve credits the a–side as featured in the film, *Rockers*.

---

***VS 305*** ***THE RECORDS: Starry Eyes / Paint Her Face***
**Label:** **Rel:** 26 Oct 1979[3] (del 1980[6]) **RRP:** £1.15[8]
Picture sleeve. Reissue of NB 2 on the Virgin label proper. Possibly unreleased.

---

***VS 306*** ***SKIDS: Working For The Yankee Dollar (doublepack – see below)***
***VS 306*** ***SKIDS: Working For The Yankee Dollar / Vanguard's Crusage***

*Record 1, side 1*
1. Working For The Yankee Dollar

*Record 1, side 2*
1. Vanguard's Crusage

*Record 2, side 1*
1. All The Young Dudes

*Record 2, side 2*
1. Hymns From A Haunted Ballroom

**Label:** V12 **Rel:** Nov[6]/7 Dec '79[3] (del '80[6]/Nov '82[10]) **RRP:** £1.05[8]
Both in picture sleeve (doublepack in gatefold). 1980 deletion date may relate to the doublepack.

---

***VS 307*** ***TOURS: Tourist Information / You Know But***
**Label:** CUS **Rel:** Nov[6]/7 Dec 1979[3] (del 1980[6]) **RRP:** £1.05[8]
Picture sleeve.

---

***VS 308*** ***THE OUT: Who Is Innocent / Linda's Just A Statue***
**Label:** V10 **Rel:** Sep[8]/7 Dec 1979[3] **RRP:** £1.05[8]
Picture sleeve. Reissued on the Rabid label (TOSH 113) in September 1982[8].

---

***VS 309*** ***MENTAL AS ANYTHING: The Nips Are Getting Bigger / Instrumental As Anything (1980 RELEASE)***

---

***VS 310*** ***INTERVIEW: To The People / Hart Crane In Mexico***
**Label:** **Rel:** Nov[6]/7 Dec 1979[3] (del 1980[6]) **RRP:** £1.05[8]
Picture sleeve.

---

***VS 311*** ***90 DEGREES: No Doctor / Fantasy Woman***
**Label:** V10 **Rel:** Nov[6]/7 Dec 1979[3] (del 1980[6]) **RRP:** £1.05[8]
Picture sleeve. Also issued on 12" – see following section for details. This and the 12" might have been poached from the Ice label, what with being co–produced by Eddy Grant and the group.

***VS 312*** ***SNAKEFINGER: Kill The Great Raven / What Wilbur***
**Label:** V10 **Rel:** Nov[6]/7 Dec 1979[3] (del 1981[6]) **RRP:** £1.05[8]
Picture sleeve. Personalised logo on labels.

---

***VS 313*** ***STEVE HILLAGE: Don't Dither, Do It / Getting In Tune***
**Label:** V10 **Rel:** Nov[6]/14 Dec 1979[3] (del 1980[6]) **RRP:** £1.05[8]
Picture sleeve.

---

***VS 314*** ***PIRANHAS: Space Invaders / Cheap 'N' Nasty***
**Label:** V10 **Rel:** Nov[8]/14 Dec 1979[3] **RRP:** £1.05[8]
Picture sleeve. Space invader logo on labels.

---

***VS 315*** ***NO RELEASE – POSSIBLY RELEASED ON DINDISC INSTEAD***

---

***VS 316*** ***NO RELEASE – POSSIBLY RELEASED ON DINDISC INSTEAD***

---

***VS 317*** ***MIKE OLDFIELD: Blue Peter / Woodhenge***
**Label:** V10 **Rel:** Nov[6]/14 Dec 1979[3] (del 1981[6]) **RRP:** £1.10[8]
Picture sleeve. A7 matrix copies have a less abrupt ending. Some normal stock coipies include promo sticker on sleeve. Two–sided Utopia acetate exists. Issued as part of the *Blue Peter* Cambodia Appeal (approximately 85% of royalties donated). (Oddly, not the same version as used as the *Blue Peter* theme.) One–sided promo version exists (VSDJ 317)

---

VS 318 is not included because, despite 45cat.com stating an intended 1979 release date for unreleased John Foxx single (*Like A Miracle* / *Film 1*) evidence suggests it was planned as a January 1980 release in any case[8].

## VS 100–12 series 12" singles

Release dates, unless specifically stated – thus (12") – are as given for the 7", so potentially not accurate. All deletion dates listed are specific to the 12" version.

---

***VS 186–12*** ***THE MOTORS: Dancing The Night Away / Whisky And Wine***
**Label:** V9 **Rel:** 9 Sep 1977[3]
Generic blue 'neon' company sleeve. Label is hybrid of the V9 design with 'neon' flash replaced by the Motors logo. The mirrored girl logo (as used on early V9 labels) replaces the Motors logo on the b–side. Company sleeve only printed on one side on some copies. Listed as limited edition[5].

---

***VS 187–12*** ***U ROY: Small Axe / Small Axe (version)***
**Label:** V9 **Rel:** Sep 1977[5]
Generic, die–cut Virgin sleeve. Listed as limited edition[5]. No 7" version.

---

***VS 188–12*** ***XTC: 3D . EP: Science Friction / She's So Square / Dance Band / Goodbye Sucker***
**Label:** V9 **Rel:** Oct 1977[5]
Picture sleeve credited as "3D . EP" on rear sleeve and spine, but not labels. *Goodbye, Sucker* uncredited. Listed as limited edition[5]. Reissued as VOLE 3.

---

***VS 189–12*** ***X–RAY SPEX: Oh Bondage, Up Yours! / I Am A Cliché***
**Label:** V9 **Rel:** Oct[5]/4 Nov 1977[3]
Generic blue 'neon' company sleeve. Listed as limited edition[5].

---

***VS 190–12*** ***POET AND THE ROOTS: All Wi Doin Is Defendin***

| | |
|---|---|
| 1. All Wi Doin Is Defendin | 1. Command Council Dub |
| 2. Five Nights Of Bleedin | 2. Defense Dub |

**Label:** V9 **Rel:** Dec1977[8]
Generic blue 'neon' company sleeve. Most likely no 7" version.

***VS 193–12*** ***GLADIATORS: Pocket Money***

1. Pocket Money
2. Money Version Disco Mix

1. Evil Doers
2. Disco Mix

**Label:** V6 **Rel:** Jan 1978[8]

Generic blue 'neon' company sleeve with current LP label design. Most likely no 7" version.

---

***VS 202–12*** ***SUPERCHARGE: I Think I'm Gonna Fall (In Love) / I Think I'm Gonna Fall (In Love) (Version)***

**Label:** V9 **Rel:** Jan[5]/3 Feb 1978[3]

Generic blue 'neon' company sleeve.

---

***VS 219–12*** ***THE MOTORS: Airport / Cold Love (Live) / Be What You Gotta Be (live)***

**Label:** V9 **Rel:** 2 Jun 1978[3]

Stickered generic blue 'neon' company sleeve – blue vinyl with blue 'neon' label design incorporating a large Motors logo.

---

***VS 220–12*** ***SEX PISTOLS: The Biggest Blow (A Punk Prayer By Ronnie Biggs) / SID VICIOUS: My Way***

**Label:** CUS **Rel:** Jun 1978[5] **RRP:** £1.49[5]

Picture sleeve. Two different versions of the 12" exist, one as listed above (VS 22012 A1 matrix) and one with a Cook, Jones and Ronnie Biggs interview at the end of side 1 (VS 22012 A3 matrix). Labels exist with both light brown and white backgrounds.

---

***VS 222–12*** ***THE MOTORS: Forget About You***

1. Forget About You

1. Picturama
2. The Middle Bit
3. Soul Surrender

**Label:** V6 **Rel:** Aug 1978[5] (del 1979[8]) **RRP:** £1.49[5]

Red vinyl in stickered generic blue 'neon' company sleeve. A few copies pressed on the red mirrored girl label, but most on the later blue 'neon' label.

---

***VS 232–12*** ***SKIDS: Wide Open***

1. The Saints Are Coming
2. Of One Skin

1. Night And Day
2. Contusion

**Label:** V12 **Rel:** Nov 1978[10] (del 1980[8]) **RRP:** £1.49[5]

Red vinyl with stickered picture sleeve: sticker says, "Go green when you pay £1.49, then rip off the cover and see red."

---

***VS 233–12*** ***XTC: Go +***

1. Dance With Me, Germany
2. Beat The Bible

1. A Dictionary Of Modern Marriage
2. Clap Clap Clap
3. We Kill The Beast

**Label:** V10 **Rel:** 1979[8] (del 1980[6]) **RRP:** £1.59[8]

Picture sleeve. Free with V 2108. No 7" version.

---

***VS 235–12*** ***FINGERPRINTZ: Dancing With Myself / Sync Unit / Sean's New Shoes***

**Label:** V10 **Rel:** Jan 1979[6] **RRP:** £1.49[15]

Green vinyl with stickered picture sleeve: sticker says, "It's not the colour of the record that matters, it's the colour of your money that counts. See Greenie enclosed. RRP £1.49".

***VS 238–12*** ***MIKE OLDFIELD: Take 4***

1. Portsmouth
2. In Dulce Jubilo

1. Wreckorder Rondo
2. Sailor's Hornpipe

**Label:** V10 **Rel:** Dec 1978[10] **RRP:** £1.49[5]
White vinyl in stickered picture sleeve.

---

***VS 239–12*** ***DON LETTS, STRATETIME KEITH, STEEL LEG AND JAH WOBBLE: Steel Leg V. The Electric Dread***

1. Steel Leg
2. Strateman And The Wide Man

1. Haile Unlikely By The Electric Dread
2. Unlikely Pub

**Label:** V10 **Rel:** Dec 1978[8] (del 1980) **RRP:** £1.49[8]
White vinyl in stickered picture sleeve.

---

***VS 243–12*** ***SUPERCHARGE: I Can See Right Thru You, Part 1 / I Can See Right Thru You, Part 2***
**Label:** no labels **Rel:** May 1979[6] (del 1980[6])
Clear vinyl disc (no labels) in die–cut sleeve with printed inner back sleeve.

---

***VS 244–12*** ***SPARKS: No One Song In Heaven / No One Song In Heaven (Long Version)***
**Label:** V10 **Rel:** Apr 1979[10]
Picture sleeve – both red and blue vinyl versions exist.

---

***VS 245–12*** ***MIKE OLDFIELD: Guilty / Guilty (Long Version)***
**Label:** V13 **Rel:** Apr 1979[8]
Blue vinyl in picture sleeve. Later 12" copies and white label test pressings on black vinyl. Different b–side to 7" version.

---

***S 246–12*** ***PHIL CORDELL: Hearts On Fire / Ginny Was A Rock 'N' Roller***
**Label:** CUS **Rel:** May 1979
White vinyl.

---

***VS 247–12*** ***THE RECORDS: Rock And Roll Love Letter / Wives And Mothers Of Tomorrow / Starry Eyes (Live)***
**Label:** CUS **Rel:** 4 May 1979[3] (12") **RRP:** 99p[15]
RRP of 99p printed on the picture sleeve.

---

***VS 248–12*** ***THE MEMBERS: Offshore Banking Business / Pennies In The Pound / Solitary Confinement***
**Label:** V10 **Rel:** Mar 1979[6]/Apr 1979[10]
Picture sleeve.

---

***VS 257–12*** ***PENETRATION: Danger Signs / Stone Heroes (Live) / Vision (Live)***
**Label:** V10 **Rel:** Apr 1979[8]
Picture sleeve.

---

***VS 258–12*** ***NOEL: Dancing is Dangerous / Dancing is Dangerous (Long Version)***
**Label:** CUS **Rel:** May 1979[8]
Die–cut picture sleeve with floppy PVC inner.

---

***VS 261–12*** ***ESSENTIAL LOGIC: Wake Up***

1. Wake Up
2. Eagle Bird

1. Quality Crayon Wax O.K.
2. Bod's Message

**Label:** CUS **Rel:** 15 Jun 1979 (12") (del 1980[6]) **RRP:** £1.59[8]
Picture sleeve. Adverts in the music press described 12" version as limited edition.

***VS 266–12*** ***ADRIAN MUNSEY: C'Est Sheep (Part 1) / C'Est Sheep (Part 2)***
**Label:** V10 **Rel:** May 1979[8] **RRP:** £1.49[8]
Picture sleeve.

---

***VS 269–12*** ***THE MEN: I Don't Depend On You / Cruel***
**Label:** pres. V10 **Rel:** 27 Jul 1979[3] (12") (del 1980[8]) **RRP:** £1.59[8]
Picture sleeve.

---

***VS 270–12*** ***SPARKS: Beat The Clock / Uncredited Track / Beat The Clock (Long Version)***
**Label:** CUS **Rel:** 27 Jul 1979[3] (12")
Die–cut picture sleeve and available in orange, blue, yellow, pink and black vinyl versions, all with large picture label centre. Track 2 on a–side is an album promotion trailer.

---

***VS 271–12*** ***THE RUTS: Babylon's Burning / Society***
**Label:** CUS **Rel:** Jun 1979[8] **RRP:** prob £1.59
Picture sleeve.

---

***VS 274–12*** ***PUBLIC IMAGE LIMITED: Death Disco / And No Bird Do Sing (1/2 Mix) / Death Disco Megamix***
**Label:** CUS **Rel:** 1979
Picture sleeve.

---

***VS 275–12*** ***DAN MACARTHUR: Dan MacArthur (Disco Dummy) / Dan MacArthur II***
**Label:** prob. CUS **Rel:** Aug 1979[6] (12") (del 1980[6]) **RRP:** £1.59[8]
Presumably in picture sleeve.

---

***VS 289–12*** ***SPARKS: Tryouts For the Human Race / Uncredited Track / Tryouts For The Human Race (Long Version)***
**Label:** CUS **Rel:** 19 Oct 1979[3] (12") (del 1980[6]) **RRP:** £1.59[8]
Die–cut picture sleeve – the inner 7" is a picture label placed under a clear vinyl section (not, technically, a picture disc), whilst the outer section is coloured vinyl (orange, blue, yellow and green copies exist). The label includes a 'hidden track, a spoof treatise on the single by Peter Cook.

---

***VS 299–12*** ***PUBLIC IMAGE LIMITED: Memories / Another***
**Label:** CUS **Rel:** 19 Oct 1979[3] (12")
Picture sleeve.

---

***VS 301–12*** ***HUDSON PEOPLE: Boogie On Downtown / Boogie On Downtown (Instrumental)***
**Label:** V10 **Rel:** 19 Oct 1979[3] (12") (del 1980[6])
Die–cut company sleeve.

---

***VS 311–12*** ***90 DEGREES, No Doctor / Fantasy Woman***
**Label:** V10 **Rel:** 7 Dec 1979[3] (12") (del 1980[6])
Generic blue 'neon' company sleeve.

## VEP 1000 series 7" EPs

***VEP 1001*** ***SUPERCHARGE: Four By Six***

| | | |
|---|---|---|
| 1. Times | 1. Get Down Boogie | **Label:** V8 |
| 2. I'll Give Anything | 2. Celebrate | **Rel:** 29 Oct 1976[3] |
| | | **RRP:** 70p[18]/85p[5] |

Picture sleeve credits EP title as "Four x Six" whilst labels credit "Four By Six".

***VEP 1002*** ***ROY ST. JOHN: The Roy St John E.P.***

1. Where Did Our Love Go
2. Nothing Like Your Loving

1. I Sure Love You
2. Dancing Through The Night

**Label:** V9
**Rel:** Mar 1977[5]
**RRP:** 70p[18]/99p[5]

Picture sleeve.

---

***VEP 1003*** ***AVANT GARDENER: Avant Gardener***

1. Gotta Turn Back
2. Strange Gurl In Clothes

1. Back Door
2. Bloodclad Boogie

**Label:** V9
**Rel:** Sep[5]/Oct '77[1]
**RRP:** 70p[18]/99p[1]

Listed in *The New Records* rather than in *The New Singles* because EPs historically listed with LPs.

---

***VEP 1004*** ***JOHN DOWIE: Another Close Shave***

1. British Tourist
2. Naked Noolies In The Moonlight
3. I Don't Want To Be Your Amputee

1. Mew Wave
2. Jim Callaghan
3. Time Warp

**Label:** V9
**Rel:** Oct[5]/Dec '77[1]
**RRP:** 70p[18]/99p[1]

Picture sleeve. Pink vinyl copies free with electric blue vinyl copies of *Short Circuit – Live at the Electric Circus* (VCL 5003). Sticker on 10" LP sleeve claims the EP topped charts (nope) and that its title was *I Hate the Dutch*, which, in reality, was part of the lyrics.

## VOLE series 12" singles

This sequence included original releases along with records otherwise released on the Virgin VS sequence and Front Line FLS sequences.

---

***VOLE 1*** ***DR. ALIMANTADO: Slavery Let I Go / Find The One***

**Label:** V9 **Rel:** Jan 1978[5] (del 1979[8])

In generic blue 'neon' company sleeve.

---

***VOLE 2*** ***U ROY: Small Axe / Small Axe (Version)***

**Label:** **Rel:** 1978

In generic blue 'neon' company sleeve. Reissue of VS 187–12.

---

***VOLE 3*** ***XTC: Science Friction EP: Science Friction / She's So Square / Dance Band***

**Label:** V9 **Rel:** prob. 1978

Reissue of VS 188–12. Said to exist in picture sleeve – only copies in generic blue 'neon' company sleeve confirmed. Presumably later repressed as VS 188–12 again because copies on that catalogue number exist on the blue/green label design.

---

***VOLE 4*** ***U BROWN: Black Star Liner / River John Mountain***

**Label:** V9 **Rel:** 1978

In generic blue 'neon' company sleeve.

---

***VOLE 5*** ***U ROY: Live At The Lyceum***

1. Runaway Girl
2. Babylon Burning

1. Chalice in the Palice
2. Wear You To The Ball

**Label:** V9 **Rel:** 1978

In generic blue 'neon' company sleeve.

---

***VOLE 6*** ***SLY DUNBAR: A Who Say / Cocaine Cocaine***

**Label:** V9 **Rel:** 1978

IIn generic blue 'neon' company sleeve. 12" issue of Front Line 7", FLS 105.

***VOLE 7*** ***ALTHEA AND DONNA: Going To Negril / The West***
**Label:** FL1 **Rel:** Aug 1978[5] **RRP:** £1.49[5]
In generic blue 'neon' company sleeve, though on the Front Line label design. "Full of fun and charm." according to *The Hartlepool Mail* for 14 October 1978. No, I am not making this up.

---

***VOLE 8*** ***POET AND THE ROOTS: It Dread Inna Inglan (For George Lindo) / Man Free (For Darcus Howe)***
**Label:** **Rel:** 1979 (del 1980[8]) **RRP:** £1.59[8]
Picture sleeve.

---

***VOLE 9*** ***JAH WOBBLE: Dreadlock Don't Deal In Wedlock / Pthilius Pubis***
**Label:** V10 **Rel:** 13 Oct 1979[3]
Picture sleeve.

## SIXPACK series 7" picture disc EPs

These were intended for export only and the Caroline Exports moonface logo is displayed on both sleeve and on the record, in the latter case alongside the Virgin logo on the two releases in the series by Virgin artists. The last two records in the series were not Virgin artists, but represented joint–releases between Caroline Exports and Rockburgh and Gull repectively. Should they be in the Virgin section? Well, inspiration failed.

The deal with this series was that you got either six tracks or at least 15 minutes of music per disc. Presumably, these were all issued during 1979, in that the Ian Matthews record comprised tracks with a 1979 publication credit.

Sleeves say, "Quality British Pressing" but the reality is that, although the records look good, they have a tendency to jump and crackle. All were released in die–cut generic sleeve with plinth and all were limited editions of 5,000 copies.

---

***SIXPACK 1*** ***CAPTAIN BEEFHEART: Six–Pack – Six–Track***

| | | |
|---|---|---|
| 1. Upon The My–O–My | 1. Sugar Bowl | **Rel:** 1979? |
| 2. Rock 'N' Roll's Evil Doll | 2. Same Old Blues | |
| 3. New Electric Ride | 3. Magic Be | |

---

***SIXPACK 2*** ***STEVE HILLAGE: Six–Pack – Six–Track***

| | | |
|---|---|---|
| 1. The Salmon Suite | 1. Not Fade Away | **Rel:** 1979? |
| 2. It's All Too Much | 2. Electrique Gypsies | |
| 3. The Golden Vibe | 3. Radio | |

---

***SIXPACK 3*** ***IAN MATTHEWS: Six–Pack – Six–Track***

| | | |
|---|---|---|
| 1. Do Right Woman | 1. Knowing The Game | **Rel:** 1979? |
| 2. Mobile Blue | 2. Polly | |
| 3. Franklin Avenue | 3. Sing Me Back Home | |

Joint Caroline Exports /Rockburgh release and not, strictly speaking a Virgin release.

---

***SIXPACK 4*** ***ARTHUR BROWN: Six–Pack – Six–Track***

| | | |
|---|---|---|
| 1. Monkey Walk | 1. We Have Got To Get Out Of This Place | **Rel:** 1979? |
| 2. I Put A Spell On You | 2. Out Of Time | |
| | 3. Crazy | |

Joint Caroline Exports /Gull release and not, strictly speaking a Virgin release.

# Promotional records (all formats)

## VDJ series

7" singles, 12" singles, LPs and even a flexidisc appeared in this sequence. Some were given away free with other records; some seem to have enjoyed a semi–official release status; some never made it past the white label test press stage. Others seem to have been pressed up purely as promotional records for radio and so on, some containing edited sections from otherwise radio–unfriendly epics. There are various gaps where it has proven impossible to find out what, if anything, was pressed or intended for those numbers. Perhaps there is still the odd VDJ sequence Wigwam, Kevin Coyne or Tom Newman 12" single complete with Disco Dynamite sleeve out there just waiting to be discovered. Who knows?

---

***VDJ 1*** ***ROYAL PHILHARMONIC ORCHESTRA WITH MIKE OLDFIELD ON GUITAR: Extract From The Orchestral Tubular Bells / Extract From The Orchestral Tubular Bells***

**Format:** 7" **Label:** V1

Labels include credit, "Arranged and Conducted By David Bedford". Despite both sides having the same title both are different extracts.

---

***VDJ 2*** ***NO ARTIST CREDITED: An Extract From White Noise 2 / An Extract From White Noise 2***

**Format:** 7" **Label:** V1

7". Despite same title and track timings, extracts are different. David Vorhaus credited as writer and producer but otherwise no artist credit.

---

***VDJ 3*** ***RUAN: Another Street Gang / Suburban Disturbance***

**Format:** 12" single **Label:** V3

Labels stamped, "PROMOTION COPY ONLY". On the short–lived beige mirrored girl LP label design rather than the yellow/red promotional label. Normal 7" version issued as VS 125.

---

***VDJ 4*** ***ARCHIE LEGGET: Jamaican Jockey / Alberto***

**Format:** 12" single **Label:** PRO

Die–cut promo sleeve. Yellow/red sleeve die–cut on front only, includes the text, "12" of Disco Dynamite". Rear sleeve includes very large mirrored girl. Normal 7" version issued as VS 129.

---

***VDJ 5*** ***UNKNOWN***

---

***VDJ 6*** ***UNKNOWN***

---

***VDJ 7*** ***MATAYA CLIFFORD: Star Fell From Heaven / Pound And Grind***

**Format:** 12" single **Label:** PRO

In die–cut promo sleeve. Normal 7" version issued as VS 127.

---

***VDJ 8*** ***UNKNOWN***

---

***VDJ 9*** ***MIKE OLDFIELD: An Extract From Ommadawn Part I / An Extract From Ommadawn Part II***

**Format:** 12" single **Label:** PRO

In die–cut promo sleeve. Side one 7.11 minutes, side two 3.25 minutes (side 2 is *On Horseback*).

---

***VDJ 10*** ***DAVID BEDFORD: An Extract From The Rime Of The Ancient Mariner – Part Two / An Extract From The Rime Of The Ancient Mariner – Part Two***

**Format:** 7" **Label:** V1

Despite same title, tracks are different.

***VDJ 11*** ***SUPERCHARGE: Get Down Boogie / Don't Let Go***
**Format:** 12" single **Label:** PRO
In die–cut promo sleeve. Normal 7" version issued as VS 134.

---

***VDJ 12*** ***BOXER: All The Time In The World / Don't Wait***
**Format:** 12" single **Label:** PRO
In die–cut promo sleeve. Normal 7" version issued as VS 135.

---

***VDJ 13*** ***U ROY: Runaway Girl / Chalice In The Palace***
**Format:** 12" single **Label:** PRO
In die–cut promo sleeve. Normal 7" version issued as VS 138.

---

***VDJ 14*** ***THE MIGHTY DIAMONDS: Have Mercy / Them Never Love Poor Marcus***
**Format:** 12" single **Label:** PRO
In die–cut promo sleeve. Normal 7" version issued as VS 137.

---

***VDJ 15*** ***UNKNOWN***

---

***VDJ 16*** ***UNKNOWN***

---

***VDJ 17*** ***TANGERINE DREAM: Stratosphere / The Big Sleep In Search Of Hades***
**Format:** 7" **Label:** V8
Labels include the text, "D.J. Copy. For promotional use only."

---

***VDJ 18*** ***UNKNOWN***

---

***VDJ 19*** ***NO ARTIST CREDITED: Musical Shark Attack (AKA Musical Dub Attack)***

1. Semi–Classical Natty Dread (Dub)
2. Musical Shark Attack (Dub)
3. Drum Sound (Dub)
4. Is Love I Deal With (Dub)
5. Social Development (Dub)
6. Jamboree (Dub)

1. Skyjuice And Festival Dumping (Dub)
2. Run For Your Life (Dub)
3. Tribute To Michael Holding (Dub)
4. Everybody Ballin' (Dub)
5. Tribute To Marcus Garvey (Dub)

**Format:** LP
**Label:** white label

Plain white labels on the only copy to be viewed during research have handwritten credit, "Musical Shark Attack". LP is a dub, instrumental version of the I–Roy LP (V 2075). Track titles above are the purest guesses based on the fact that this album has eleven tracks, as does V 2075. Several Internet sources credit the LP as "Musical Dub Attack" with artist listed as The Revolutionaries.

---

***VDJ 20*** ***CAN: Don't Say No / Return***
**Format:** 7" **Label:** V9

---

***VDJ 21*** ***UNKNOWN***

---

***VDJ 22*** ***DELROY WASHINGTON: Give All The Praise To Jah / Stand Up And Be Happy***
**Format:** 12" single **Label:** V7 **Rel:** Aug 1977[5]
In generic blue 'neon' company sleeve. According to *Music Master 1979* this was released to the general public, though as a limited edition.

---

***VDJ 23*** ***STEVE HILLAGE: Leylines To Glassdom / GLENN PHILLIPS: Lies***
**Format:** 7" **Label:** V9
Picture sleeve. Given away at Hillage concerts (on which Glenn Phillips was support act) and at Virgin retail outlets. In Bristol, copies were given to discotheques for free distribution to punters in advance of the Hillage concert. The Hillage track is not the same as the version on *Green* (V 2098).

***VDJ 24*** ***SEX PISTOLS: Submission***
**Format:** 7" **Label:** V9
One–sided 7" single free with the export version of *Never Mind the Bollocks, Here's the Sex Pistols* (V 2086/SPOTS 001). B–side label white and blank.

---

***VDJ 25*** ***TANGERINE DREAM: Encore / Hobo March (NOT PRESSED?)***
Normal VS 199 copies have a "VDJ 25" matrix number scratched out in the run–off with "VS 199" matrix added. At some point the decision must have been made for this to be a proper release instead and the VDJ number was used for the Steve Hillage 12" listed below.

---

***VDJ 25*** ***STEVE HILLAGE: Getting Better / Palm Trees (Love Guitar)***
**Format:** 12" single **Label:** V7
In generic, blue 'neon' company sleeve. Normal stock 7" version issued as VS 212.

---

***VDJ 26*** ***SOLID SENDERS: Live***

| | | |
|---|---|---|
| 1. Walking on the Edge | 1. Highway 81 | **Format:** LP |
| 2. Paradise | 2. Neighbour Neighbour | **Label:** V10 |
| 3. All Abroad | 3. Rock Me Baby | |

Free with early copies of *Solid Senders* (V 2105). Export copies for the US market included the "Sales Point Wilco" sticker plus another sticker saying, "This is a British Double Slice" and going on to say that the album included one studio and one live album plus a free poster.

---

***VDJ 27*** ***DEVO: A Flimsy Wrap***
**Format:** 7" flexi
33⅓ rpm, one–sided flexidisc free with early copies of *Q: Are We Not Men? A: We Are Devo* (V 2106). Pressed by Lyntone with matrix number LYN 6260. There must have been quite a few left over because it seems to have also been free with early copies of *Secret Agent Man* (VS 280) as well as with the export version of the Stiff label compilation album, *B Stiff* (ODD 1), which was shrinkwrapped for the US market with sticker saying, "this album includes a free single". This pairing is not as odd as it sounds because by this time Virgin's sales team was also responsible for Stiff product.

---

***VDJ 28*** ***FINGERPRINTZ: Do You Want To Know A Secret / Who's Your Friend***
**Format:** 12" single **Label:** V10

---

***VDJ 29*** ***THE RECORDS: High Heels***

| | |
|---|---|
| 1. Abracadabra (Have You Ever Seen Her) | 1. 1984 |
| 2. See My Friends | 2. Have You Seen Your Mother, Baby, Standing In the Shadows |

**Format:** 12" single **Label:** CUS
Free with *Shades in Bed* (V 2122). Rumours of a 7" version relate to the US LP freebie.

---

***VDJ 30*** ***XTC: Chain Of Command / Limelight***
**Format:** 7" **Label:** V10
Free with the first 15,000 copies of *Drums and Wires* (V 2129). Label says, "Free single not for sale".

## Custom catalogue numbers

**_No cat. no. XTC: Live At Eric's_**

1. Radios In Motion
2. Cross Wires
3. Let's Have Fun
4. Fireball XL5
5. Science Friction
6. I'm Bugged
7. New Town Animal In A Furnished Cage
8. Hang On To The Night

1. All Along The Watchtower
2. She's So Square
3. Do What You Do
4. Spinning Top
5. Neon Shuffle
6. Traffic Light Rock
7. Unknown track

Cassette only. Above is a best guess at track break. Recorded 13 August 1977 at Eric's, Liverpool. Virgin Tapes promotional–only issue came with a generic Virgin Tapes cassette inlay. The cassette is a Maxell C60. *Traffic Light Rock* was released on the free *Record Mirror* EP – see directly below.

---

**_No cat. no. VARIOUS ARTISTS: Presented Free by Record Mirror_**

1. Monolight (Tangerine Dream)
2. Traffic Light Rock (XTC)

1. Whisky And Wine (The Motors)
2. Control Tower (U–Roy)

**Label:** V9
**Rel:** Dec 1977[14]

7" EP free with *Record Mirror*. Record says the Tangerine Dream track is from "UD2506", which is wrong on two counts. First, *Encore* was VD 2506 and, second, this is an overdubbed version of the section of *Monolight* that appears on *Encore*. XTC track is otherwise unreleased live track, recorded 13 August 1977 at Eric's, Liverpool (from the promotional *Live at Eric's* cassette – see directly above). No catalogue number on labels – run–off matrix number is VR 08–10274–SHOL 2550.

---

**_No cat. no. XTC: XTC Interview_**

1. Interview for the release of White Music

Cassette only. Virgin Tapes promotional–only issue with generic Virgin Tapes cassette inlay. The cassette is a Maxell C46.

---

**_LYN 3261 SEX PISTOLS: Lentilmas – A Seasonal Offering To You From Virgin Records_**

Lyntone 7" flexidisc given to journalists at Christmas 1977. Some accompanied by a Christmas card.

---

**_RM/BURG 1 VARIOUS ARTISTS: Half Pounder_**

1. Radios In Motion (XTC)
2. No More Fighting (Althea And Donna)
3. Unidentified (Flying Being) (Steve Hillage)
4. Fly Away (The Gladiators)
5. Kate (Colin Towns)

1. Breathless (The Motors)
2. Up In The Balcony (Yellow Dog)
3. Ghetto Rock (Tapper Zukie)
4. Are We Dreaming? (Kevin Coyne)
5. Planet Called Earth (The Diamonds)

**Label:** V9
**Rel:** 1978

LP with inner sleeve. Label is an amended blue 'neon' design with added "Record Mirror" credits. Exclusive free album for *Record Mirror* readers. Credited as "Half Pounder" on sleeve but credited as "Hamburger Half Pounder" on labels. Inner sleeves include illustrated discographies for all artists on the album, inluding cassette details.

---

**_No cat. no. SEX PISTOLS: The Interview_**

7" two–sided flexidisc recorded at Middlesborough Rock Garden in August 1977. According to the *Record Collector Rare Record Price Guide 2014*, 1,000 copies were pressed in 1979. I haven't been able to verify that this record actually exists, but it's here just in case.

***RMOS 1*** ***VARIOUS ARTISTS: Oversell***

1. Soho a Go Go (The Members)
2. Paint Her Face (The Records)
3. Night Nurse (Fingerprintz)
4. Get Ready (The Gladiators)
5. Cloudburst Flight (Tangerine Dream)

1. Integral Plot (Skids)
2. Gut Feeling (Devo)
3. They Never Love In This Time (Culture)
4. I Think I'm Gonna Fall In Love (Supercharge)
5. King Pharoah (Twinkle Bros)
6. Barbara's Song (Julie Covington)

**Label:** CUS
**Rel:** 1979

Joint LP release by Virgin and *Record Mirror* – the label states "Exclusive free album for Record Mirror readers – not for resale". *Soho a Go Go* by The Members is listed twice on the label by mistake. The Tangerine Dream track is an edited version of the album track from *Force Majeure*. The Supercharge track does not include the brackets that appear in other releases. The Records track is erroneously titled on the sleeve as "Paint Your Face" but is correctly listed on the label. The NB 2 catalogue number is listed for the Records track, so the LP must predate the December 1979 reissue of *Starry Eyes*.

***No cat. no.*** ***COWBOYS INTERNATIONAL: Many Times***

Clear, blank, unnumbered 7" flexidisc free with picture sleeve copies of *Nothing Doing*, VS 267. It is possible that this was assigned one of the otherwise unknown VDJ catalogue numbers.

***VSDJ 317*** ***MIKE OLDFIELD: Blue Peter***

One–sided promotional 7" with the original abrupt ending. Quite why Virgin suddenly adopted a different (and one–off) format for denoting a promotional record when other promotional records appeared in the VDJ sequence is a mystery.

## Caroline

The Caroline name enjoyed a dual existance as both Virgin's export arm and as the name for Virgin's mid–priced budget label. Caroline Exports adverts appeared regularly in the music press stating, "Worldwide wholesalers of UK and European gramophone records, cassette tapes, clothes and posters. Virgin Records material our speciality". Curiously, Caroline adverts for wholesale exports existed in the back pages of the music press whilst Virgin adverts advertised a "personalised export service" under the name of "Virgin Records (Exports)" in their main adverts. The eagle–eyed might have noticed that both shared the same Woodfield Road address.

As regards Caroline the record label, there were two main catalogue sequences, both budget priced. The first C 1500 sequence records were issued at £1.49, a price that was most likely pegged to Island's budget HELP series. The later CA 2000 catalogue sequence was initially priced at £1.99 per album. Most Caroline LPs included a mirrored girl price sticker (C 1503 has been spotted with a sticker that says "Caroline only 1.49 retail", but without mirrored girl graphic). Toward the end of its existence, two double albums were issued, priced at £3.25 each. It is worth noting that singles from Caroline label LPs were issued on the Virgin label proper. No cassette or 8–track versions issued.

## C 1500 series LPs

There is one point of confusion with this catalogue sequence, which is that Gong's *Camembert Electrique* was issued twice on two different catalogue numbers. Even more odd is that the first issue on Caroline as C 1505 seems to have coincided with the album's release on the Virgin label's 'ultra budget' series as VC 502, with RRP of 59p. There are possible solutions. Firstly, the vast majority of C 1505 copies seem to crop up for sale in countries other than the UK, so perhaps the Caroline release was contemporary to the Virgin issue and was intended for sale outside of the UK at the higher budget price of £1.49, whilst the VC 502 issue was issued in the UK at the much lower price of 59p. Either that or the album was originally intended for release on Caroline (in that the VC 502 issue has the C 1505 matrix amended in the run–off) but was switched to the Virgin instead. In this scenario, it would then have been reissued on Caroline once the Virgin version had sold 150,000 copies and been deleted as planned.

---

***C 1501*** ***TONI CONRAD AND FAUST: Outside The Dream Syndicate***

| Side 1 | Side 2 | |
|---|---|---|
| 1. From The Side Of Man And Womankind | 1. From The Side Of The Machine | **Rel:** 1973 |
| | | **RRP:** £1.46[4] |

---

***C 1502*** ***HOMESICK JAMES/SNOOKY PRIOR: Homesick James And Snooky Prior***

| Side 1 | Side 2 | |
|---|---|---|
| 1. Crossroads | 1. The Woman I Love | **Rel:** 1974 |
| 2. Nothin' But Trouble | 2. I Feel Alright | **RRP:** £1.49[4]/ £1.46[5] |
| 3. Shake Your Money Maker | 3. Drivin' Dog | |
| 4. Cross Town | 4. She Knows How To Love Me | |
| 5. Careless Love | 5. Homesick Blues Again | |
| 6. After You Were There Won't Be Nobody Else | | |

***C 1503*** ***COXHILL/MILLER: Miller/Coxhill/Coxhill/Miller***

1. Chocolate Field
2. One For You
3. Portland Bill

1. Will My Thirst Play Me Tricks?/The Ant About To Be Crushed Ponders Not The Where Withal Of Bootleather
2. Maggots
3. Bath '72
4. Wimbledon Baths
5. Gog Ma Gog

**Rel:** 1973
**RRP:** £1.49[4]

---

***C 1504*** ***DUDU PUKWANA AND SPEAR: In The Townships***

1. Baloyi
2. Ezilalini
3. Zakude

1. Sonia
2. Angel Nemali
3. Nobomvu
4. Sekela Khuluma

**Rel:** May 1974[1]
**RRP:** £1.49[1/4]

---

***C 1505*** ***GONG: Camembert Electrique***

See VC 502 for track listing.

**Rel:** not advised
**RRP:** pres. £1.49

This was near simultaneously released as VC 502 and was later issued again as C 1520.

---

***C 1506*** ***MAX: Max***

1. Stephanie
2. Rolling Up
3. Cell Block E
4. Shapes And Spaces

1. Witch Woman
2. Troublemaker
3. Dance Of Death
4. All I Know

**Rel:** May[11]/ Aug 1974[4]
**RRP:** £1.49[4]

Insert. Max Handley was deputy editor of Richard Branson's *Student* magazine. Ah, nepotism. Perhaps, but a very good album nonetheless. *Music Master 1976* and *Music Master 1979* both credit the album to "Max Handley" although credits on sleeve and labels include no mention of surname.

---

***C 1507*** ***COXHILL/MILLER: The Story So Far ... Oh Really?***

1. G Song
2. F Bit
3. Songs Of March
4. More G Songs
5. Does This
6. The Greatest Offshore Race In The World (From The Film Of The Same Name)

1. Reprise For Those Who Prefer It Slower
2. Tubercular Balls
3. Soprano Derivativa
4. Oh, DO I Like To Be Beside The Seaside?
5. In Memoriam: Meister Eckhart. From The Welfare State Epic Of The Same Name Starring Randolph Scott
6. A Fabulous Comedian

**Rel:** Oct[4]/Nov'74[11]
**RRP:** £1.46[12]/ £2.45[4]

*Music Master 1976* incorrectly prices this in line with the V 2000 full price series. The *Melody Maker* price would appear to be that charged at Virgin's own shops. Correct RRP is £1.49.

---

***C 1508*** ***FRED FRITH: Guitar Solos***

1. Hello Music
2. Glass c/w Steel
3. Ghosts
4. Out Of Their Heads (On Locoweed)

1. Not Forgotten
2. Hollow Music
3. Heat c/w Moment
4. No Birds

**Rel:** Oct[4]/Nov'74[11]
**RRP:** £2.45[4]

*Music Master 1976* incorrectly prices this in line with the V 2000 full price series. See notes for C 1507 above.

### *C 1509* *LADY JUNE: Lady June's Linguistic Leprosy*

| Side 1 | Side 2 | |
|---|---|---|
| 1. Some Day Silly Twenty Three | 1. Bars | **Rel:** Nov[4/11]/ Dec 1974[1] |
| 2. Reflections | 2. The Letter | **RRP:** £1.49[1] |
| 3. Am I | 3. Mangel/Wurzel | |
| 4. Everythingsnothing | 4. To Whom It May Not Concern | |
| 5. Tunion | 5. Optimism | |
| 6. The Tourist | 6. Touch–Downer | |

Insert.

---

### *C 1510* *EGG: The Civil Surface*

| Side 1 | Side 2 | |
|---|---|---|
| 1. Germ Patrol | 1. Prelude | **Rel:** Nov[4/11/12]/ Dec 1974[1] |
| 2. Wind Quartet 1 | 2. Wring Out The Ground Loosely Now | **RRP:** £1.49[1]/ £1.46[4] |
| 3. Enneagram | 3. Nearch | |
| | 4. Wind Quartet 2 | |

---

### *C 1511* *LINK WRAY: Interstate 10 (NOT RELEASED)*

Originally assigned to Link Wray's *Interstate 10* and notified to *Music Master* with April 1975 release date[6] but not ultimately released.

---

### *C 1511* *FRIENDS: Friends*

| Side 1 | Side 2 | |
|---|---|---|
| 1. 5/8 Tune | 1. Nursery Rhyme | **Rel:** Jul[4]/Aug '75[5] |
| 2. Black Vibrations | 2. Loose Tune | **RRP:** £1.49[15]/ £2.29[5] |

Included sleeve sticker with list of musicians, plus the price of £1.49, topped off with a quote from *Jazz Forum*, "...electronic jazz record of the year". *Music Master 1979* lists this under "John Abercrombie" (with RRP but no release date) and under "Friends" (with release date but no RRP). RRP probably as at 1978, when it looks as though this record was readvised to *Music Master* along with various Virgin/ECM releases that included Abercrombie.

---

### *C 1512* *DUDU PUKWANA: Flute Music (NOT RELEASED)*

Originally assigned to Dudu Pukwana's *Flute Music* and notified to *Music Master* with March 1975 release date[4] but not ultimately released on this catalogue number. Instead released at higher RRP as CA 2005.

---

### *C 1512* *DAEVID ALLEN: Banana Moon*

| Side 1 | Side 2 | |
|---|---|---|
| 1. It's The Time Of Your Life | 1. Stoned Innocent Frankenstein ... | **Rel:** Jul[4]/Aug '75[1] |
| 2. Memories | 2. ... And His Adventures In The Land Of Flip | **RRP:** £1.49[1] |
| 3. All I Want Is Out Of Here | 3. I'm A Bowl | |
| 4. Fred The Fish And The Chip On His Shoulder | | |
| 5. White Neck Blooze | | |
| 6. Codeine Coda | | |

Track 6, side 1 is a continuous loop. The original French Byg label issue has a track timing of 12.32 for this, whilst this reissue ups this by a few hours. Perhaps 'research' indicated this is how long it would take the average addled hippy to spot that the record was stuck.

---

### *C 1513* *TALISKER: Dreaming Of Glenisla*

| Side 1 | Side 2 | |
|---|---|---|
| 1. Dreaming Of Glensia | 1. Mrs. Macleod Ramsay And Soldier's Song | **Rel:** Oct[4]/Nov '75[1] |
| 2. Diddlin' For The Bairns And Lament For Dairmid | 2. Ca' The Yows | **RRP:** £1.59[1] |
| 3. Drum Salute And Lament For Mal Dean | 3. Mingulay Boat Song | |
| | 4. Heel An' Toe, Foot An' Moo' | |
| | 5. Homeward | |

***C 1514*** ***LOL COXHILL/WELFARE STATE: Lol Coxhill/Welfare State***

1. The First Bit
2. Egal O.K.
3. Le Tombeau De Ravel
4. Labrinth:
   i. Gumbley's Creole Trombone
   ii. Blossom Time
   iii. Expedition To The Lair Of The Terrifying SpiderBoy...Who Fortunately Was Not At Home
   iv. An Awfully Romantic Duet For Possibly Blackbird And Definitely Saxophone
5. Miscellaneous:
   i. Tuba Gallicalis
   ii. Egg Dance
   iii. Mad Tom
6. Welwyn Garden:
   i. Mole Song
   ii. Little German Band
   iii. Bring Out Your Skeletons
   iv. Lady Howard Calypso
   v. Parade
   vi. Tribal Drumming From The Nim Ram River Region

1. Big German Band
2. Rag
3. Ghosts
4. Luke Jamboree
5. Skipton March
6. Arena
7. Child Of The Evening
8. Anna Maria
9. W.S. Samba
10. Yet Another Egal O.K.

**Rel:** Mar[5]/May '76[1]
**RRP:** £1.59[5]/ £2.59[1]

*The New Records* price is incorrect.

---

***C 1515*** ***LOL COXHILL: Fleas In Custard***

1. Duet For Soprano Saxophone And Guitar

1. Hitherto Unrevealed Facts
2. Hints For Beginners
3. Three A.M. Modulations
4. Synalto
5. Voices Of The Enlightened
6. Hurry Along Please
7. Don't Call Us....

**Rel:** Feb[5]/Apr '76[1]
**RRP:** £1.59[1]

---

***C 1516*** ***GLOBAL VILLAGE TRUCKING COMPANY: Global Village Trucking Company***

1. On The Judgement Day
2. Lasga's Farm
3. Love Your Neighbour
4. Short Change/Tall Story
5. Smiling Revolution

1. Love Will Find A Way
2. If You Don't Mind (Me Saying)
3. The Inevitable Fate Of Ms Danya Sox
4. Watch Out There's A Mind About

**Rel:** Mar[5]/Apr '76[1]
**RRP:** £1.59[1]

Insert. On release, keyboard player, the Hon. James Lascelles, was about 8th in line to the UK throne.

---

***C 1517*** ***STEPHAN MICUS: Archaic Concerts***

1. Concert For Gender, Shakuhachi And Zither

1. Concert For AngKlung, Acoustic Guitar And Zither

**Rel:** Apr 1976[5]
**RRP:** £1.59[5]

Yellow sleeve sticker stating "Recommended Retail Price £1.59" with the Virgin mirrored girl logo.

***C 1518*** ***FRITH/BAILEY/FITZGERALD/REICHEL: Guitar Solos 2***

1. Water/Struggle/The North (Fred Frith)
2. Only Reflect (Fred Frith)
3. Brixton Winter 1976 (G. F. Fitzgerald)

1. Avantlore (Hans Reichel)
2. Vain Yookte (Hans Reichel)
3. Donnerkuhle (Hans Reichel)
4. Virginal (Derek Bailey)
5. Praxis (Derek Bailey)
6. The Lost Chord (Derek Bailey)

**Rel:** Jun 1976[5]
**RRP:** £1.59[5]

---

***C 1519*** ***GLENN PHILLIPS: Lost At Sea***

1. I've Got A Bullet With Your Name On It
2. I Feel Better Already
3. Guruvir
4. A Storm
5. Dogs

1. Lenore
2. You Know I Do (Lenore Part II)
3. The Flu
4. Jimmy Klein
5. Hubbler
6. My Favourite Song

**Rel:** Feb 1977[5]
**RRP:** £1.99[5]

1975 publication date relates to original US release.

---

***C 1520*** ***GONG: Camembert Electrique***

See VC 502 for track listing.

**Rel:** Mar[5]/Apr '77[1]
**RRP:** £1.99[1]

Reissue of C 1505 and VC 502. Copies included a green sticker with the recommended retail price.

---

***C 1521*** ***VARIOUS ARTISTS: Front Line***

See VC 503 for track listing.

**Rel:** Mar[5]/Apr '77[1]
**RRP:** £1.99[1]

## CA 2000 series LPs

***CA 2001*** ***CAROL GRIMES: Warm Blood***

1. That's What It Takes
2. High Hill Country Rain
3. Taxes On The Farmer
4. All For One
5. Ray, Ray, Ray
6. Lost My Faith (In Everything But You)

1. Warm Blood
2. You're The Only One
3. Somebody Sleeping In My Bed
4. Southern Boogie
5. Don't Want You On My Mind
6. Wait For Me Down By The River

**Rel:** May 1974[1]
**RRP:** £1.99[1/4]
**Del** 1977[5]

---

***CA 2002*** ***B. B. SEATON: Dancing Shoes***

1. Hold On (My People)
2. Everybody Loves A Winner
3. Who's That Lady?
4. No More Tribalism
5. Brothers Stand Up
6. Brothers Beware

1. Dancing Shoes
2. Thing About You
3. Making Love Is So Much Fun
4. I Believe (When I Fall In Love It Will Be Forever)
5. Anyday Now
6. How Can I Exist?

**Rel:** Jul 1974[4/11]
**RRP:** £1.99[4]
**Del** 1975[5]

---

***CA 2003*** ***KLAUS SCHULZE: Blackdance***

1. Ways Of Changes
2. Some Velvet Phasing

1. Voices Of Syn

**Rel:** Aug [4]/ Sep 1974[1/11]
**RRP:** £1.99[1/4]

***CA 2004 JABULA: Jabula***

1. Jabula Happiness
2. Baile They Are Gone
3. Listen To Me Crying
4. Naledi
5. Badishi – Herdboys

1. Thandi
2. Siakala – We Are Sad
3. Our Fathers
4. Let Us Be Free

**Rel:** Feb[4]/Mar '75[1]
**RRP:** £1.95[1]

*V* (VD 2502) lists this for February 1975 release.

---

***CA 2005 DUDU PUKWANA AND SPEAR: Flute Music***

1. Flute Music
2. Shekele
3. Ko–Didi

1. Sondela
2. Freeze
3. You Cheated Me
4. Flute Music

**Rel:** Mar 1975[4]
**RRP:** pres. £1.99

*Music Master 1976* lists this (twice) as C 1512 – credited to both "Dudu Pukwana" and "Dudu Pukwana & Spear".

---

***CA 2006 KLAUS SCHULZE: Timewind***

1. Bayreuth Return

1. Wahnfried 1883

**Rel:** Aug[4]/Oct '75[1]
**RRP:** £1.99[1]

Credited in *The New Records* to "Klaus Schulze & Timewind". Timewind was the name for the short-lived duo of Schulze and Michael Hoenig. This LP was awarded the Grand Prix International du Disque in France.

---

***CA 2007 GILGAMESH: Gilgamesh***

1. One And More/Phil's Little Dance – For Phil Millers Trousers
2. Worlds Of Zin
3. Eyes Were Lady And Friend
4. Not Withswtanding

1. Arriving Twice
2. Island Of Rhodes/Paper Boat – For Doris/As If Your Open
3. For Absent Friends
4. We Are All/Someone Else's Food/ Jamo And Other Boating Disasters – From The Holiday Of The Same Name
5. Just C

**Rel:** Jul[4]/ Aug '75[1]
**RRP:** £1.99[1]

Promotional copies seem to be easier to find than stock copies.

---

***CA 2008 ROY ST. JOHN: Declaration Immegration***

1. Immigration Declaration
2. Slow Me Down
3. The Facts Of Life
4. Cool And Lazy
5. California Migrant
6. She Got The River

1. Take A Chance On Loving Me Tonight
2. Maid Of Orleans
3. Out In The Backyard
4. Gaudelia
5. Aztec Stomp
6. Waiting For The Lights To Change

**Rel:** Feb[5]/Apr '76[1]
**RRP:** £2.25[5]/ £1.59[1]

Erroneously listed as CA 2007 in *The New Records*. The *Music Master 1979* price is the correct one.

---

***CA 2009 JABULA SPEAR: Thunder Into Our Hearts***

1. Thunder Into Our Hearts
2. Soweto My Love
3. Ithumeleng Ba Mamelodi

1. Tears Of Afrika
2. Baleka – Run Away
3. Journey To Afrika
4. Harvest Part II

**Rel:** Jul 1976[1/5]
**RRP:** £2.25[1]

Sleeve credits "Jabula" but labels credit "Jabula Spear". Orange sleeve sticker with RRP.

***CA 2010 PHILIP GLASS: Music In Twelve Parts – Parts 1 And 2***

| | | |
|---|---|---|
| 1. Music In 12 Parts – Part 1 | 1. Music In 12 Parts – Part 2 | **Rel:** May[5]/Jul '76[1]<br>**RRP:** £2.25[1] |

Early sleeves included a red sticker showing the recommended retail price. Original copies in matt, textured sleeve, later copies in smooth, gloss sleeve. Sleeve credits "Music in Twelve Parts – Parts 1 & 2" whilst labels replace "Twelve" with "12".

***CA 2011 I ROY: Crisus Time***

| | | |
|---|---|---|
| 1. Roots Man Time | 1. Don't Touch I Man Locks | **Rel:** Aug[5]/Oct '76[1] |
| 2. African Talk | 2. Satta | **RRP:** £2.25[1] |
| 3. Crisus Time | 3. African Herbsman | |
| 4. Equality And Justice | 4. Love Your Neighbour | |
| 5. Hypocrite Blackout | 5. Send Us A Little Power Oh Jah | |
| 6. Musical Injection | 6. Moving On Strong | |

## CAD 3000 series 2–LPs

***CAD 3001 CAN: Unlimited Edition***

| | | |
|---|---|---|
| *Side 1* | *Side 2* | **Rel:** Apr[5]/Jul '76[1] |
| 1. Gomorrha | 1. EFS No. 27 | **RRP:** £3.25[1] |
| 2. Doko E | 2. TV Spot | |
| 3. LH 702 | 3. EFS No. 7 | |
| 4. I'm Too Leise | 4. The Empress And The Ukraine King | |
| 5. Musette | 5. EFS No. 10 | |
| 6. Blue Bag (Inside Paper) | 6. Mother Upduff | |
| | 7. EFS No. 36 | |
| *Side 3* | *Side 4* | |
| 1. Cutaway | 1. Fall Of Another Year | |
| 2. Connection | 2. EFS No. 8 | |
| | 3. Transcendental Express | |
| | 4. Ibis | |

Sleeve sticker says, "Can Double Album Recommened Retail Price £3.25".

***CAD 3002 HENRY COW: Concerts***

| | | |
|---|---|---|
| *Side 1* | *Side 2* | **Rel:** Jun[5]/Aug '76[1] |
| 1. Beautiful As The Moon... | 1. Bad Alchemy | **RRP:** £3.25[1] |
| 2. Nirvana For Mice | 2. Little Red Riding Hood Hits The Road | |
| 3. Ottawa Song | 3. Ruins | |
| 4. Gloria Gloom | | |
| 5. ...Terrible As An Army With Banners | | |
| *Side 3* | *Side 4* | |
| 1. Oslo | 1. Groningen | |
| | 2. Udine | |
| | 3. Groningen Again | |

Side 1 recorded for John Peel's Top Gear, broadcast 18 August 1975. Album later reissued by Henry Cow's Broadcast label as BC 2.

# Oval

Oval Music was established in 1972 by Charlie Gillett and Gordon Nelki. Gillett played many records from the US Southern States on BBC Radio London and the feedback led the pair to travel to Louisiana and New Orleans to find material for a UK compilation LP. They found plenty of material but couldn't find a UK label willing to release the LP until, in 1973, Virgin took on the distribution.

That might have been it, except that Oval started to receive tapes from various people that had been impressed by the album. One was Jimmy O'Neill, but for reasons unknown (other than being a pun on the Rolling Stones track title) the subsequent single was put out under the name of Jimmy Shelter. The Virgin connection continued when O'Neill signed to Virgin with his band Fingerprintz.

Oval set about re–releasing material by Barbara Lynn and the Sir Douglas Quintet prior to putting out a trio of reggae singles. Shortly after this, the relationship with Virgin came to and end and Oval moved distribution to A&M. All records released during the Virgin years included the credit, "Distributed by Virgin Records" on either label or sleeve.

## OVL 3000 series LP

***OVL 3001*** ***VARIOUS ARTISTS: Another Saturday Night***

1. Before I Grow Old (Tommy McLain)
2. Cajun Fugitive (I'm A Lonesome Fighter) (Belton Richard)
3. Try To Find Another Man (Tommy McLain And Clint West)
4. Jole Blon (Vince Bruce)
5. Who Needs You So Bad (Gary Walker)

Oh Lucille (Belton Richard)

1. Another Saturday Night (Clint West)
2. Un Autre Soir D'Ennui (Another Sleepless Night) (Belton Richard)

3, The Promised Land (Johnnie Allen)

4. Two Steps De Bayou Teche (Austin Pitre)
5. Downhome Music (Rufus Jagneaux)
6. Laisser Les Cajuns Dancer (Belton Richard)

**Rel:** 1974[4]
**RRP:** £1.46[12]

Mail–order price listed as £1.35 in the *Melody Maker* for 16 November 1974.

## OVLM 5000 series LPs

***OVLM 5001*** ***SIR DOUGLAS QUINTET: Mendocino***

1. Mendocino
2. I Don't Want
3. I Wanna Be Your Mama Again
4. At the Crossroads
5. If You Really Want Me To, I'll Go

1. And It Didn't Even Bring Me Down
2. Lawd, I'm Just A Country Boy In This Great Big Freaky City
3. She's About a Mover
4. Texas Me
5. Oh Baby, It Just Don't Matter

**Rel:** Nov 1975[4]
**RRP:** not advised

---

***OVLM 5002*** ***BARBARA LYNN: Here Is Barbara Lynn***

1. You'll Lose A Good Thing
2. Take Your Love And Run
3. Maybe We Can Slip Away
4. Sure Is Worth It
5. Only You Know How To Love Me
6. I'll Suffer

1. You're Losing Me
2. Sufferin' City
3. Multiplying Pain
4. Why Can't You Love Me
5. Mix It Up
6. This Is The Thanks I Get

**Rel:** Oct 1976[5]
**RRP:** £2.79[5]

## OVAL 1000 series 7" singles

The first three singles were all released on different label designs, the first two being different shades of blue and the last being an orange 'sunburst' design. The orange label design was subsequently used throughout the label's association with Virgin. As far as is known, neither of the first two singles were pressed on the later label design.

---

***OVAL 1001*** ***JOHNNIE ALLEN: Promised Land / SHELTON DUNAWAY: Betty And Dupree***
**Rel:** 6 Dec 1974[3] **RRP:** 50p or 55p
A–side subcredited, "Featuring BELTON RICHARD on Accordion".

---

***OVAL 1002*** ***CELEBRATED ARTISTS BAND: Who Do You Think You Are / Keyhole In The Door***
**Rel:** 17 Jan 1975[3] (del 1977[5]) **RRP:** 50p or 55p

---

***OVAL 1003*** ***JIMME SHELTER: Achin' In My Heart / Cold On Me***
**Rel:** 13 Jun 1975[3] **RRP:** 55p[18]

---

***OVAL 1004*** ***TOMMY McLAIN: Before I Grow Too Old / CLINT WEST: Sweet Suzannah***
**Rel:** 1 Aug[3]/15 Aug 1975[3] **RRP:** 60p[18]

---

***OVAL 1005*** ***PETE FOWLER: One Heart, One Song / The Miner's Strike***
**Rel:** 1 Aug[3]/3 Oct 1975[3] (del 1977[5]) **RRP:** 60p[18]

---

***OVAL 1006*** ***BARBARA LYNN: Letter To Mommy And Daddy / You'll Lose A Good Thing***
**Rel:** 22 Aug[3]/12 Sep 1975[3] **RRP:** 60p[18]

---

***OVAL 1007*** ***THE SIR DOUGLAS QUINTET: Mendocino / I Wanna Be Your Mama Again***
**Rel:** 3 Oct 1975[3] (del 1977[5]) **RRP:** 60p[18]

---

***OVAL 1008*** ***DENNIS BROWN: Go Now / Why Must I?***
**Rel:** 20 Feb[3]/Mar 1976[5] (del 1978[5]) **RRP:** 60p[18]

---

***OVAL 1009*** ***MICHAEL ROSE: Guess Who's Coming To Dinner / Guess Who's Coming To Dub***
**Rel:** 20 Feb[3]/Mar 1976[5] **RRP:** 60p[18]
*Music Master 1979* lists distribution via Island/EMI with no mention of Virgin.

---

***OVAL 1010*** ***HORACE ANDY: I'm In Love (Got To Get You) / I'm In Dub***
**Rel:** 20 Feb[3]/Mar 1976[5] (del 1978[8]) **RRP:** 60p[18]
*Music Master 1979* lists distribution via Island/EMI with no mention of Virgin. Label states that this is a "DEB/Morpheus/Opal Records" production and the record seems to have been released the same year as *Got To Get You* b/w *You* as a D.E.B. Music production on the Morpheus label (MOR 1010).

---

***OVAL 1011*** ***NO RELEASE***

---

***OVAL 1012*** ***TOMMY McLAIN: Sweet Dreams / Think It Over***
**Rel:** 6 Aug 1976[3] **RRP:** 70p[18]
*Music Master 1979* lists as Oval/Virgin with distribution via Island/EMI. Listed along with earlier single releases on the rear of the *Here Is Barbara Lynn* LP sleeve

## WATT and JCOA

Jazz Composer's Orchestra Association was a not–for–profit label put together by Mike Mantler and Carla Bley. US pressings were heavily imported by Virgin for sale through its shops and mail–order business. When Mantler and Bley set up a new record label, WATT, it was jointly distributed with Virgin in the UK and by ECM in mainland Europe. Shortly afterwards Virgin also gave selected JCOA back catalogue items full UK release on a joint JCOA/Virgin label. This was followed up by a spate of new recordings on JCOA before the label seemed to be abandoned in favour of the new WATT label. At some point after April 1977 Virgin ceased to release WATT label records in the UK, though still distributed the label in the UK along with other ECM releases.

The 16 November 1974 edition of *Melody Maker* lists mail–order prices for WATT and J 2000 LPs at £1.95, J 3001 at £2.35 and J 4001 at £3.30.

## WATT series LPs

***WATT/1*** ***CARLA BLEY: Tropic Appetites***

1. What Will Be Left Between Us And The Moon
2. Tonight? (For Japan)
3. In India (To Irene)
4. Enormous Tots (To People's Music Works)
5. Caucasian Bird Riffles (For Sheila)

1. Funnybird Song (To Swallow)
2. Indonesian Dock Sucking Supreme (To Peking Widow)
3. Song Of The Jungle Stream (To Besha And To Tadd Dameron)
4. Nothing (for WATT)

**Rel:** Jun[11]/Aug '74[1]
**RRP:** £2.50[1/4]

**Cassette:** TCWATT 1 **Rel:** Jul 1974[11]/Aug 1974[17]

Track dedications appear on sleeve but not labels: brackets above are for clarity and are not on sleeve. Labels credit Carla Bley; sleeve includes subcredit, "words by Paul Haines with Julie Tippetts Howard Johnson Michael Mantler David Holland Toni Marcus Paul Motian and Unidentified Cat".

---

***WATT/2*** ***MICHAEL MANTLER: No Answer***

1. Number Six
   i. Part One
   ii. Part Two
   iii. Part Three
   iv. Part Four

1. Number Twelve
   i. Part One
   ii. Part Two
   iii. Part Three
   iv. Part Four

**Rel:** Jun[4/11]/Aug 1974[1]
**RRP:** £2.50[1/4]

**Cassette:** TCWATT 2 **Rel:** Jul[11]/Aug 1974[17]

Sleeve subcredits are, "with Jack Bruce Carla Bley Don Cherry" and "words by Samuel Beckett from How It Is".

---

***WATT/3*** ***MICHAEL MANTLER/CARLA BLEY: 13 3/4***

1. 13

1. 3/4

**Rel:** Nov[4]/Jan '76[1]
**RRP:** £2.99[1]

Label listed as "Virgin WATT" in *The New Records*.

---

***WATT/4*** ***MICHAEL MANTLER/EDWARD GOREY: The Hapless Child***

1. The Sinking Spell
2. The Object Lesson
3. The Insect God

1. The Doubtful Guest
2. The Remembered Visit
3. The Hapless Child

**Rel:** Apr[5]/May '76[1]
**RRP:** £3.25[1]

Sleeve subtitled, "and other inscrutable stories" and the credits, "Music by Michael Mantler Words by Edward Gorey". Spine credits artist as "MICHAEL MANTLER / EDWARD GOREY" and title as "The Hapless Child", though labels credit "Michael Mantler" with title credit, "The Hapless Child and Other Inscrutable Stories". Listed in *The New Records* as "Hapless Child & Other Gorey Songs".

***WATT/5*** ***MICHAEL MANTLER: Silence***

1. I Walk With My Girl
2. I Watch The Clouds
3. It Is Curiously Hot
4. When I Run

1. Sometimes I See People
2. Around Me Sits The Night
3. She Was Looking Down
4. For Instance
5. A Long Way
6. After My Work Each Day
7. On Good Evenings

**Rel:** Jan[5]/Apr '77[1]
**RRP:** £3.49[5]/ £2.99[1]

Sleeve subcredits are, "with Carla Bley Robert Wyatt Kevin Coyne Chris Spedding Ron McClure" and "an adaption of the play by Harold Pinter". Label listed as "Virgin" in *The New Records.*

## J 2000 series LPs

***J 2001*** ***DON CHERRY/THE JAZZ COMPOSERS ORCHESTRA: Relativity Suite***

1. Tantra
2. Mali Doussn'gouni
3. Desireless

1. The Queen Of Tung–Ting Lake
2. Trans–Love Airways
3. Infinite Gentleness
4. March Of The Hobbits

**Rel:** Nov[4/11]/ Dec 1974[1/11]
**RRP:** £2.50[1]

---

***J 2002*** ***ROSWELL RUDD: The Jazz Composers Orchestra Plays Numatik Swing Band***

1. Vent
2. Breathahoward
3. Circulation

1. Lullaby for Greg
2. Aerosphere

**Rel:** Feb 1975[4]
**RRP:** not advised
**Del** 1977[5]

---

***J 2003*** ***GRACHAN MONCUR III/JAZZ COMPOSERS ORCHESTRA: Echoes Of Prayer***

1. Band 1
   i. Prologue
   ii. Reverend King's Wings I
   iii. Medgar's Menace I
   iv. Drum Transition
   v. Garvey's Ghost (Space Station)
2. Band 2
   i. Angela's Angel I
   ii. Drum Transition

1. Band 3
   i. Right On I
   ii. Angela's Angel II
   iii.Right On II
   iv. Reverend King's Wings II
   v. Medgar's Menace II
   vi. Drum Transition
   vii. African Percussion Ensemble
2. Band 4
   i. Right On III
   ii. Angela's Angel III (Jamboree)
   iii. Drum Transition
   iv. Amen Cadence
   v. Epilogue: Excuse Me, Mr Justice

**Rel:** Nov 1975[4]
**RRP:** not advised

---

***J 2004*** ***CLIFFORD THORNTON/THE JAZZ COMPOSERS ORCHESTRA: Gardens Of Harlem***

1. Ogún Bára
2. O Desãyo
3. Agbadzá

1. Changó Obarí
2. Aïn Salah
3. Gospel Ballade
4. Sweet Oranges
5. Blues City

**Rel:** Feb[5]/Apr '76[1]
**RRP:** £2.99[1]

---

***J 2005*** ***LEROY JENKINS/THE JAZZ COMPOSERS ORCHESTRA: For Players Only***

1. For Players Only (Part One)

1. For Players Only (Part Two)

**Rel:** Feb[5]/Apr '76[1]
**RRP:** £2.99[1]

## JD 3000 series 2–LP

***JD 3001*** ***JAZZ COMPOSERS ORCHESTRA: The Jazz Composer's Orchestra***

*Side 1*
1. Communications #8
2. Communications #9

*Side 2*
1. Communications #10
2. Preview

**Rel:** Sep 1974[4/11]
**RRP:** £2.94[4]

*Side 3*
1. Communications #11 – Part 1

*Side 4*
1. Communications #11 – Part 2

Set part numbers in run–off and on labels: set parts JDA 311 and JDA 312. Spine and labels credit artist as "Jazz Composers Orchestra" (no apostrophe) and label credits title as "The Jazz Composers Orchestra" (again no apostrophe). Sleeve credits title as "The Jazz Composer's Orchestra" (with apostrophe) with subcredits, "Cecil Taylor Don Cherry Roswell Rudd Pharoah Sanders Larry Coryell Gato Barbieri" and "Music composed and conducted by Michael Mantler".

## JT 4000 series 3–LP

***JT 4001*** ***JAZZ COMPOSERS ORCHESTRA: Escalator Over the Hill***

*Side 1*
1. Hotel Overture

*Side 2*
1. This Is Here...
2. Like Animals
3. Escalator Over The Hill
4. Stay Awake
5. Ginger And David
6. Song To Anything That Moves

**Rel:** Sep 1974[4/11]
**RRP:** £3.92[4/11]

*Side 3*
1. Eoth Theme
2. Businessmen
3. Ginger And David Theme
4. Why
5. It's Not What You Do
6. Detective Writer Daughter
7. Doctor Why
8. Slow Dance
9. Smalltown Agonist

*Side 4*
1. End Of Head
2. Over Her Head
3. Little Pony Soldier
4. Oh Say Can You Do?
5. Holiday In Risk
6. Holiday In Risk Theme

*Side 5*
1. A.I.R.
2. Rawalpindi Blues

*Side 6*
1. End Of Rawalpindi
2. End Of Animals
3. ...And It's Again

Libretto booklet in embossed gatefold sleeve. Sleeve credits "A Chronotransduction by Carla Bley Paul Haynes" though labels credit "Jazz Composers Orchestra". Side 1 backed by side 6, side 2 backed by side 5 and side 2 backed by side 3. This is the only Virgin release with auto–coupling sequencing for record players with autochange function presumably it was pressed from US metalwork. Set part numbers appear in run–off and on labels: record one set part JTA 411, record two JTA 412 and record three JTA 413.

## Atra

Atra released one LP and (probably) 24 singles prior to entering into joint distribution with Virgin. Virgin was involved for a very short time between late 1975 and early 1976. Only the first two Atra 1000 sequence LPs were distributed by Virgin – or jointly distributed by Virgin and Atra via Island, to be strictly accurate. The singles listed below were released during the period that Virgin jointly distributed Atra label LPs, but it is possible that Atra handled distribution of singles themselves –Virgin is not mentioned as distributor in *Music Master 1979*. So the singles are included here 'just in case'.

The deal with Atra was not ultimately a happy one and things came to a sudden and violent climax on 1 March 1976 when the label's owners pulled Richard Branson out of bed in his own home and proceded to have him beaten up over monies allegedly owed to the company by Virgin. In view of the fact that Branson later admitted that Atra was undoubtedly owed money (though less than £500 and not the £5,000 demanded by the brothers), it can perhaps be viewed as adding insult to injury that Atra's star signing, Keith Hudson, released his next album on Virgin.

## ATRALP 1000 series LPs

***ATRALP 1001 KEITH HUDSON: Torch Of Freedom***

| Side 1 | Side 2 | |
|---|---|---|
| 1. (a) Lost All Sense Of Direction; (b)Jah Jah | 1. (a) Turn The Heater On; (b) So Cold Without You | **Rel:** Oct 1975[4] |
| 2. (a) Don't Look At Me So; (b) Look At Me | 2. (a) Five More Years Of Yr Time; (b) My Time | **RRP:** not advised |
| (a) Don't Let The Teardrops Fool You; (b)Teardrops | 3. (a) Torch Of Freedom; (b) Freedom Movements | **Del** Aug 1976[5] |
| 4. Like I'm Dying | | |

Record subtitled "Phase 1" on labels. All tracks, except the last track on side 1, are split into two parts, hence the odd break in track naming convention above. White label test pressings (on two one–sided, white label records) exist in a different sleeve design to that used on the released version.

---

***ATRALP 1002 IIND STREET DREADS: Pick A Dub***

| Side 1 | Side 2 | |
|---|---|---|
| 1. Pick A Dub | 1. In The Rain | **Rel:** Oct[4]/Nov '75[4] |
| 2. Black Heart | 2. Part 1–2 Dub Wise | **RRP:** not advised |
| 3. Michale Talbot Affair | 3. Black Right | |
| 4. Don't Move | 4. Satta | |
| 5. Blood Brother | 5. I'm All Right | |
| 6. Dreader Than | 6. Depth Charge | |

Sleeve and labels credit the group as above (pronounced "Second Street Dreads"). First name on Track 3, side 1, misspelled as above on sleeve and label.

## ATRA series 7" singles

***ATRA 24 BUNNY BROWN: I Love The Way You Love / I Love The Way You Love***

**Rel:** 5 Dec 1975[3].

---

***ATRA 25 ALTON ELLIS: Papa / Papa***

**Rel:** 5 Dec 1975[3]

---

***ATRA 26 ALTON ELLIS: Rasta Spirit / WILD BUNCH INC.: Jal Dub (PRE–VIRGIN)***

***ATRA 27*** ***LOCKS LEE: What Can I Do / Dreader Version***
**Rel:** 21 Nov 1975[3]
A Kiss Records Production and both labels include the Kiss logo directly under the Atra 'Ankh' logo.

---

***ATRA 28*** ***KEITH HUDSON: Lost All Sense Of Direction / Jah Jah***
**Rel:** 21 Nov 1975[3]
A–side label includes the credit "Phase 1".

---

***ATRA 29*** ***ERVIN ANDREWS: Just A Lonely Man / Lonely Man II (Instrumental)***
**Rel:** 5 Dec 1975[3] (del 1977[8]/1978[5])

---

***ATRA 30*** ***DANNY CLARKE: The Longest Liver / CLINTONES ALL STARS: I Live (POSSIBLY POST–VIRGIN)***
**Rel:** 1976

## The Front Line

There had been a smattering of reggae releases appearing on Caroline and Virgin since 1974 but it was during the last half of 1977 that very large orders started coming in from Nigeria (U–Roy's LPs were especially popular) so Richard Branson went to Jamaica to find more artists to help satisfy demand. As he said in his autobiography, "I knew that there must be more toasters out in Jamaica and I decided we should go out there and corner the market".

The Sex Pistols were on the verge of breaking up so Branson took John Lydon with him to try to persuade him not to leave the group. They set up shop in the Sheraton Hotel in Kingston and held open auditions. John Lydon had the executive decision as to which artists to sign and it has to be said that his choice was pretty much spot on. Branson, Lydon and Ken Berry (who was in charge of the infamous briefcase containing $30,000) returned to the UK with almost twenty more artists on the roster.

The Front Line imprint was set up, according to Simon Draper in Terry Southern's book, *Virgin*, to prevent this host of reggae signings from swamping the Virgin label proper. *The Front Line* name had already been used as the title for the highly influential budget sampler LP and the striking image of a bleeding fist, clenching barbed wire from that album was subsequently used on marketing materials, such as on posters advertising U–Roy's *Natty Rebel.*

For the best part of a year Virgin enjoyed large sales of Front Line material in Nigeria, but then it all came to a sudden and – as far as Virgin's finances were concerned – an almost disastrous end. Branson, in his autobiography, says, "We had to abandon most of the reggae bands we had signed ... since a military coup had banned all imports ... and destroyed our sales", which explains the sudden end of the Front Line imprint. That almost everything was sent to Nigeria might also explain why it is so hard to find copies in the UK and, hence, the rather steep price when copies do turn up for sale.

## FL 1000 series LPs

One of the things that has caused consternation amongst reggae discographers is that there are so many gaps in the main FL 1000 catalogue sequence. It has generally been assumed that these related to planned records that were subsequently unissued. They actually have a more simple explanation, though this doesn't actually help to fill them with absolute certainty, except in one case (FL 1038). The catalogue numbers were unused in the UK but were used in Nigeria for reggae records previously issued on the Virgin label proper. These records seem to have been pressed in Nigeria rather than in the UK, but it is possible that UK pressings for the Nigerian market might yet turn up.

The only FL 1000 series release – indeed the only Front Line album – to be issued on cassette was Althea and Donna's *Uptown Top Ranking.*

---

***FL 1001*** ***I ROY: Heart Of A Lion***

| | | |
|---|---|---|
| 1. Heart Of A Lion | 1. Jordan River | **Label:** FL1 |
| 2. Sister Nelly | 2. Fire Stick | **Rel:** Feb 1978[5] |
| 3. Casmas Town | 3. Peace In The City | **RRP:** £4.10[5] |
| 4. Tonight | 4. Tiddle Le Bop | **Del** 1980[6] |
| 5. Catty Rock | 5. Move Up Roots Man | |

Nigerian–manufactured copies known to exist on the same catalogue number.

***FL 1002*** ***GLADIATORS: Proverbial Reggae***

| Side 1 | Side 2 | |
|---|---|---|
| 1. Jah Works | 1. Stick A Bush | **Label:** FL1 |
| 2. The Best Things In Life | 2. Stop Before You Go | **Rel:** Mar[5]/Apr '78[1] |
| 3. Dreadlocks The Time Is Now | 3. Can You Imagine How I Feel | **RRP:** £4.10[1/5] |
| 4. Fly Away | 4. We'll Find The Blessing | |
| 5. Marvel Not | 5. Music Makers From Jamaica | |

---

***FL 1003*** ***U BROWN: Mr. Brown Something***

| Side 1 | Side 2 | |
|---|---|---|
| 1. Turning Table | 1. Natty Dread Upon Mountain Top | **Label:** FL1 |
| 2. Natty Dread A Take Over | 2. Tottenham Rock | **Rel:** 1978 |
| 3. Natural Sound | 3. Natty Dread Unite | **RRP:** pres. £4.10 |
| 4. Peace And Love | 4. Rocking Vibration | |
| 5. Know Yourself | 5. Mr. Brown Something | |

---

***FL 1004*** ***PRINCE HAMMER: Bible***

| Side 1 | Side 2 | |
|---|---|---|
| 1. Jah Is My Refuge | 1. Sister Bella | **Label:** FL1 |
| 2. Selassie School | 2. Bible | **Rel:** 1978 |
| 3. Forty Days | 3. Wicked Woman | **RRP:** pres. £4.10 |
| 4. Morwell Esquire | 4. The Lion | |
| 5. Flash Your Dread | 5. Mourning For You | |

---

***FL 1005*** ***JAH LLOYD THE BLACK LION: The Humble One***

| Side 1 | Side 2 | |
|---|---|---|
| 1. St. Anne Collie | 1. Cocaine | **Label:** FL1 |
| 2. Special Request | 2. Book Of Truth | **Rel:** Jun 1978[5] |
| 3. The Humble One | 3. Jah Lion | **RRP:** £4.10[5] |
| 4. Children Of Man | 4. Upful Rasta Man | |
| 5. Time Of Weeping | 5. Dis Ya Sounds | |

---

***FL 1006*** ***TAPPER ZUKIE: M. P. L. A.***

| Side 1 | Side 2 | |
|---|---|---|
| 1. Pick Up The Rockers | 1. Ital Pot | **Label:** FL1 |
| 2. M.P.L.A. | 2. Marcus | **Rel:** Aug 1978[5] |
| 3. Don't Get Crazy | 3. Chalice To Chalice | **RRP:** £4.10[5] |
| 4. Go De Natty | 4. Don't Deal With Babylon | |
| 5. Stop The Gun Shooting | 5. Freedom | |

Reissue of KLP 9022, originally released January 1977[5] on Klik. Klik label issue listed as still on catalogue when the Front Line version was issued.

---

***FL 1007*** ***NO RELEASE***

---

***FL 1008*** ***SLY DUNBAR: Simple Sly Man***

| Side 1 | Side 2 | |
|---|---|---|
| 1. Cocaine Cocaine | 1. Sun Is Shining | **Label:** FL1 |
| 2. Top Rank | 2. A Who Say | **Rel:** Jun 1978[5] |
| 3. Mr. Bassie | 3. Nigger Whitie | **RRP:** £4.10[5] |
| 4. Dope Addict | 4. Dance And Shake Your Tambourine | |

---

***FL 1009*** ***TAPPER ZUKIE: Peace In The Ghetto***

| Side 1 | Side 2 | |
|---|---|---|
| 1. Peace In The Arena | 1. Dangerous Woman | **Label:** FL1 |
| 2. The City Of Mount Zion | 2. Get On The Double | **Rel:** Apr 1978[5] |
| 3. Ghetto Rock | 3. Praise Jah In Gladness | **RRP:** £4.10[5] |
| 4. Tribute To Steve Biko | 4. Peace In The City | |
| | 5. Bimbo Bimbo | |

---

***FL 1010*** ***THE ICEBREAKERS WITH THE DIAMONDS: Planet Mars Dub***

| Side 1 | Side 2 | |
|---|---|---|
| 1. Dub With Garvey | 1. Grand Rock | **Label:** FL1 |
| 2. Sweet Answer | 2. Two Brothers | **Rel:** Jun 1978[5] |
| 3. Work Out | 3. Finger Out | **RRP:** £4.10[5] |
| 4. Who Cares? | 4. Ital Rock | |
| 5. Run Away | 5. Planet Mars | |

According to the *Half Pounder* promotional compilation LP (RM BURG 1), this was scheduled for release on 26 May 1978.

---

***FL 1011*** ***BIG YOUTH: Isaiah – First Prophet Of Old***

| Side 1 | Side 2 | |
|---|---|---|
| 1. World in Confusion | 1. Lord Jah Bless | **Label:** FL1 |
| 2. Writing On The Wall | 2. Reaping Time | **Rel:** Jun 1978[5] |
| 3. Zion | 3. Love We A Deal With | **RRP:** £4.10[5] |
| 4. Isaiah First Prophet Of Old | 4. Upful One | |

---

***FL 1012*** ***ALTHEA AND DONNA: Uptown Top Ranking***

| Side 1 | Side 2 | |
|---|---|---|
| 1. No More Fighting | 1. The West | **Label:** FL1 |
| 2. Jah Rastafari | 2. Jah Music | **Rel:** Apr 1978[5] |
| 3. Make A Truce | 3. If You Don't Love Jah | **RRP:** £4.10[5] |
| 4. Oh Dread | 4. Sorry | |
| 5. Uptown Top Ranking | 5. They Wanna Just | |

**Cassette:** FLC 1012 **Rel:** pres. Apr 1978 **RRP:** not advised

The only Front Line label LP given cassette release. Cassette listed on the *Half Pounder* promotional compilation (RM BURG 1) so cassette issued assumed to be sometime between release of Althea and Donna's LP in April and May, when the *Half Pounder* promotional LP seems to have issued.

---

***FL 1013*** ***PRINCE FAR I: Message From The King***

| Side 1 | Side 2 | |
|---|---|---|
| 1. Message From The King | 1. Concrete Column | **Label:** FL1 |
| 2. The Dream | 2. Dry Bone | **Rel:** 1978 |
| 3. Commandment Of Drugs | 3. Foggy Road | **RRP:** not advised |
| 4. Moses, Moses | 4. Wisdom | |
| 5. Blackman Land | 5. Armageddon | |

---

***FL 1014*** ***BIG YOUTH: Dreadlocks Dread***

| Side 1 | Side 2 | |
|---|---|---|
| 1. Train To Rhodesia | 1. Marcus Garvey Dread | **Label:** FL1 |
| 2. House Of Dread Locks | 2. Big Youth Special | **Rel:** 1978 |
| 3. Lightning Flash (Weak Heart Drop) | 3. Dread Organ | **RRP:** not advised |
| 4. Natty Dread She Want | 4. Black Man Message | |
| 5. Some Like It Dread | 5. You Don't Care | |
| | 6. Moving On | |

Reissue of KLP 9001, originally released March 1976[6] on Klik – though with the last two tracks on side two reversed. Klik issue listed as still on catalogue when the Front Line version was issued.

---

***FL 1015*** ***RANKING TREVOR: In Fine Style***

| Side 1 | Side 2 | |
|---|---|---|
| 1. Masculine Gender | 1. Chanting Home | **Label:** FL1 |
| 2. Rub A Dub Style | 2. Ready Sister | **Rel:** 1978 |
| 3. Original Piece | 3. Natty And The Root Man | **RRP:** not advised |
| 4. Got To Keep Blow | 4. Seven The Hard Way | |
| 5. Love Life And Inity | 5. There's Fe Live In A Babylon | |

---

***FL 1016*** ***CULTURE: Harder Than The Rest***

| Side 1 | Side 2 | |
|---|---|---|
| 1. Behold | 1. Tell Me Where You Get It | **Label:** FL1 |
| 2. Holy Mount Zion | 2. Free Again | **Rel:** 1978 |
| 3. Stop The Fussing And Fighting | 3. Work On Natty | **RRP:** not advised |
| 4. Iron Sharpening Iron | 4. Love Shine Bright | |
| 5. Vacancy | 5. Play Skilfully | |

White label test pressings known to exist.

### *FL 1017 POET AND THE ROOTS: Dread Beat An' Blood*

1. Dread Beat An' Blood
2. Five Nights Of Bleeding
3. Doun Di Road
4. Song Of Blood

1. It Dread Inna Inglan (For) George Lindo
2. Come Wi Goh Dung Deh
3. Man Free (For Darcus Howe)
4. All Wi Doin Is Defendin

**Label:** FL1
**Rel:** 1978
**RRP:** not advised

The 1984 reissue in the Crucial Cuts series (VX 1002) was credited to "Linton Kwesi Johnson".

---

### *FL 1018 U–ROY: Version Galore*

1. Your Ace From Space
2. On The Beach
3. Version Galore
4. True Confession
5. Tide Is High
6. Things You Love

1. The Same Song
2. Happy Go Lucky Girl
3. Rock Away
4. Wear You To The Ball
5. Don't Stay Away
6. Hot Pop

**Label:** FL1
**Rel:** 1978
**RRP:** £3.99[6]
**Del** Nov 1981[6]

Reissue of Trojan label LP, TBL 161. White label test pressings known to exist.

---

### *FL 1019 THE ABYSSINIANS: Arise*

1. Oh Lord
2. This Land Is For Everyone
3. Mightiest Of All
4. Meditation
5. Wicked Men

1. Jah Loves
2. Dem A Come
3. South African Enlistment
4. Hey You
5. Let My Days Be Long

**Label:** FL1
**Rel:** 1978
**RRP:** £4.69[5]

Lyric sheet.

---

### *FL 1020 GREGORY ISAACS: Cool Ruler*

1. Native Woman
2. John Public
3. Party In The Slum
4. Uncle Joe
5. World Of The Farmer

1. One More Time
2. Let's Dance
3. Don't Pity Me
4. Created By The Father
5. Raving Tonight

**Label:** FL1
**Rel:** Feb 1979[9]
**RRP:** £4.69[5]

---

### *FL 1021 PRINCE FAR I: Long Life*

1. Daughters Of Zion
2. Right Way
3. Black Starliner Must Come
4. Praise Him With Psalms
5. In Your Walking Remember Jah Jah

1. Farmyard
2. Love One Another
3. Who Have Eyes To See
4. So Long

**Label:** FL1
**Rel:** 1978
**RRP:** £4.69[5]

---

### *FL 1022 NIGERIAN–ONLY RELEASE OF VIRGIN LABEL LP*

---

### *FL 1023 U ROY: Jah Son Of Africa*

1. Jah Son Of Africa
2. Rivers Of Babylon
3. Tom Drunk
4. Peace And Love In The Ghetto

1. Running Around Town With Tom, Dick And Harry
2. I Got To Tell You Goodbye
3. Herbman Skanking
4. Africa For The Africans
5. Love In The Arena

**Label:** FL1
**Rel:** 1978
**RRP:** £4.69[5]
**Del:** 1980[6]

Red vinyl.

---

### *FL 1024 NIGERIAN–ONLY RELEASE OF VIRGIN LABEL LP*

**_FL 1025_** **_VIVIAN WEATHERS: Bad Weather_**

| | | |
|---|---|---|
| 1. Going To The Blues | 1. People A Talk | **Label:** FL1 |
| 2. Hip Hug | 2. Star Of Sufferation | **Rel:** 1978 |
| 3. The Way You Walk | 3. Gypsy Love | **RRP:** £4.69[5] |
| 4. A Fool And His Baby | 4. The Letter | |
| 5. Street Talk | 5. Move Ghetto Children | |

**_FL 1026_** **_NIGERIAN–ONLY RELEASE OF VIRGIN LABEL LP_**

**_FL 1027_** **_NIGERIAN–ONLY RELEASE OF VIRGIN LABEL LP_**

**_FL 1028_** **_I ROY: Ten Commandments_**

| | | |
|---|---|---|
| 1. Commandment I – Exodus | 1. Commandment VI – Three Little Birds | **Label:** FL1 |
| 2. Commandment II – Put It On | 2. Commandment VII – Natural Mystic | **Rel:** 1978 |
| 3. Commandment III – The Heathen | 3. Commandment VIII – Jamming | **RRP:** prob. £4.69 |
| 4. Commandment IV – Waiting In Vain | 4. Commandment IX – So Much Things To Say | |
| 5. Commandment V – One Love | 5. Commandment X – Guiltiness | |

**_FL 1029_** **_TAPPER ZUKIE: In Dub_**

| | | |
|---|---|---|
| 1. Tapper Zukie In Dub | 1. Rush I Some Dub | **Label:** FL1? |
| 2. Pick Up The Dub | 2. Cool This Dub | **Rel:** not advised |
| 3. Dub M.P.L.A. | 3. Jah Jah Dub | **RRP:** prob. £4.69 |
| 4. Beautiful Dub | 4. Judgement Dub | |
| 5. Prophesy Dub | 5. Loving Dub | |
| 6. Falling Dub | 6. Rub This Dub | |

Track listing sourced from original Stars label issue, so might not represent the Front Line track listing.

**_FL 1030_** **_U BROWN: Can't Keep A Good Man Down_**

| | | |
|---|---|---|
| 1. Weather Balloon | 1. Step It Inna Greenwich Farm | **Label:** FL1 |
| 2. Tie And Dye | 2. Blow Brother Joe | **Rel:** Feb 1979[6] |
| 3. Step It Inna Freedom Street | 3. Row Mr. Fisherman | **RRP:** £4.69[6] |
| 4. Wicked Have To Run | 4. Can't Keep A Good Man Down | |
| 5. Hiding Place | 5. Trad Along Jah | |

**_FL 1031_** **_JAH LLOYD: Black Moses_**

| | | |
|---|---|---|
| 1. Greenbay incident | 1. Rudy Come Back | **Label:** FL1? |
| 2. Reggae Feeling | 2. Hold Them Natty Dread | **Rel:** 1979 |
| 3. Black Moses | 3. Sounds Of Psalms | **RRP:** prob. £4.69 |
| 4. Dispencer | 4. Sweat And Tears | |
| 5. IMF | 5. Punk Reggae | |

**_FL 1032_** **_TAPPER ZUKIE: Tapper Roots_**

| | | |
|---|---|---|
| 1. Oh Lord! | 1. Tapper Roots | **Label:** FL1? |
| 2. Satta | 2. First Street Rock | **Rel:** 1979 |
| 3. Don't Shoot The Youth | 3. Green Bay Murder | **RRP:** prob. £4.69 |
| 4. Rastaman Skank | 4. Freedom Street | |
| 5. Riding West | 5. Simpleton Leave Violence | |

**_FL 1033_** **_I ROY: World On Fire_**

| | | |
|---|---|---|
| 1. Dog War | 1. African Song | **Label:** FL1 |
| 2. Set the Captives Free | 2. Ism And Schism | **Rel:** 1979 |
| 3. Package Deal | 3. World On Fire | **RRP:** prob. £4.69 |
| 4. It's Alright | 4. Radical Music | **Del** 1981[6] |
| 5. Stronger Strong | 5. Ali | |

***FL 1034*** ***VARIOUS ARTISTS: Hottest Hits (From The Vaults Of Treasure Island)***

1. Those Guys (The Sensations)
2. Come On Little Girl (The Melodians)
3. Loving Pauper (Dobby Dobson)
4. Midnight Hour (Silver Tones)
5. Heartaches (Vic Taylor)
6. Cry Tough (Alton and the Flames)

1. Queen Majesty (The Techniques)
2. Right Track (Phillis Dillon)
3. I'll Never Fall In Love (The Sensations)
4. The Tide Is High (The Paragons)
5. Things You Say You Love (The Jamaicans)
6. It's Raining (The Three Tops)

**Label:** FL1
**Rel:** Feb 1979[6]
**RRP:** £4.69[6]

---

***FL 1035*** ***GLADIATORS: Naturality***

1. Naturality
2. Struggle
3. Write To Me
4. Counting My Blessing
5. Get Ready

1. Praises To The Most High
2. Nyahbingi Marching On
3. Dry Your Weeping Eyes
4. Greatest Love
5. Exodus

**Label:** FL1
**Rel:** Feb 1979[6]
**RRP:** £4.69[6]

---

***FL 1036*** ***NIGERIAN–ONLY RELEASE OF VIRGIN LABEL LP***

---

***FL 1037*** ***NIGERIAN–ONLY RELEASE OF VIRGIN LABEL LP***

---

***FL 1038*** ***U–ROY: Natty Rebel (NIGERIAN–ONLY RELEASE)***

Nigerian–only issue of V 2059. Nigerian label design is a cross between the two UK label designs with brown fist on yellow background and "Front Line" in red. See V 2059 for track listing.

---

***FL 1039*** ***NIGERIAN–ONLY RELEASE***

---

***FL 1040*** ***CULTURE: Cumbolo***

1. They Never Love In This Time
2. Innocent Blood
3. Cumbolo
4. Poor Jah People
5. Natty Never Get Weary

1. Natty Dread Naw Run
2. Down In Jamaica
3. This Train
4. Pay Day
5. Mind Who You Beg For Help

**Label:** FL2
**Rel:** 1979
**RRP:** prob. £4.69

---

***FL 1041*** ***TWINKLE BROTHERS: Praise Jah***

1. Praise Jah
2. King Pharaoh
3. Africa
4. Dread In The Ghetto
5. Jahoviah

1. Keep On Trying
2. Shu Be Dup
3. In This Time
4. Gone Already
4. Come Home

**Label:** FL2
**Rel:** 1979
**RRP:** prob. £4.69

---

***FL 1042*** ***SLY DUNBAR: Sly, Wicked And Slick***

1. Rasta Fiesta
2. Sesame Street
3. Lovers Bop
4. Senegal Market Place

1. Mr. Music
2. Queen Of The Minstrels
3. Dirty Harry
4. Oriental Taxi

**Label:** FL2
**Rel:** May 1979[6]
**RRP:** £4.69[6]

---

***FL 1043*** ***NIGERIAN–ONLY RELEASE OF VIRGIN LABEL LP***

---

***FL 1044*** ***GREGORY ISAACS: Soon Forward***

1. Universal Tribulation
2. Mr. Brown
3. Down the Line
4. Lonely Girl
5. Bumping And Boring

1. My Relationship
2. Slave Market
3. Black Liberation Struggle
4. Jah Music
5. Soon Forward

**Label:** FL2
**Rel:** Aug 1979[9]
**RRP:** prob. £4.99

***FL 1045*** ***THE MIGHTY DIAMONDS: Deeper Roots (Back To The Channel)***

*Side 1*
1. Reality
2. Blackman
3. Dreadlocks Time
4. Diamonds And Pearls
5. One Brother Short

*Side 2*
1. Bodyguard
2. 4000 Years
3. Master Plan
4. Two By Two
5. Be Aware

*Free album, side 1*
1. Reality Dub
2. Blackman Dub
3. Dreadlocks Time Dub
4. Diamonds And Pearls Dub
5. One Brother Short Dub

*Free album, side 2*
1. Bodyguard Dub
2. 4000 Years Dub
3. Master Plan Dub
4. Two By Two Dub
5. Be Aware Dub

**Label:** FL2
**Rel:** 1979
**RRP:** prob. £4.99

With free dub album and sleeve sticker.

---

***FL 1046*** ***NO RELEASE***

---

***FL 1047*** ***CULTURE: International Herb***

1. The international Herb
2. Jah Rastafari
3. It A Guh Dread
4. Rally Around Jahoviah's Throne
5. The Land We Belong

1. Ethiopians Waan Guh Home
2. Chiney Man
3. I Tried
4. The Shepherd
5. Too Long In Slavery

**Label:** FL2
**Rel:** Sep 1979[6]
**RRP:** £4.99[6]

---

***FL 1048*** ***GLADIATORS: Sweet So Till***

1. Sweet So Till
2. No Disturbance
3. A Day We Go
4. Let Jah Be Praised

1. Red And Green And Gold
2. Back Yard Meditation
3. Press Along
4. Merrily
5. Holiday Ride

**Label:** FL2
**Rel:** Nov 1979[6]
**RRP:** £4.99[6]

## FCL 5000 series 10" LP

Originally intended for the VCL 5000 series but shifted to Front Line.

***FCL 5001*** ***TWINKLE BROTHERS: Love***

1. Free Africa
2. Solid As The Rock
3. Watch The Hypocrites

1. Love
2. I Love You So
3. South Africa

**Label:** FL1
**Rel:** Jun 1978[5]
**RRP:** £2.99[5]

Inner sleeve. Run–offs have "VCL–5002–A–2"/"VCL–5002–B–2" matrix numbers crossed out with "FCL 5001" matrix numbers added. Later issued as a 12" LP with extra dub tracks (FLX 4003).

## FLB 3000 series LPs

***FLB 3001*** ***VARIOUS ARTISTS: The Front Line II***

1. Jah Works (The Gladiators)
2. Natty Dread Upon A Mountain Top (U–Brown)
3. I Love You So (Twinkle Brothers)
4. Foggy Road (Prince Far I)
5. Mr. Bassie (Sly Dunbar)
6. Sister Bella (Prince Hammer)
7. Make A Truce (Althea and Donna)

1. Dread Beat And Blood (Poet And The Roots)
2. Rub A Dub Style (Ranking Trevor)
3. Holy Mount Zion (Culture)
4. Tribute To Steve Biko (Tapper Zukie)
5. Love We A Deal (Big Youth)
6. Jordan River (I–Roy)
7. Cocaine (Jah Lloyd)

**Label:** FL1
**Rel:** not advised
**RRP:** not advised

Sleeve subtitled, "Your last chance..." The first sampler in this series was issued first on Virgin (VC 503) and once the ultra–budget issue had sold requisite number was reissued on Caroline (C 1521).

***FLB 3002*** ***VARIOUS ARTISTS: Front Line III***

| | | |
|---|---|---|
| 1. Lonely Girl (Gregory Isaacs) | 1. Get Ready (The Gladiators) | **Label:** FL2 |
| 2. Mr. Music (Sly Dunbar) | 2. I Got To Tell You Goodbye (U Roy) | **Rel:** Sep 1979[6] |
| 3. 4000 Years (The Mighty Diamonds) | 3. I Tried (Culture) | **RRP:** £2.15[6] |
| 4. Fire In A Wire (I Roy) | 4. Borno Dub (Prince Far I In Dub) | |
| 5. Jahoviah (Twinkle Brothers) | 5. South African Enlistment (The Abyssinians) | |

## FLX 4000 series LPs

***FLX 4001*** ***I ROY: Cancer***

| | | |
|---|---|---|
| 1. Cancer | 1. Tribute To Herbie Mann | **Label:** FL1? |
| 2. Bubblin Jug | 2. The Gold Coast | **Rel:** Mar 1979[6] |
| 3. Devils Bug | 3. Columbian Red | **RRP:** £4.99[6] |
| 4. Andy Capp | 4. Virgin Affair | **Del** 1981[6] |
| 5. Lead Belly | 5. Walk Like A Dragon | |

***FLX 4002*** ***PRINCE FAR I: Cry Tuff Dub Encounter Part 2***

| | | |
|---|---|---|
| 1. Suru–Lere Dub | 1. Ogun Dub | **Label:** FL2 |
| 2. Anambra Dub | 2. Bendel Dub | **Rel:** May 1979[6] |
| 3. Kaduna Dub | 3. Ondo Dub | **RRP:** £3.49[6] |
| 4. Oyo Dub | 4. Gongola Dub | |
| 5. Borno Dub | | |

***FLX 4003*** ***TWINKLE BROTHERS: Love***

| | | |
|---|---|---|
| 1. Free Africa | 1. Love | **Label:** FL2 |
| 2. Solid As The Rock | 2. Love (Dub) | **Rel:** 1979 |
| 3. Solid As The Rock (Dub) | 3. I Love You So | **RRP:** not advised |
| 4. Watch The Hypocrites | 4. I Love You So (Dub) | |
| 5. Watch The Hypocrites (Dub) | 5. South Africa | |

Originally issued as 10" LP (FCL 5001) minus dub tracks.

***FLX 4004*** ***U–ROY: With Words of Wisdom***

| | | |
|---|---|---|
| 1. Honey Come Forward | 1. The Merry Go Round | **Label:** FL2 |
| 2. Treasure Isle Skank | 2. Wake The Town | **Rel:** Sep 1979[6] |
| 3. Rule The Nation | 3. What Is Catty | **RRP:** £4.99[6] |
| 4. Drive Her Home | 4. Everybody Bawling | **Del** 1980[6] |
| 5. Tom Drunk | 5. Ain't That Loving You | |
| 6. Words Of Wisdom | 6. Behold | |

## FLD 6000 series 2–LPs

Both releases sold at the current price of a single album, but each included a free dub LP. The only slight oddity is that the free LP included with *The General* was given a different title, *Spider's Web*.

***FLD 6001*** ***THE MIGHTY DIAMONDS: Deeper Roots (plus free LP)***

| *Side 1* | *Side 2* | |
|---|---|---|
| 1. Reality | 1. Bodyguard | **Label:** FL2 |
| 2. Blackman | 2. 4000 Years | **Rel:** Aug 1979[6] |
| 3. Dreadlocks Time | 3. Master Plan | **RRP:** £4.99[6] |
| 4. Diamonds And Pearls | 4. Two By Two | |
| 5. One Brother Short | 5. Be Aware | |

*Free album, side 1*
1. Reality Dub
2. Blackman Dub
3. Dreadlocks Time Dub
4. Diamonds And Pearls Dub
5. One Brother Short Dub

*Free album, side 2*
1. Bodyguard Dub
2. 4000 Years Dub
3. Master Plan Dub
4. Two By Two Dub
5. Be Aware Dub

Originally issued as FL 1045 with free LP, this was reissued on this new catalogue sequence and again marketed as including a free dub album. As per FL 1045 some copies have a suspicious–looking curcular stain on the front cover that suggests a sticker advertising inclusion of the free LP.

---

***FLD 6002*** ***I–ROY: The General + free LP: Spider's Web***

*Side 1*
1. African Continent
2. Reggae Rockers
3. Bad Boy Corner
4. Quarter Pound Of Ishens
5. The General

*Side 2*
1. To The Bump
2. Fire In A Vatican
3. Hill And Gully
4. Killermanjaro
5. Fire In A Wire

**Label:** FL2
**Rel:** Sep 1979[6]
**RRP:** not advised
**Del** 1981[6]

*Side 3, Spider's Web*
1. Killer's Coal Range
2. Death On The Rio Grande
3. The Spider's Web
4. Iron Lady
5. Fiddler's Bug

*Side 4, Spider's Web*
1. Warlord Of Zenda
2. Mind Your Own Business
3. M.Y.O.B.
4. African Continent
5. Free Zimbabwe

Free LP titled *Spider's Web* on labels, which also say "Free Dub album with 'The General'". This may account for one of the missing VDJ catalogue numbers. Sleeve includes the credit "Free Dub Album".

## FLS 100 series 7" singles

***FLS 101*** ***I ROY: Fire Stick / Casmas Town***
**Label:** FL1 **Rel:** 10 Mar 1978[3]

---

***FLS 102*** ***GLADIATORS: Stick A Bush / Music Makers From Jamaica***
**Label:** FL1 **Rel:** 10 Mar 1978[3]

---

***FLS 103*** ***JAH LLOYD THE BLACK LION: This Ya Sound / Upfull Rastaman***
**Label:** FL1 **Rel:** 1978

---

***FLS 104*** ***TWINKLE BROTHERS: Free Africa / Special Brew***
**Label:** FL1 **Rel:** 1978

---

***FLS 105*** ***SLY DUNBAR: A Who Say / Cocaine Cocaine***
**Label:** FL1 **Rel:** 1978
Also released on 12" as VOLE 7 on the Virgin blue 'neon' label design.

---

***FLS 106*** ***PRINCE HAMMER: Bible / Morwell Esquire***
**Label:** FL1 **Rel:** May 1978[5] **RRP:** 80p[5]

---

***FLS 107*** ***ALTHEA AND DONNA: Puppy Dog Song / Sorry***
**Label:** FL1 **Rel:** May 1978[5] **RRP:** 80p[5]
Picture sleeve.

---

***FLS 108*** ***JOYELLA BLADE: Cairo / Cairo Dub***
**Label:** FL1 **Rel:** May 1978[5] **RRP:** 80p[5]

***FLS 109*** ***TAPPER ZUKIE: She Want A Phensic (Dangerous Woman) / Rastaman Skank***
**Label:** FL1 **Rel:** Jun 1978[5] **RRP:** 80p[5]

---

***FLS 110*** ***ALTHEA & DONNA: Going To Negril / The West***
**Label:** FL1 **Rel:** 25 Aug 1978[3] **RRP:** 80p[5]
Also released on 12" as VOLE 7 (with a 7.8 min. version of the a–side) on the Front Line label design.

---

***FLS 111*** ***GLADIATORS: Dreadlocks The Time Is Now / Pocket Money***
**Label:** FL1 **Rel:** Jul 1978[5] **RRP:** 80p[5]

---

***FLS 112*** ***PRINCE FAR I: No More War / No More War (version)***
**Label:** FL1 **Rel:** Jul 1978[5] **RRP:** 80p[5]

---

***FLS 113*** ***THE ABYSSINIANS: Hey You / This Land Is For Everyone***
**Label:** FL1 **Rel:** Sep 1978[5] **RRP:** 90p[5]
Double a–side. *Hey You* has an "A" matrix suffix and *This Land is for Everyone* a "B" matrix suffix.

---

***FLS 114*** ***VIVIAN WEATHERS: Hip Hug / Hip Dub***
**Label:** FL1 **Rel:** 29 Sep 1978[3]

---

***FLS 115*** ***TAPPER ZUKIE: First Street Rock / Oh Lord***
**Label:** FL1 **Rel:** 1978 **RRP:** 90p[5]
Double a–side. *First Street Rock* has an "A" matrix suffix and *Oh Lord* a "B" matrix suffix.

---

***FLS 116*** ***CULTURE: Natty Get Weary / Natty Get Weary (Dub)***
**Label:** FL1 **Rel:** 24 Nov 197[3] **RRP:** 90p[5]

---

***FLS 117*** ***TWINKLE BROTHERS: Distant Drums / Distant Drums Dub***
**Label:** FL1 **Rel:** 8 Dec 1978[3] **RRP:** 90p[8]
Radio edit copies were pressed, but distributed with normal stock labels. The one copy viewed has the original 4.10 track timing crossed out in biro with 2.57 written underneath

---

***FLS 118*** ***GLADIATORS: Struggle / Praises To The Most High***
**Label:** FL2 **Rel:** 27 Apr 1979[3] **RRP:** 90p[8]

---

***FLS 119*** ***TWINKLE BROTHERS: Keep On Trying / Keep On Dubing***
**Label:** FL2 **Rel:** 27 Apr 1979[3] **RRP:** 95p[8]
Yes, the spelling on the b–side is confirmed as "Dubing". 7" and 12" versions have different b–sides. Also issued on 12" – see following section for details.

---

***FLS 120*** ***NO RELEASE***
Despite a documented release date of April 1979 (RRP 90p)[8], it is likely that no 7" version was issued – indeed, only listed as a 12" release in *The New Singles*. See following section for details of the 12".

---

***FLS 121*** ***NO RELEASE***
Only issued on 12" – see following section for details.

---

***FLS 122*** ***NO RELEASE***
Only issued on 12" – see following section for details.

---

***FLS 123*** ***NO RELEASE***
Only issued on 12" – see following section for details.

---

***FLS 124*** ***NO RELEASE***
Only issued on 12" – see following section for details.

***FLS 125*** ***CULTURE: International Herb / Down In Jamaica***
**Label:** FL2 **Rel:** 26 Oct 1979[3] **RRP:** £1.05[8]
Picture sleeve.

---

***FLS 126*** ***GLADIATORS: Holiday Ride / No Disturbance***
**Label:** FL2 **Rel:** 19 Oct 1979[3] (del 1980[6]) **RRP:** £1.05[8]

## FLS 100–12 series 12" singles

***FLS 119–12*** ***TWINKLE BROTHERS: Keep On Trying / King Pharoah***
**Label:** FL2 **Rel:** Apr 1979[8] **RRP:** 95p[8]
Die–cut generic blue 'neon' sleeve. 7" and 12" versions have different b–sides.

---

***FLS 120–12*** ***SLY DUNBAR: Rasta Fiesta / Dirty Harry***
**Label:** FL2 **Rel:** 27 Apr 1979[3] (12") (del 1980[6])
Die–cut generic blue 'neon' sleeve.

---

***FLS 121–12*** ***GREGORY ISAACS, Soon Forward / GREGORY ISAACS AND PRINCE FAR I: Uncle Joe / Come Off Me Toe***
**Label:** FL2 **Rel:** 1979

---

***FLS 122–12*** ***THE MIGHTY DIAMONDS: Bodyguard / One Brother Short***
**Label:** FL2 **Rel:** 27 Jul 1979[3] (12") (del 1980[6]) **RRP:** £1.49[8]
Picture sleeve.

---

***FLS 123–12*** ***TWINKLE BROTHERS: Jahoviah / TWINKLE BROTHERS FEATURING SIR LEE: Free Africa***
**Label:** FL2 **Rel:** Oct 1979[6] (del 1980[6]) **RRP:** £1.05[8]
Die–cut generic blue 'neon' sleeve. If RRP is correct, this was priced the same as a 7" single.

---

***FLS 124–12*** ***I ROY: Fire In A Wire / Hill And Gully***
**Label:** FL2 **Rel:** Sep 1979[8] **RRP:** £1.05[8]

## VOLE series 12" single – slight reprise

The VOLE series was on the Virgin label proper, but VOLE 7 was on the Front Line label design. FLS 105 was also issued as a 12" in the VOLE series, but on the then normal Virgin label design.

---

***VOLE 7*** ***ALTHEA AND DONNA: Going To Negril / The West***
**Label:** FL1 **Rel:** Aug 1978[5] **RRP:** £1.49[5]
12" release of the Front Line 7" FLS 110 on the Front Line label design.

# Butt

The Butt label, manufactured and distributed by Vineyard Productions, according to sleeves, doesn't seem to have much to do with Virgin at first glance. Except that both sleeve and labels include a familiar moonface logo, as first used in *Student* magazine and then appropriated by Caroline Exports. 1980s releases make the connection a bit more obvious with the inclusion of the credit, "Export distribution by Caroline Exports [U.K.]". That Vineyard Productions and Butt are Caroline Exports spin–off companies is extremely likely, especially when a quick look at Vineyard Productions' address shows that it is one and the same as Caroline Exports' new address – 56 Stanford Road, London, NW 10.

Curiously, records were pressed by Lyntone rather than by CBS, which at this point manufactured Virgin's product, and, by the look of things, Virgin's normal UK distribution channels were not used.

Caroline Exports was involved in the release of several other records – the *Six–Pack – Six–Track* series of 7" picture disc and the luminous vinyl compilation LP, *Dead on Arrival* all include the Caroline Exports moonface logo on sleeves. Details for these can be found in the Virgin listings because these were either on the Virgin label proper or also included the Virgin logo.

## NOTT series LPs

***NOTT 001*** ***ELECTRIC BANANA: The Seventies***

| | | |
|---|---|---|
| 1. Good TImes | 1. James Marshall | **Rel:** 1978 |
| 2. Easily Done | 2. Do My Stuff | **RRP:** not advised |
| 3. I Could Not Believe My Eyes | 3. Whiskey Song | |
| 4. Sweet Orphan Lady | 4. Maze Song | |
| 5. The Loser | 5. Take Me Home | |
| 6. Walk Away | | |

All tracks are published by De Wolfe and all had been included previously on music library LPs. Sleeve includes Caroline Export, Butt and De Wolfe logos side by side. A sticker on the sleeve stated, "Electric Banana are The Pretty Things give or take a bit!"

---

***NOTT 002*** ***THE LONG HELLO: The Long Hello***

| | | |
|---|---|---|
| 1. The Theme From (Plunge) | 1. Fairzahel Gardens | **Rel:** pres. 1978 |
| 2. The O Flat Session | 2. Looking At You | **RRP:** not advised |
| 3. Morris To Cape Roth | 3. I've Lost My Cat | |
| 4. Brain Seizure | | |

Reissue of the 1976 numbered, limited edition private pressing by various ex–members of Van der Graaf Generator, Rare Bird and friends.

## BUTT series LP

***BUTT 001*** ***JADE WARRIOR: Reflections***

| | | |
|---|---|---|
| 1. English Morning | 1. A Winter's Tale | **Rel:** 1979 |
| 2. Lady Of The Lake | 2. Yellow Eyes | **RRP:** not advised |
| 3. Borne On The Solar Wind | 3. Dark River | |
| 4. Morning Hymn | 4. House Of Dreams | |
| 5. Bride Of Summer | | |
| 6. Soldier's Song | | |

Insert and inner sleeve.

## Ice

Virgin signed up Eddy Grant's Ice label, which had up to now been manufactured and distributed by Pye, in mid–August 1979. This was a bit of a shock because only two weeks previously, on 4 August, *Music Week* had announced that the label had been signed by WEA, complete with a photo of WEA's Tony Calder and Eddy Grant celebrating the deal. According to Calder, quoted in the 18 August edition of *Music Week*, Grant had been unhappy with one particular (but major) clause in the contract, and one that WEA had felt disinclined to alter. In practical terms, from point of view of this discography, this had the effect of delaying the next round of 7" and 12" singles releases by a week.

What, if anything, was intended for the the missing catalogue numbers in the GUY sequence is unknown. All that is known is that they were not used. There is the slight possibility that planned singles were transferred to the Virgin label, though that would be the purest guess – and the only known Virgin single with an Eddy Grant connection is 90 Degrees' *No Doctor*, which is all very well, but there are three gaps!

## ICE series LP

***ICE 4*** ***EDDY GRANT: Walking On Sunshine***

| | | |
|---|---|---|
| 1. Walking On Sunshine | 1. My Love, My Love | **Rel:** Sep 1979[11] |
| 2. Living On The Front Line | 2. Just Imagine I'm Loving You | **RRP:** not advised |
| 3. The Front Line Symphony | 3. Dance In Guyana | |
| | 4. Say I Love You | |
| | 5. We Are | |

**Cassette:** TICE 4 **Rel:** pres Sep or Oct 1979 **RRP:** not advised

Above release date as documented in the 18 August 1979 edition of *Music Week*. In the 4 August edition of *Music Week* the planned release date via the WEA deal is documented as 7 September 1979. Whether Virgin managed to stick to the planned date is unknown, but September it remained.

## GUY series 7" singles

***GUY 27*** ***EDDY GRANT: Walking On Sunshine / Sunshine Jam***

**Rel:** 24 Aug 1979[11] **RRP:** not advised

One copy viewed has a 17 August 1979 release date stamped on the a–side label, which is the date originally planned via the WEA deal (as documented in the 4 August edition of *Music Week*). The revised release date via Virgin is as documented in the 18 August edition of *Music Week*. As for the release date of 16 March 1979, as listed in *The New Singles*, it is unknown as to whether there was a release via Pye at this point, or whether the release was postponed until August. For what it's worth, all copies viewed during research have had Virgin credits on labels.

---

***GUY 31*** ***THE MEXICANO: Move Up Starsky / Jamaican Child***

**Rel:** 1979 **RRP:** not advised

## Guy series 12" singles

***GUY 27–12*** ***EDDY GRANT: Walking On Sunshine / Sunshine Jam***

**Rel:** 24 Aug 1979[11] **RRP:** not advised

In generic, Ice die–cut sleeve. Originally planned and actual release dates as per GUY 27 above.

---

***GUY 31–12*** ***THE MEXICANO: Move Up Starsky / Jamaican Child***

**Rel:** 1979 **RRP:** not advised

Blue vinyl in generic, Ice die–cut sleeve.

# DinDisc

The DinDisc label was set up by Virgin along with the DinSong publishing company to prevent a wave of new product from swamping the Virgin label proper. It is probable that all of the following singles were originally allocated VS 100 series catalogue numbers. Evidence? Well, perhaps not evidence, as such, but it is slightly suspicious that between August 1979 and the end of the year there are seven DinDisc releases either released or advised and six unused catalogue numbers in the VS 100 sequence? Meanwhile, the brace of 1980s releases are included just to avoid an annoying gap.

## DIN series 7" singles

***DIN 1*** ***THE REVILLOS: Where's The Boy For Me? / The Fiend***
**Rel:** 28 Sep 1979[3] **RRP:** 90p[8]
Picture sleeve.

---

***DIN 2*** ***ORCHESTRAL MANOEUVRES IN THE DARK: Electricity / Almost***
**Rel:** 28 Sep 1979[3] **RRP:** prob. 90p
Picture sleeve. A–side is a re–recording of the track issued on Factory as FAC 6. The b–side was a remixed version. Reissued early 1980 on same catalohue number with slightly revised rear sleeve design and LP versions of both tracks. This explains why various sources claim 1979 release whilst others claim 1980.

---

***DIN 3*** ***DUGGIE CAMPBELL: Enough To Make You Mine / Steamin'***
**Rel:** Oct[8]/2 Nov 1979[3] **RRP:** £1.15[8]
Picture sleeve. B–side also listed as "China Grove" though unconfirmed. Above title is confirmed.

---

***DIN 4*** ***MARTHA AND THE MUFFINS: Insect Love / Cheesies And Gum***
**Rel:** Oct[9]/2 Nov 1979[3] (del 1981[6]) **RRP:** £1.15[8]
Foldout picture sleeve in floppy PVC outer sleeve.

---

***DIN 5*** ***THE REVILLOS: Motor Bike Beat / No Such Luck (1980 RELEASE)***

---

***DIN 6*** ***ORCHESTRAL MANOEUVRES IN THE DARK: Red Frame/White Light / I Betray My Friends (1980 RELEASE)***
12" version (DIN 6–12) has same track listing.

---

***DIN 7*** ***THE BRIANS: My Famous Brother / Brian's Sister Sue***
**Rel:** 30 Nov 1979[3] **RRP:** prob. £1.15
Picture sleeve.

## Odds and sods

The NB 7" single catalogue 'sequence' originally belonged to No Bad Records, which was set–up by Skids' manager, Sandy Muir. The Skids single was distributed locally only until Virgin signed the Skids and took over distribution of the single. On the second and third NB releases, No Bad credits are conspicuous by their absence and The Skids' Richard Jobson states that the Skids record was the only one released on No Bad (email: 2 January 2012).

Will Birch, from The Records, is quoted on 45cat.com as saying that the group demanded their own record label when signing to Virgin and that "NB" stood for "No Bullshit". Presumably, at this point someone at Virgin spotted that there was already a record with the NB prefix so merely assigned the next number – perhaps it is ironic that, what with the 'no bullshit' theme, it should be number two.

But what about the third single, which includes no hint of anything other than a Virgin credit on the sleeve? Haven't got a clue is the answer! Whatever the circumstances, and in lieu of exact information, all three NB singles are listed together for neatness if for no other reason.

The rest of the singles included in this section include either Virgin copyright, publishing, distribution or marketing credits – or various combinations thereof – on sleeve, label or both. And perhaps more telling is that the trade listed most as being Virgin releases. Whatever the gullible public will fall for is all for nothing if the retail trade doesn't know from where to order the record.

### No Bad/The Record Company

***NB 1*** ***THE SKIDS: Charles / Reasons / Test Tube Babies (7")***
**Label:** No Bad **Rel:** Apr 1978[6]
Picture sleeve. Later listed as distributed by Lightning.

---

***NB 2*** ***THE RECORDS: Starry Eyes / Paint Her Face (7")***
**Label:** CUS **Rel:** 1978 **RRP:** 90p[5]
Picture sleeve. Label credited as "The Record Company" on the sleeve with "Virgin Records Ltd." credit beneath. No company credited on the labels, though a 20 Great POrtland Street address. Subsequently reissued as VS 305. On the *Oversell* compilation LP (RMOS 1) the sleeve mistakenly credits the b–side as "Paint Your Face", though the label credit is correct.

---

***NB 3*** ***SPYS: The Young Ones / Heavy Scene (7")***
**Label:** CUS **Rel:** Feb 1979[8] **RRP:** 90p[8]
Picture sleeve includes only a "Virgin Records Ltd." credit. Catalogue number credited as "N.B.3." on sleeve with a more usual "NB 3" on labels. As with NB 2, no company is credited on the labels.

### Quiet Records

***SCH 1*** ***DOUBLE LIFE: Angel Street / The Tourist (7")***
**Label:** Quiet **Rel:** 14 Jul 1978[3]
On the Quiet Records label. Picture sleeve. *The New Singles* lists the catalogue number erroneously as "VS SCH 1". Sleeve and labels state, "Marketed by Virgin Records Ltd".

---

***SCH 2*** ***OLIVER ST JOHN: Give Me Your Hand / First Taste Of Love (7")***
**Label:** Quiet **Rel:** 15 Jul 1979[3]
On the Quiet Records label. Picture sleeve. Sleeve states, "Marketed by Virgin Records Ltd" and credits the publisher as Quiet Records. The labels, however, state the publisher as Virgin, with no mention of marketing.

## Disques Clouseau

***MERDE 1*** ***PATRICK DUVET AND HIS SWEET PERVERSIONS: Sex And Drugs And Rock 'N' Roll / Wake Up And Make Love With Me (7")***
**Label:** Disques Clouseau **Rel:** 27 Apr 1979[3]
On the Disques Clouseau label, which is a one–off, made–up label intended purely for this piss–take of the then extremely popular Patrick Juvet. Picture sleeve. *The New Singles* erroneously lists the a–side as "Sex Et Drugs Et Rock 'n' Roll". Labels include a Virgin copyright credit.

---

***MERDE 1–12*** ***PATRICK DUVET AND HIS SWEET PERVERSIONS: Sex And Drugs And Rock 'N' Roll / Wake Up And Make Love With Me (12")***
**Label:** Disques Clouseau **Rel:** not advised
Picture sleeve.

## Smirksongs

***DHSS 1*** ***THE SMIRKS: Angry With Myself / Penetration / American Patriots (7")***
**Label:** CUS **Rel:** 1979
On the Smirksongs label. PIcture sleeve. Two tracks on a–side. Labels have a "Virgin Music (Publishers) Ltd" credit but sleeve does not. Labels credit copyright and publishing to "Smirksongs".

---

***DHSS 2*** ***THE SMIRKS: To You / New Music (7")***
**Label:** CUS **Rel:** 15 Jun 1979[3]
On the Smirksongs label. PIcture sleeve. Sleeve states, "Distributed by Virgin Records". Labels have a "Virgin Music (Publishers) Ltd" credit for copyright and a "Virgin Records Ltd" credit for publishing.

## Fast Product

***VF 1*** ***THE HUMAN LEAGUE: The Dignity Of Labour (12" EP + free 7" flexidisc)***

| | | |
|---|---|---|
| 1. The Dignity Of Labour Part 1 | 1. The Dignity Of Labour Part 3 | **Lbl:** Fast Product |
| 2. The Dignity Of Labour Part 2 | 2. The Dignity Of Labour Part 4 | **Rel:** 1979 |

PIcture sleeve and free 7" flexidisc, F10X VF 1 (see flexidisc details below). An odd one, this. The band had recently been signed to Virgin, but Bob Last, of the Fast Product label, with which the group had previously been signed, persuaded Virgin's Simon Draper to release the record on Fast Product instead of Virgin. However, it doesn't take much to spot that this is very much a Virgin release whatever the label name says. For a start the catalogue number bears no relation to Fast Product's catalogue sequence and most likely stands for "Virgin Fast 1" (as in pulling a fast 1 perhaps). Next, Virgin gets three credits on the labels, one for the record company and two for the publishing company.

---

***F10X VF 1*** ***THE HUMAN LEAGUE: no track details (7" flexidisc)***
**Lbl:** Fast Product **Rel:** 1979
Free with VF 1 above. One–sided flexidisc, playing at 33⅓ and pressed by Lyntone.

## One–off catalogue number

***NUKE 235*** ***FAST BREEDER AND RADIO ACTORS: Nuclear Waste / Digital Love (7")***
**Label:** Nuke **Rel:** 2 Jun 1978[3]
Picture sleeve and insert. Includes a "Virgin Records Ltd" credit as publisher. Later reissued by both Charly and DB, both in picture sleeves. Includes current Virgin artist, Steve Hillage, Virgin producer, Mike Howlett, along with Sting, who was signed to Virgin Music (Publishing) Ltd. The rumour at the time was that Sid Vicious was originally asked to sing, but turned the offer down. True? Who knows.

# ECM and JAPO

ECM and JAPO were independent West German jazz labels. ECM was established by Manfred Eicher in 1969, whilst JAPO was established by Manfred Scheffner as a mail–order label in 1967, soon after which Scheffner moved into shop–based retail. Both labels were closely connected – many JAPO LPs were produced by ECM's Manfred Eicher and the records were published by ECM–Verlag. ECM reissued at least one JAPO album and the company eventually took over JAPO in its entirity.

Up until 1976 ECM releases were distributed in the UK by the same Island/EMI set up that distributed Virgin's releases, whilst JAPO releases were distributed by CRD, a Middlesex–based distribution company that specialised in European imports. In early 1976 Virgin took over distribution of new titles and back catalogue for both labels. It may or may not be coincidental that 1976 was the same year that ECM won *DownBeat* magazine's Critics Poll for 'Producer of the Year'.

Track listings are not included for ECM or JAPO label LPs because these were West German pressings and Virgin acted purely as UK distributor. Strictly speaking, these records should not be listed because the discography covers UK releases only. However, contemporary trade publications often listed these LPs as UK releases, so we're relaxing the rules a little – but *just* a little. Think of these listings as a bit of a bonus rather than beefing about probable back catalogue omissions and the fact that no end date for Virgin distribution could be confirmed.

## ECM LPs

### Back catalogue distributed by Virgin

Further back catalogue items were almost certainly distributed by Virgin but the following are the only records where evidence exists in trade publications.

---

***ECM 1003*** ***PAUL BLEY WITH GARY PEACOCK: Paul Bley With Gary Peacock***
**Rel:** 1970 **RRP:** £2.85[4]
Listed in *Music Master 1985* as "ECM/Virgin". Above price at 1975, when Island/EMI distributed. No price increase documented when Virgin took over distribution. *Music Master 1985* gives a deletion date of 1983, which is at least two years after Virgin ceased distributing ECM records in the UK.

---

***ECM 1010*** ***PAUL BLEY: Ballads***
**Rel:** 1971 **RRP:** £2.85[4]

---

***ECM 1023*** ***PAUL BLEY: Open To Love***
**Rel:** 1975
*Music Master 1985* gives a deletion date of 1983 – see ECM 1003 above.

---

***ECM 1062*** ***COLLIN WALCOTT: Cloud Dance***
**Rel:** Jan 1976[7]

### New releases distributed by Virgin

The biggest problem with documenting ECM releases distributed by Virgin accurately is that not all records released by ECM during the period are listed in UK trade publications and, as mentioned, no definitive end date can be identified. All that is known is that no further ECM records appear listed as Virgin label releases in either *The NewRecords* or one or other of the *Music Master* publications after May 1979.

Where release date (including month) is specified, those records are documented in trade publications as being distributed by Virgin. The gaps are filled on the (possibly erroneous) assumption that all new releases during the identified period were distributed in the UK by Virgin.

---

***ECM 1069*** ***KENNY WHEELER: Gnu High***
**Rel:** Mar[5]/Apr 1976[1] **RRP:** £3.50[1]

---

***ECM 1070*** ***KEITH JARRETT: Arbour Zena***
**Rel:** Jun[5]/Jul 1976[1] **RRP:** £3.85[1]
*The New Records* incorrectly lists the title as "Mysteries". *Mysteries* is listed in the same edition as being on the Impulse label (IMPL 8026) at £2.99, so *The New Records* obviously got a bit confused ... and well they might, what with Keith Jarrett putting out around eight LPs a year at this point.

---

***ECM 1071*** ***TOMASZ STANKO: Balladyna***
**Rel:** May[5]/Jul 1976[1] **RRP:** £3.85[1]

---

***ECM 1072*** ***GARY BURTON QUINTET: Dreams So Real***
**Rel:** Jul[5]/Aug 1976[1] **RRP:** £3.85[1]
Subtitled, *Music of Carla Bley.*

---

***ECM 1073*** ***PAT METHENY: Bright Size Life***
**Rel:** Apr 1976[5] **RRP:** £3.85[5]

---

***ECM 1074*** ***JACK DEJOHNETTE'S DIRECTIONS: Untitled***
**Rel:** Sep 1976[5] **RRP:** £3.85[5]

---

***ECM 1075*** ***JAN GARBAREK – BOBO STENSON QUARTET: Dansere***
**Rel:** Apr 1976[5] **RRP:** £3.85[5]

---

***ECM 1076*** ***BARRE PHILLIPS: Mountainscapes***
**Rel:** Sep 1976[5] **RRP:** £3.85[5]

---

***ECM 1077*** ***EDWARD VESALA: Nan Madol***
**Rel:** Jul[5]/Aug 1976[1] (del 1980[6]) **RRP:** £3.85[1]
This was a reissue of an album first issued in 1974 on the JAPO label.

---

***ECM 1078*** ***ENRICO RAVA: The Plot***
**Rel:** Apr[5]/May 1977[1] **RRP:** £3.85[1]

---

***ECM 1079*** ***JACK DEJOHNETTE: Pictures***
**Rel:** Mar[5]/Apr 1977[1] **RRP:** £3.85[1]/£3.99[5]

---

***ECM 1080*** ***JOHN ABERCROMBIE, RALPH TOWNER: Sargasso Sea***
**Rel:** Oct 1976[5] **RRP:** £3.99[5]

---

***ECM 1081*** ***ART LANDE/MARK ISHAM/BILL DOUGLASS/GLENN CRONKHITE: Rubisa Patrol***
**Rel:** Oct 1976[5] **RRP:** £3.99[5]

---

***ECM 1082*** ***ARILD ANDERSON: Shimri***
**Rel:** Mar[5]/Apr 1977[1] **RRP:** £3.85[1]/£3.99[5]

---

***ECM 1083*** ***TERJE RYPDAL: After The Rain***
**Rel:** Dec 1976[5] **RRP:** £3.99[5]

---

***ECM 1084*** ***EBERHARD WEBER: The Following Morning***
**Rel:** Feb[5]/Mar 1977[1] **RRP:** £3.85[1]/£3.99[5]

***ECM 1085*** ***KEITH JARRETT: The Survivor's Suite***
**Rel:** Nov 1977[5] **RRP:** £4.25[5]

---

***ECM 1086/1087*** ***KEITH JARRETT: Hymns Spheres (2–LP)***
**Rel:** Dec 1976[5] **RRP:** £6.99[5]
Listed in *Music Master 1979* as ECMD 1086 (though above catalogue number confirmed). Presumably, the ECMD catalogue prefix was devised by Virgin to more easily distinguish double ECM albums from single albums.

---

***ECM 1088*** ***EDWARD VESALA: Satu***
**Rel:** Feb 1977[5] **RRP:** £3.99[5]

---

***ECM 1089*** ***EGBERTO GISMONTI: Dança Das Cabeças***
**Rel:** Apr 1977[5] **RRP:** £3.99[5]

---

***ECM 1090/1091*** ***KEITH JARRETT: Staircase/Hourglass/Sundial (2–LP)***
**Rel:** May 1977[5] **RRP:** £6.99[5]
Listed in *Music Master 1979* as ECMD 1090 (though above catalogue number confirmed). See ECM 1086/1087 above.

---

***ECM 1092*** ***GARY BURTON QUARTET WITH EBERHARD WEBER: Passengers***
**Rel:** Apr[5]/May 1977[1] **RRP:** £3.85[1]/£3.99[5]

---

***ECM 1093*** ***JAN GARBAREK: Dis***
**Rel:** May[5]/Jun 1977[1] **RRP:** £3.85[1]/£3.99[5]

---

***ECM 1094*** ***STEVE KUHN GROUP: Motility***
**Rel:** Apr[5]/May 1977[1] **RRP:** £3.85[1]/£3.99[5]

---

***ECM 1095*** ***RALPH TOWNER: Solstice Sound And Shadows***
**Rel:** Nov 1977[5] **RRP:** £4.25[5]

---

***ECM 1096*** ***COLLIN WALCOTT: Grazing Dreams***
**Rel:** Aug[5]/Oct 1977[1] **RRP:** £4.25[1]

---

***ECM 1097*** ***PAT METHENY: Watercolours***
**Rel:** May[5]/Jun 1977[1] **RRP:** £3.85[1]

---

***ECM 1098*** ***JULIAN PRIESTER AND MARINE INTRUSION: Polarisation***
**Rel:** May[5]/Jun 1977[1] **RRP:** £3.85[1]/£3.99[5]

---

***ECM 1099*** ***JOHN TAYLOR/NORMA WINSTONE/KENNY WHEELER: Azimuth***
**Rel:** Aug[5]/Oct 1977[1] **RRP:** £4.25[1]
*The New Records* miscredits Norma Winstone as "Norman".

---

***ECM–X–1100*** ***KEITH JARRETT: Sun Bear Concerts (10–LP box set)***
**Rel:** 1978
Includes a booklet. Listed in *Music Master 1979* as "ECMX 1" (though above catalogue number confirmed on record labels). Presumably, the ECMX 1 catalogue number was devised by Virgin to more easily distinguish the boxed set from single albums in the normal ECM 1000 sequence.

---

***ECM 1101*** ***GARY PEACOCK/KEITH JARRETT/JACK DEJOHNETTE: Tales Of Another***
**Rel:** Aug[5]/Oct 1977[1] **RRP:** £4.25[1]

---

***ECM 1102*** ***KENNY WHEELER: Deer Wan***
**Rel:** Jan 1978[5] **RRP:** £4.59[5]

***ECM 1103*** ***JACK DEJOHNETTE'S DIRECTIONS: New Rags***
**Rel:** Aug[5]/Oct 1977[1] **RRP:** £4.25
Label listed as "Virgin" in *The New Records*, though various other ECM records in the same edition list ECM only.

---

***ECM 1104*** ***RICHARD BEIRACH: Hubris***
**Rel:** Jan 1978[5] **RRP:** £4.59[5]/£4.99[5]
*Music Master 1979* lists the LP twice with two different prices.

---

***ECM 1105*** ***JOHN ABERCROMBIE/DAVE HOLLAND/JACK DEJOHNETTE: Gateway 2***
**Rel:** 1978 **RRP:** £4.99[5]

---

***ECM 1106*** ***ART LANDE AND RUBISA PATROL: Desert Marauders***
**Rel:** 1978 **RRP:** £4.99[5]

---

***ECM 1107*** ***EBERHARD WEBER COLOURS: Silent Feet***
**Rel:** 1978 **RRP:** £4.99[5]

---

***ECM 1108*** ***PAUL MOTIAN TRIO: Dance***
**Rel:** Jan 1978[5] **RRP:** £4.59[5]/£4.99[5]
*Music Master 1979* lists the LP twice with two different prices.

---

***ECM 1109*** ***DAVE HOLLAND: Emerald Tears***
**Rel:** 1978 **RRP:** £4.99[5]

---

***ECM 1110*** ***TERJE RYPDAL: Waves***
**Rel:** Jan 1978[5] **RRP:** £4.59[5]

---

***ECM 1111*** ***GARY BURTON: Times Square***
**Rel:** 1978 **RRP:** £4.99[5]

---

***ECM 1112*** ***KEITH JARRETT/DENNIS RUSSELL DAVIES: Ritual***
**Rel:** 1978 **RRP:** pres. either £4.59 or £4.99

---

***ECM 1113*** ***TOM VAN DER GELD AND CHILDREN AT PLAY: Patience***
**Rel:** Jan 1978[5] **RRP:** £4.59[5]

---

***ECM 1114*** ***PAT METHENY GROUP: Pat Metheny Group***
**Rel:** 1978 **RRP:** £4.99[5]

---

***ECM 1115*** ***KEITH JARRETT: My Song***
**Rel:** 1978 **RRP:** £4.99[5]

---

***ECM 1116*** ***EGBERTO GISMONTI: Sol Do Meio Dia***
**Rel:** 1978 **RRP:** £4.99[5]

---

***ECM 1117*** ***JOHN ABERCROMBIE: Characters***
**Rel:** 1978 **RRP:** £4.99[5]

---

***ECM 1118*** ***JAN GARBAREK: Places***
**Rel:** 1978 **RRP:** £4.99[5]

---

***ECM 1119*** ***GARY PEACOCK: December Poems***
**Rel:** Mar 1979[7] **RRP:** £4.99[7]

---

***ECM 1120*** ***BILL CONNORS: Of Mist And Melting***
**Rel:** 1978 **RRP:** £4.99[7]

***ECM 1121*** ***RALPH TOWNER/EDDIE GOMEZ/JACK DEJOHNETTE: Batik***
**Rel:** 1978 **RRP:** £3.99[5]

---

***ECM 1122*** ***ENRICO RAVA QUARTET: Enrico Rava Quartet***
**Rel:** 1978 **RRP:** £4.99[5]

---

***ECM 1123*** ***BARRE PHILLIPS: Three Day Moon***
**Rel:** 1978 **RRP:** £4.99[5]

---

***ECM 1124*** ***STEVE KUHN: Non–Fiction***
**Rel:** 1978 **RRP:** £4.99[5]

---

***ECM 1125*** ***TERJE RYPDAL/MIROSLAV VITOUS/JACK DEJOHNETTE: Terje Rypdal/Miroslav Vitous/Jack DeJohnette***
**Rel:** 1979 **RRP:** pres. £4.99

---

***ECM 1126*** ***ART ENSEMBLE OF CHICAGO: Nice Guys***
**Rel:** 1979 **RRP:** pres. £4.99

---

***ECM 1127*** ***ARILD ANDERSEN QUARTET: Green Shading Into Blue***
**Rel:** 1978 **RRP:** £4.99[5]

---

***ECM 1128*** ***JACK DEJOHNETTE: New Directions***
**Rel:** 1978 **RRP:** £4.99[5]

---

***ECM 1129*** ***STEVE REICH: Music For 18 Musicians***
**Rel:** 1978 **RRP:** £4.99[5]

---

***ECM 1130*** ***AZIMUTH: The Touchstone***
**Rel:** 1978 **RRP:** £4.99[5]

---

***ECM 1131*** ***PAT METHENY: New Chautauqua***
**Rel:** May 1979[7] **RRP:** £4.99[7]

## JAPO LPs

### Back catalogue distributed by Virgin

Further back catalogue was almost certainly distributed by Virgin, but the following is the only LP where evidence is available. Just to confuse matters, *Nan Madol* by Edward Vesala (original released as JAPO 60007 in 1974) was subsequently reissued as ECM 1077 in 1976 and it is ECM's reissue that Virgin distributed in the UK.

---

***JAPO 60001*** ***MAL WALDREN: The Call***
**Rel:** 1979[7] **RRP:** £5.30[7]
This was a 1971 release but the first documented Virgin distribution of this album in the UK is 1979.

### New releases distributed by Virgin

The biggest problem with documenting JAPO releases distributed by Virgin accurately is that not all records released by JAPO during the period are listed in UK trade publications and, as with ECM, no definitive end date can be identified. The assumption is that the deals with ECM and JAPO covered the same time period. No further JAPO records appear listed as Virgin label releases in either *The New Records* or one or other of the *Music Master* publications after an unspecified point in 1979.

Where release date with month is specified, those records are documented as being distributed by Virgin. The gaps have been filled up on the (possibly erroneous) assumption that all new releases during the identified period were distributed in the UK by Virgin, which is by no means assured.

---

***JAPO 60010*** ***ENRICO RAVA: Quotation Marks***
**Rel:** Aug 1976[1] **RRP:** £3.85[1]

---

***JAPO 60011*** ***MAGOG: Magog***
**Rel:** Mar 1976[5] **RRP:** £3.85[5]

---

***JAPO 60012*** ***OM: Kirikuki***
**Rel:** 1976 **RRP:** not advised

---

***JAPO 60013*** ***MANFRED SCHOOF QUINTET: Scales***
**Rel:** Dec 1976[5] **RRP:** £3.99[5]

---

***JAPO 60014*** ***LARRY KARUSH/GLEN MOORE: May 24, 1976***
**Rel:** Dec 1976[5] **RRP:** £3.99[5]

---

***JAPO 60015*** ***HERBERT JOOS: Daybreak***
**Rel:** Mar 1977[5] **RRP:** £3.99[5]

---

***JAPO 60016*** ***OM: Rautionaha***
**Rel:** Apr[5]/May 1977[1] **RRP:** £3.85[1]/£3.99[5]
*The New Records* miscredits the artist as "Um".

---

***JAPO 60017*** ***STEPHAN MICUS: Implosions***
**Rel:** Jul 1977[5]/Aug 1977[1] **RRP:** £3.99[5]/£4.25[1]
Label listed as "Virgin" in *The New Records.*

---

***JAPO 60018*** ***KEN HYDER'S TALISKER: Land Of Stone***
**Rel:** Nov 1977[5] **RRP:** £4.25[5]

---

***JAPO 60019*** ***MANFRED SCHOOF QUINTET: Light Lines***
**Rel:** 1978 **RRP:** not advised

---

***JAPO 60020*** ***RENA RAMA: Landscapes***
**Rel:** 1977 **RRP:** not advised

---

***JAPO 60021*** ***GLOBE UNITY: Improvisations***
**Rel:** 1978 **RRP:** not advised

---

***JAPO 60022*** ***OM WITH DOM UM ROAMOA: Om With Dom Um Roamoa***
**Rel:** Jan 1978[5] **RRP:** £4.59[5]

---

***JAPO 60023*** ***LENNART ÅBERG: Partial Solar Eclipse***
**Rel:** 1977 **RRP:** not advised

---

***JAPO 60024*** ***CONTACT TRIO: New Marks***
**Rel:** 1978 **RRP:** not advised

---

***JAPO 60025*** ***JACK DEJOHNETTE/PIERRE FAVRE/FREDY STUDER/DOM UM ROMAO/DAVID FRIEDMAN/GEORGE GRUNTZ: Percussion Profiles***
**Rel:** 1978 **RRP:** not advised

---

***JAPO 60026*** ***STEPHAN MICUS: Till The End Of Time***
**Rel:** 1978 **RRP:** not advised

## Virgin artists on other labels

Just in case you're wondering, the Harvest live compilation, *The Roxy, London WC2 (Jan – Apr 77)*, isn't included because the X–Ray–Spex performance precedes the band's signing with Virgin.

---

### *GT 4997* *VARIOUS ARTISTS: Greasy Truckers (2–LP)*

*Side 1 – CAMEL*
1. God Of Light Revisited Parts One, Two And Three

*Side 2 – HENRY COW*
1. Off The Map
2. Cafe Royal
3. Keeping Warm In Winter/Sweet Heart of Mine

*Side 3 – GLOBAL VILLAGE TRUCKING CO*
1. Look Into Me
2. Earl Stonham (The Gunslinger)
3. You're A Floozy Madame Karma (But I Love Your Lowdown Ways)
4. Everybody Needs A Good Friend

*Side 4 – GONG*
1. General Flash Of The United Hallucinations
2. Part 32 Floating Anarchy

**Label:** Greasy Truckers
**Rel:** 1973
**RRP:** £2.00[12]

Insert. Early copies with large, orange sleeve sticker. Released in conjunction with Greasy Truckers but has that indefinable 'look and feel' of a Virgin release. So did Virgin want to sign Camel?

---

### *CHR 1079* *VARIOUS ARTISTS: Over The Rainbow (LP)*

1. Wheelin 'N' Dealin (Sassafras)
2. Grand Hotel (Procol Harum)
3. Brickyard Blues (Frankie Miller And Procol Harum)
4. I Am The Walrus (Sassafras)

1. Hokey Pokey (Richard And Linda Thompson)
2. Halfway Between Heaven And Earth (Hatfield And The North)
3. Discover The Lover (John Martyn)
4. Saviour (Kevin Coyne)

**Label:** Chrysalis
**Rel:** May 1975[5]

**Cassette:** ZCHR 1079 **Rel:** not advised **RRP:** not advised

Subtitled "The Last Concert Live!" Includes otherwise unreleased live performances from Kevin Coyne and Hatfield and the North (although the Hatfield track was later included on *Afters*, this is a slightly different edit). Recorded March 16th 1975 at the Rainbow Theatre – an uncredited John Peel announces. Concert promoted by Chrysalis and Virgin. Tickets were £1 and were only available from the Rainbow box office or from Virgin shops. Doors opened at 2.30 PM and Sassafras was first on.

---

### *MCA PSR 413* *TANGERINE DREAM: Betrayal (Sorcerer Theme) / Search (7")*

**Label:** MCA **Rel:** 1977

Promotional–only 7" on MCA. From the MCA soundtrack LP, Sorcerer (MCL 1646).

---

### *MCF 2806* *TANGERINE DREAM: Sorcerer (LP)*

1. Main Title
2. Search
3. The Call
4. Creation
5. Vengeance
6. The Journey

1. Grind
2. Rain Forest
3. Abyss
4. The Mountain Road
5. Impressions Of Sorcerer
6. Betrayal (Sorcerer Theme)

**Label:** MCA
**Rel:** Jul 1977[5]
**RRP:** £3.35[5]

**Cassette:** TC–MCF 2806 **Rel:** Jul 1977[5] **RRP:** £3.60[5]

Soundtrack licensed to MCA – original copies are on the black rainbow label design. Repromoted March 1978 with £3.89[5] RRP because the film was renamed *Wages Of Fear*. The repromoted version included a large sleeve sticker saying "New Film Title Wages Of Fear" and just to confuse the issue *Music Master 1979* credited the repromoted album as "Wages Of Fear" even though still titled *Sorcerer*. The cassette was repromoted with a RRP of £4.10[5]

***SHSP 4084*** ***IVOR CUTLER: Life In A Scotch Sitting Room, Volume 2 (LP)***

| Side 1 | Side 2 | |
|---|---|---|
| 1. Episode 2 | 1. Episode 7 | **Label:** Harvest |
| 2. Episode 3 | 2. Episode 12 | **Rel:** Mar 1978[5] |
| 3. Episode 9 | 3. Jungle Tip – Leopard | **RRP:** £3.89[5] |
| 4. Jungle Tip – Owl | 4. Episode 8 | |
| 5. Episode 1 | 5. Episode 6 | |
| 6. Episode 11 | 6. Episode 4 | |
| 7. Jungle Tip – Lion | 7. Jungle Tip – Boa | |
| 8. Episode 5 | 8. Episode 13 | |
| 9. Episode 14 | 9. Episode 0 | |

**Cassette:** TC–SHSP 4084 **Rel:** Mar 1978[5] **RRP:** £4.10[5]

LP includes several pieces previously released on his Virgin albums. Virgin's Al Clark gets a credit ("Deep gratitude") and Virgin as a whole gets a thank you for permission to use the tracks..

---

***K 66077*** ***VARIOUS ARTISTS: Hope And Anchor Front Row Festival (2–LP)***

| *Side 1* | *Side 2* | |
|---|---|---|
| 1. Dr. Feelgood (Wilko Johnson Band) | 1. Billy (The Pleasers) | **Label:** WB |
| 2. Straighten Out (The Stranglers) | 2. Science Friction (XTC) | **Rel:** Apr 1978[5] |
| 3. Styrofoam (Tyla Gang) | 3. Eastbound Train (Dire Straits) | **RRP:** £5.99[5] |
| 4. Don't Munchen It (The Pirates) | 4. Bizz Fizz (Burlesque) | |
| 5. Speed Kills (Steve Gibbons Band) | 5. Let's Submerge (X-Ray Spex) | |
| 6. I'm Bugged (XTC) | 6. Crazy (999) | |
| 7. I Hate School (Suburban Studs) | | |

| *Side 3* | *Side 4* |
|---|---|
| 1. Demolition Girl (The Saints) | 1. Underground Romance (Philip Rambow) |
| 2. Quite Disappointing (999) | 2. Rock And Roll Radio (The Pleasers) |
| 3. Creature Of Doom (The Only Ones) | 3. On The Street (Tyla Gang) |
| 4. Gibson Martin Fender (The Pirates) | 4. Johnny Cool (Steve Gibbons Band) |
| 5. Sound Check (Steel Pulse) | 5. Twenty Yards Behind (Wilko Johnson Band) |
| 6. Zero Hero (Roogalator) | 6. Hanging Around (The Stranglers) |

**Cassette:** K4 66077 **Rel:** Apr 1978[5] **RRP:** £5.99[5]

2–LP initially on blue vinyl. Insert. Issued by jointly by WB and Albion Records. Includes *I'm Bugged* and *Science Friction* by XTC. The Wilko Johnson Band, Roogalator and X–Ray–Spex do not have Virgin credits so presumably were not signed to Virgin at the time. Recorded between Tuesday, 22 November and Thursday, 15 December 1977. Issued as a double–play cassette.

---

***CN 3393/S*** ***MIKE OLDFIELD: In Concert – 206 / In Concert – 207 (2–LP set)***

| *Side 1* | *Side 2* | |
|---|---|---|
| *1. (Brian Matthews Introduction)* | 1. Incantations (Continued) | **Label:** BBC Trans. Services |
| 2. Incantations | 2. *(Brian Matthews Previews Second Half Of Concert)* | |

| *Side 3* | *Side 4* |
|---|---|
| *1. (Brian Matthews Introduction)* | 1. Guilty |
| 2. Tubular Bells | 2. Tubular Bells |
| | 3. Guilty (Reprise) |

2–LP set in individual generic die–cut BBC Transcription Services sleeves with two inserts. Set part numbers are 206 and 207. Separate matrix numbers – 145473–S to 145476–S – included on labels. First insert has background information about Mike Oldfield with track details on the rear. The other comprises radio cue sheets, one side per record. Both cue sheets include the text, "Programmes 206 & 207 may be used as two separate one–hour concerts or – as originally recorded – as one two–hour show." Recorded at Wembley Arena, 2nd May, 1979. Insert provides the information that the record was made available for broadcast for week 36, 1979.

# Appendices: summary listings

## Quadraphonic releases

| | |
|---|---|
| QV 2001 | MIKE OLDFIELD: Tubular Bells (SQ Quad) |
| QV 2043 | MIKE OLDFIELD: Ommadawn (SQ Quad) |
| QVQS 2043 | MIKE OLDFIELD: The QS Quadrophonic Ommadawn (QS Quad) |
| V 2090 | DAVID BEDFORD: Instructions For Angels (Matrix H Quad compatible: only available in this format – sleeve lists "V2090/Matrix H Quad") |
| VBOX 1 | MIKE OLDFIELD: Boxed (SQ Quad versions of *Tubular Bells*, *Hergest Ridge*, *Ommadawn* and *Collaborations*: *Collaborations* was only available in this format on vinyl) |
| VD 2505 | KEVIN COYNE: In Living Black And White (SQ Quad: all copies in this format) |
| VD 2511 | MIKE OLDFIELD: Exposed (SQ Quad: all copies in this format) |

## Picture discs

Sparks and Noel 12" singles that appear to be picture discs really have large picture labels.

| | |
|---|---|
| SIXPACK 1 | CAPTAIN BEEFHEART: Six–Pack – Six–Track (picture disc only) |
| SIXPACK 2 | STEVE HILLAGE: Six–Pack – Six–Track (picture disc only) |
| SIXPACK 3 | IAN MATTHEWS: Six–Pack – Six–Track (picture disc only: not Virgin, but a joint release between Rockburgh Records and Caroline Exports) |
| SIXPACK 4 | ARTHUR BROWN: Six–Pack – Six–Track (picture disc only: not Virgin, but a jointrelease between Gull Records and Caroline Exports) |
| V 2126 | NOEL: Is There More To Life Than Dancing (probably picture disc only) |
| VP 2001 | MIKE OLDFIELD: Tubular Bells |
| VP 2086 | SEX PISTOLS: Never Mind The Bollocks, Here's The Sex Pistols |
| VP 2106 | DEVO: Q: Are We Not Men? A: We Are Devo |
| VP 2107 | JULIE COVINGTON: Julie Covington (perhaps unreleased) |
| VS 273 | JANE AIRE AND THE BELVEDERES: Call Me Every Night |

## Coloured, luminous and clear vinyl releases

| | |
|---|---|
| FL 1023 | U ROY: Jah Son Of Africa |
| GUY 31–12 | THE MEXICANO: Move Up Starsky (blue) |
| V 2098 | STEVE HILLAGE: Green (green) |
| V 2101 | THE MOTORS: Approved By The Motors (red) |
| V 2109 | PENETRATION: Moving Targets (luminous) |
| V 2111 | TANGERINE DREAM: Force Majeure (clear) |
| V 2115 | SPARKS: No 1 in Heaven (yellow) |
| V 2116 | SKIDS: Scared To Dance (blue) |
| VCL 5003 | VARIOUS ARTISTS: Short Circuit Live At The Electric Circus (blue) |
| VD 2508 | VARIOUS ARTISTS: Dead On Arrival (luminous) |
| VDT 101 | MIKE OLDFIELD: Incantations (one record red, one record blue – one known) |
| VEP 1004 | JOHN DOWIE: Another Close Shave (pink) |
| VR 1 | STEVE HILLAGE: Rainbow Dome Musick (clear) |
| VS 196 | JULIE COVINGTON: Only Women Bleed (orange; red rumoured to exist) |
| VS 217 | YELLOW DOG: Wait Until Midnight (yellow, some orange copies) |
| VS 219–12 | THE MOTORS: Airport (blue) |
| VS 223 | DEVO: Come Back Jonee (grey) |
| VS 224 | YELLOW DOG: Little Gods (luminous) |
| VS 227 | SKIDS: Sweet Suburbia (white) |
| VS 232–12 | SKIDS: Wide Open (red) |
| VS 235–12 | FINGERPRINTZ: Dancing With Myself (green) |
| VS 238–12 | MIKE OLDFIELD: Take 4 (white) |

VS 239–12 DON LETTS, STRATETIME KEITH, STEEL LEG AND JAH WOBBLE: Steel Leg V. The Electric Dread (white)
VS 241 SKIDS: Into The Valley (white)
VS 242 THE MEMBERS: The Sound Of The Suburbs (clear)
VS 243–12 SUPERCHARGE: I Can See Right Thru You (clear)
VS 244 SPARKS: No One Song In Heaven (green)
VS 244–12 SPARKS: No One Song In Heaven (red and blue versions)
VS 245–12 MIKE OLDFIELD: Guilty (blue)
VS 246 PHIL CORDELL: Hearts On Fire (red)
VS 246–12 PHIL CORDELL: Hearts On Fire (white)
VS 252 FINGERPRINTZ: Who's Your Friend? (blue)
VS 253 COWBOYS INTERNATIONAL: Aftermath (orange)
VS 255 KEVIN COYNE: I'll Go Too (green)
VS 259 XTC: Life Begins At The Hop (clear)
VS 270–12 SPARKS: Beat The Clock (orange, yellow, blue and pink versions)
VS 289–12 SPARKS: Tryouts For The Human Race (orange, blue, yellow and green versions with paper label under clear vinyl centre section)

## 12" singles

FLS 119–12 TWINKLE BROTHERS: Keep On Trying
FLS 120–12 SLY DUNBAR: Rasta Fiesta
FLS 121–12 GREGORY ISAACS, Soon Forward
FLS 122–12 THE MIGHTY DIAMONDS: Bodyguard
FLS 123–12 TWINKLE BROTHERS: Jahoviah
FLS 124–12 I ROY: Fire In A Wire
GUY 27–12 EDDY GRANT: Walking On Sunshine
GUY 31–12 THE MEXICANO: Move Up Starsky
MERDE 1–12 PATRICK DUVET AND HIS SWEET PERVERSIONS: Sex And Drugs And Rock 'N' Roll
METAL 1 PUBLIC IMAGE LIMITED: Metal Box (3 x 12" single)
VDJ 3 RUAN: Another Street Gang
VDJ 4 ARCHIE LEGGET: Jamaican Jockey
VDJ 7 MATAYA CLIFFORD: Star Fell From Heaven
VDJ 9 MIKE OLDFIELD: An Extract From Ommadawn
VDJ 11 SUPERCHARGE: Get Down Boogie
VDJ 12 BOXER: All The Time In The World
VDJ 13 U ROY: Runaway Girl
VDJ 14 THE MIGHTY DIAMONDS: Have Mercy
VDJ 22 DELROY WASHINGTON: Give All The Praise To Jah
VDJ 25 STEVE HILLAGE: Getting Better
VDJ 29 THE RECORDS: High Heels
VF 1 THE HUMAN LEAGUE: The Dignity Of Labour
VOLE 1 DR. ALIMANTADO: Slavery Let I Go
VOLE 2 U ROY: Small Axe
VOLE 3 XTC: Science Friction EP
VOLE 4 U BROWN: Black Star Liner
VOLE 5 U ROY: Live At The Lyceum
VOLE 6 SLY DUNBAR: A Who Say
VOLE 7 ALTHEA AND DONNA: Going To Negril
VOLE 8 POET AND THE ROOTS: It Dread Inna Inglan (For George Lindo)
VOLE 9 JAH WOBBLE: Dreadlock Don't Deal In Wedlock
VS 186–12 THE MOTORS: Dancing The Night Away
VS 187–12 U ROY: Small Axe
VS 188–12 XTC: 3D EP
VS 189–12 X-RAY SPEX: Oh Bondage, Up Yours!
VS 190–12 POET AND THE ROOTS: All Wi Doin Is Defendin
VS 193–12 GLADIATORS: Pocket Money
VS 202–12 SUPERCHARGE: I Think I'm Gonna Fall (In Love))

| | |
|---|---|
| VS 219–12 | THE MOTORS: Airport |
| VS 220–12 | SEX PISTOLS: The Biggest Blow (A Punk Prayer By Ronnie Biggs) |
| VS 222–12 | THE MOTORS: Forget About You |
| VS 232–12 | SKIDS: Wide Open |
| VS 233–12 | XTC: Go + |
| VS 235–12 | FINGERPRINTZ: Dancing With Myself |
| VS 238–12 | MIKE OLDFIELD: Take 4 |
| VS 239–12 | DON LETTS, STRATETIME KEITH, STEEL LEG AND JAH WOBBLE: Steel Leg V. The Electric Dread |
| VS 243–12 | SUPERCHARGE: I Can See Right Thru You, Part 1 |
| VS 244–12 | SPARKS: No One Song In Heaven |
| VS 245–12 | MIKE OLDFIELD: Guilty |
| VS 246–12 | PHIL CORDELL: Hearts On Fire |
| VS 247–12 | THE RECORDS: Rock And Roll Love Letter |
| VS 248–12 | THE MEMBERS: Offshore Banking Business |
| VS 257–12 | PENETRATION: Danger Signs |
| VS 258–12 | NOEL: Dancing is Dangerous |
| VS 261–12 | ESSENTIAL LOGIC: Wake Up |
| VS 266–12 | ADRIAN MUNSEY: C'Est Sheep |
| VS 269–12 | THE MEN: I Don't Depend On You |
| VS 270–12 | SPARKS: Beat The Clock |
| VS 271–12 | THE RUTS: Babylon's Burning |
| VS 274–12 | PUBLIC IMAGE LIMITED: Death Disco |
| VS 275–12 | DAN MACARTHUR: Dan MacArthur (Disco Dummy) |
| VS 289–12 | SPARKS: Tryouts For the Human Race |
| VS 299–12 | PUBLIC IMAGE LIMITED: Memories |
| VS 301–12 | HUDSON PEOPLE: Boogie On Downtown |
| VS 311–12 | 90 DEGREES, No Doctor |

## Flexidiscs

| | |
|---|---|
| F10X VF 1 | THE HUMAN LEAGUE: no track details |
| LYN 3261 | SEX PISTOLS: Lentilmas – A Seasonal Offering To You From Virgin Records |
| VDJ 27 | DEVO: A Flimsy Wrap |
| No cat. no. | COWBOYS INTERNATIONAL: Many Times |
| No cat. no. | SEX PISTOLS: The Interview (may not exist) |

## 8-track cartridges

8–tracks marked * are known to have been issued in hard plastic case with paper wraparound inlay. If the Henry Cow and Link Wray 8–tracks were really issued (which is doubtful despite listings in one trade publication) then they too would have been issued in the same format. Later 8–tracks from 1974 onward were issued, sealed, in card slipcases.

| | |
|---|---|
| 8XV 2001 | MIKE OLDFIELD: Tubular Bells* |
| 8XV 2004 | FAUST: Faust IV* |
| 8XV 2005 | HENRY COW: The Henry Cow Legend (may not exist) |
| 8XV 2006 | LINK WRAY: Beans And Fatback (may not exist) |
| 8XV 2008 | HATFIELD AND THE NORTH: Hatfield And The North (may not exist) |
| 8XV 2010 | TANGERINE DREAM: Phaedra |
| 8XV 2013 | MIKE OLDFIELD: Hergest Ridge |
| 8XV 2015 | CAPTAIN BEEFHEART AND THE MAGIC BAND: Unconditionally Guaranteed |
| 8XV 2017 | ROBERT WYATT: Rock Bottom |
| 8XV 2019 | GONG: You |
| 8XV 2020 | DAVID BEDFORD: Star's End (may not exist) |
| 8XV 2023 | CAPTAIN BEEFHEART AND MAGIC BAND: Bluejeans And Moonbeams |
| 8XV 2025 | TANGERINE DREAM: Rubycon |
| 8XV 2026 | THE ROYAL PHILHARMONIC ORCHESTRA/MIKE OLDFIELD/DAVID BEDFORD: The Orchestral Tubular Bells |

8XV 2029 CLEAR LIGHT SYMPHONY: Clear Light Symphony
8XV 2032 WHITE NOISE: White Noise 2 (may not exist)
8XV 2033 KEVIN COYNE: Matching Head And Feet
8XV 2034 ROBERT WYATT: Ruth Is Stranger Than Richard
8XV 2043 MIKE OLDFIELD: Ommadawn
8XV 2044 TANGERINE DREAM: Ricochet
8XV 2068 TANGERINE DREAM: Stratosphere
8XVD 2501 KEVIN COYNE: Marjory Razorblade*

## Cassettes

There may be more. Virgin often waited a bit – sometimes years — to see if it was worthwhile putting out cassette versions of albums. In at least some of those instances the company didn't seem to bother telling anyone about their having sneaked out a cassette. Also it is possible that some of the following tapes only exist in the imagination of various trade publications. Heigh ho.

FLC 1012 ALTHEA AND DONNA: Uptown Top Ranking
TCV 2001 MIKE OLDFIELD: Tubular Bells
TCV 2002 GONG: Radio Gnome Invisible Part 1 Flying Teapot
TCV 2004 FAUST: Faust IV
TCV 2005 HENRY COW: The Henry Cow Legend
TCV 2006 LINK WRAY: Beans And Fatback
TCV 2007 GONG: Radio Gnome 2 Angels Egg
TCV 2008 HATFIELD AND THE NORTH: Hatfield And The North
TCV 2009 CHILI CHARLES: Busy Corner
TCV 2010 TANGERINE DREAM: Phaedra
TCV 2011 HENRY COW: Unrest
TCV 2012 KEVIN COYNE: Blame It On The Night
TCV 2013 MIKE OLDFIELD: Hergest Ridge
TCV 2014 SLAPP HAPPY: Slapp Happy
TCV 2015 CAPTAIN BEEFHEART AND THE MAGIC BAND: Unconditionally Guaranteed
TCV 2016 EDGAR FROESE: Aqua
TCV 2017 ROBERT WYATT: Rock Bottom
TCV 2018 COMUS: To Keep From Crying
TCV 2019 GONG: You
TCV 2020 DAVID BEDFORD: Star's End
TCV 2021 IVOR CUTLER: Dandruff
TCV 2022 TOM NEWMAN: Fine Old Tom
TCV 2023 CAPTAIN BEEFHEART AND MAGIC BAND: Bluejeans And Moonbeams
TCV 2024 SLAPP HAPPY/HENRY COW: Desperate Straights
TCV 2025 TANGERINE DREAM: Rubycon
TCV 2026 THE ROYAL PHILHARMONIC ORCHESTRA/MIKE OLDFIELD/DAVID BEDFORD: The Orchestral Tubular Bells
TCV 2027 HENRY COW/SLAPP HAPPY: In Praise Of Learning
TCV 2028 CHILI CHARLES: Quickstep
TCV 2029 CLEAR LIGHT SYMPHONY: Clear Light Symphony
TCV 2030 HATFIELD AND THE NORTH: The Rotters' Club
TCV 2031 STEVE HILLAGE: Fish Rising
TCV 2032 WHITE NOISE: White Noise 2
TCV 2033 KEVIN COYNE: Matching Head And Feet
TCV 2034 ROBERT WYATT: Ruth Is Stranger Than Richard
TCV 2035 WIGWAM: Nuclear Nightclub
TCV 2036 PEKKA POHJOLA: B The Magpie (probably does not exist)
TCV 2037 IVOR CUTLER: Velvet Donkey
TCV 2040 EDGAR FROESE: Epsilon In Malaysian Pale
TCV 2041 CAN: Landed (listed in *Music Master* but as yet unconfirmed)
TCV 2043 MIKE OLDFIELD: Ommadawn
TCV 2044 TANGERINE DREAM: Ricochet
TCV 2046 GONG: Shamal

| | |
|---|---|
| TCV 2049 | BOXER: Below the Belt |
| TCV 2052 | THE MIGHTY DIAMONDS: Right Time |
| TCV 2059 | U ROY: Natty Rebel |
| TCV 2061 | PETER TOSH: Legalize It |
| TCV 2066 | STEVE HILLAGE: L |
| TCV 2068 | TANGERINE DREAM: Stratosphere |
| TCV 2071 | CAN: Flow Motion |
| TCV 2074 | GONG: Gazeuse |
| TCV 2081 | PETER TOSH WITH WORDS SOUND AND POWER: Equal Rights |
| TCV 2086 | SEX PISTOLS: Never Mind The Bollocks, Here's The Sex Pistols |
| TCV 2089 | THE MOTORS: 1 |
| TCV 2094 | DEREK AND CLIVE: Come Again |
| TCV 2095 | XTC: White Music |
| TCV 2097 | TANGERINE DREAM: Cyclone |
| TCV 2098 | STEVE HILLAGE: Green |
| TCV 2100 | MAGAZINE: Real Life |
| TCV 2101 | THE MOTORS: Approved By The Motors |
| TCV 2102 | THE DIAMONDS: Planet Earth (listed in Music Master but as yet unconfirmed) |
| TCV 2106 | DEVO: Q: Are We Not Men? A: No, We Are Devo |
| TCV 2107 | JULIE COVINGTON: Julie Covington |
| TCV 2109 | PENETRATION: Moving Targets |
| TCV 2111 | TANGERINE DREAM: Force Majeure |
| TCV 2112 | DEREK AND CLIVE: Ad Nauseum |
| TCV 2114 | PUBLIC IMAGE LIMITED: First Issue |
| TCV 2115 | SPARKS: No 1 In Heaven (not confirmed, but almost certainly issued) |
| TCV 2116 | SKIDS: Scared To Dance |
| TCV 2121 | MAGAZINE: Secondhand Daylight |
| TCV 2122 | THE RECORDS: Shades In Bed |
| TCV 2123 | INTERVIEW: Big Oceans |
| TCV 2130 | SHOOTING STAR: Shooting Star |
| TCV 2131 | PENETRATION: Coming Up For Air |
| TCV 2132 | THE RUTS: The Crack |
| TCV 2133 | THE HUMAN LEAGUE: Reproduction |
| TCV 2134 | JANE AIRE AND THE BELVEDERES: Jane Aire And The Belvederes |
| TCV 2135 | STEVE HILLAGE: Open |
| TCV 2138 | SKIDS: Days In Europa |
| TCV 2141 | MIKE OLDFIELD: Platinum |
| TCV 2144 | SID VICIOUS: Sid Sings |
| TCV 2777 | STEVE HILLAGE: Motivation Radio |
| TCVD 2501 | KEVIN COYNE: Marjory Razorblade |
| TCVD 2502 | VARIOUS ARTISTS: V |
| TCVD 2506 | TANGERINE DREAM: Encore |
| TCVD 2510 | SEX PISTOLS: The Great Rock 'N' Roll Swindle |
| TCVD 2511 | MIKE OLDFIELD: Exposed |
| TCVDT 101 | MIKE OLDFIELD: Incantations |
| TCVX 1 | MIKE OLDFIELD: Boxed |
| TCWATT/1 | CARLA BLEY: Tropic Appetites |
| TCWATT/2 | MICHAEL MANTLER: No Answer |
| TICE 4 | EDDY GRANT: Walking On Sunshine |
| No cat. no. | XTC: Live At Eric's (promo only) |
| No cat. no. | XTC: XTC Interview (promo only) |

## Caroline label artists on Virgin VS 100 series 7" singles

All singles by Caroline artists were released on the Virgin label proper. All tracks below are taken from Caroline label LPs, apart from those marked *, which were only available on single.

| | |
|---|---|
| VS 106 | MAX: Stephanie / All I Know |
| VS 109 | CAROL GRIMES: You're The Only One / Southern Boogie |

VS 111 — B. B. SEATON: Dancing Shoes / Moon River*
VS 118 — JABULA: Jabula Happiness / Baile They Are Gone
VS 123 — DAEVID ALLEN: It's The Time Of Your Life / Fred The Fish (And The Chip On His Shoulder)
VS 146 — B. B. SEATON: Moon River* / No More Tribalism
VS 147 — ROY ST. JOHN: Way You Look Tonight* / Cincinnati*

## UK–only Virgin set numbers assigned to ECM multi–LPs

ECMD 1086 — KEITH JARRETT: Hymns Spheres (2–LP: ECM 1086/1087)
ECMD 1090 — KEITH JARRETT: Staircase/Hourglass/Sundial (2–LP: ECM 1090/1091)
ECMX 1 — KEITH JARRETT: Sun Bear Concerts (10–LP box set: ECM–X–1100)

## Known export–only packages/releases

EXPACK 001 — VARIOUS ARTISTS: Dead On Arrival (stickered, shrinkwrapped 2–LP, VD 2508, on luminous vinyl with poster)
ODD 1 — DEVO: B Stiff (Stiff label LP with Virgin VDJ 27 flexi, shrinkwrapped and exported by Caroline Exports)
SIXPACK 1 — CAPTAIN BEEFHEART: Six–Pack – Six–Track (7" picture disc)
SIXPACK 2 — STEVE HILLAGE: Six–Pack – Six–Track (7" picture disc)
SIXPACK 3 — IAN MATTHEWS: Six–Pack – Six–Track (7" picture disc: not Virgin, but a joint release between Rockburgh Records and Caroline Exports)
SIXPACK 4 — ARTHUR BROWN: Six–Pack – Six–Track (7" picture disc: not Virgin, but a joint release between Gull Records and Caroline Exports)
SPOTS 001 — SEX PISTOLS: Never Mind The Bollocks, Here's The Sex Pistols (stickered, shrinkwrapped LP, V 2086, with one–sided single, VDJ 24) and poster)
V 2105 — SOLID SENDERS: Solid Senders (stickered, shrinkwrapped with free live LP, VDJ 26, and poster)

## Releases with the Caroline Exports [U.K.] logo

BUTT 001 — JADE WARRIOR: Reflections
NOTT 001 — THE ELECTRIC BANANA: The Seventies
NOTT 002 — THE LONG HELLO: The Long Hello
SIXPACK 1 — CAPTAIN BEEFHEART: Six–Pack – Six–Track (7" picture disc)
SIXPACK 2 — STEVE HILLAGE: Six–Pack – Six–Track (7" picture disc)
SIXPACK 3 — IAN MATTHEWS: Six–Pack – Six–Track (7" picture disc: joint release between Rockburgh Records and Caroline Exports)
SIXPACK 4 — ARTHUR BROWN: Six–Pack – Six–Track (7" picture disc: joint release between Gull Records and Caroline Exports)
VD 2508 — VARIOUS ARTISTS: Dead On Arrival (2–LP, luminous vinyl, export catalogue number EXPACK 001)

## Virgin Films

The only full–length film released by Virgin Films in the 1970s was *Space Movie*, directed by Tony Palmer, which was distributed by Warner in 1979. The music was by Mike Oldfield with production credits for Richard Branson and Simon Draper. According to the *Record Collector Rare Record Guide 2012* there exist four one–sided acetates of music from the soundtrack, which includes music from *The Orchestral Tubular Bells*, *Ommadawn* and *Incantations*, plus *Portsmouth* and some otherwise unissued material originally recorded for *Incantations*. Parts of the shelved *The Orchestral Hergest Ridge* are also included. A soundtrack album was planned, though this was also shelved. This most likely explains the otherwise unused VD 2509 catalogue number, which would fit from point of view of dates.

Filming for Virgin Films went on in 1978 and 1979 for *The Great Rock And Roll Swindle*. Despite a 1979 release for the soundtrack LP the film was not put on general distribution until 1980.

## The Great British Record Label series

Each book in the Great British Record Label series has received a great deal of praise thanks to a combination of attention to detail and the fact that the author's knowledge and love of British record labels both mainstream and oddball shines through. The intention was – and remains – to make each book in the series the definitive work on the label. *Bristol Folk*, by the same author, predates this series, but already pointed the way!

### The Famous Charisma Discography

The first book in the series was produced to celebrate the 40th anniversary of Charisma, possibly the greatest independent British record label that has ever existed. Tony Stratton Smith, the label's owner, used his maxim of "Anything good of its kind" to put together an enviable roster of artists as diverse as Genesis, Van der Graaf Generator, Sir John Betjeman, John Arlott, Malcolm McLaren, Bo Hansson, Lindisfarne and Hawkwind.

**Paperback: ISBN 978–0–9563531–1–5/Kindle: ISBN 978–0–9563531–4–6 ePub version coming soon**

### The Saydisc and Village Thing Discography

This discography provides an in–depth view of the wonderfully–eclectic Saydisc label and related Village Thing, Matchbox, Roots, Amon Ra and Ahura Mazda labels. The release celebrated the 45th anniversary of Saydisc and the 40th anniversary of Village Thing, the original 'folkadelia' label, and the author was given special access to the label archives. The book includes access to many previously–unpublished photographs.

**Paperback: ISBN 978–0–9563531–2–2 Kindle and ePub versions coming soon***

### Transacord: Sounds of Steam (with free limited edition CD)

Possibly Britain's best–loved specialist label, Transacord was run by the celebrated British Film Sound Recordist, Peter Handford. The label started life in 1953 and released its first railway recording in 1955. The heyday was in the 1960s, when Argo took over the business end of things and Transacord records started selling in silly quantities. The book includes a limited edition, free CD with two tracks never before available on CD.

**Paperback: ISBN 978–0–9563531–3–9 Kindle and ePub versions coming soon***

### Bristol Folk: a Discographical History

Bristol Folk has proved very popular with fans of British folk, blues and 'psych' or 'acid folk'. Why Bristol? Well, Bristol's nationally recognised folk scene was a magnet for established names, such as Al Stewart, Stefan Grossman, the Incredible String Band and John Renbourn, whilst Bristol's own enviable roster of artists included Ian Anderson, Pigsty Hill Light Orchestra, Adge Cutler and the Wurzels, Shelagh McDonald, Stackridge, Al Jones, Steve Tilston, Dave Evans, Keith Christmas, and more. 34 pages of illustrations include record sleeves, photographs (many previously unpublished), promotional materials and memorabilia from private collections and archives to which the author had special access. Fred Wedlock contributed a postscript shortly before his untimely death.

**Paperback: ISBN 978–0–9563531–0–8 Kindle and ePub versions coming soon***

### Coming soon – and just arrived!

Volumes in the pipeline cover Harvest, Manticore, Purple, Swan Song, Immediate, WWA, Nepentha and others. Breaking news – the B&C discography has recently been published and there is another railway–related book on the way, this one courtesy of Ian McDonald.

**All available from www.bristol–folk.co.uk**

*digital versions are text only

www.ingramcontent.com/pod-product-compliance
Ingram Content Group UK Ltd.
Pitfield, Milton Keynes, MK11 3LW, UK
UKHW020317250726
13967UKWH00004B/1767

9 781909 953000